Culture and Craftsmanship in the Belgian Tradition

*wild*BREWS:

Beer Beyond the Influence of Brewer's Yeast

Jeff Sparrow

**With foreword by
Peter Bouckaert**

A Division of the
Brewers Association
Boulder, Colorado

Brewers Publications
A division of the Brewers Association
PO Box 1679, Boulder, CO 80306-1679
BrewersAssociation.org

Printed in the United States of America.

10 9 8 7 6 5 4

ISBN-13: 978-0-937381-86-1
ISBN-10: 0-937381-86-1

Library of Congress Cataloging-in-Publication Data

Sparrow, Jeff, 1965-
  Wild brews : beer beyond the influence of brewer's yeast /
by Jeff Sparrow ; with foreword by Peter Bouckaert.
       p. cm.
  Includes bibliographical references and index.
  ISBN-13: 978-0-937381-86-1
  ISBN-10: 0-937381-86-1
  1. Beer--Belgium. 2. Brewing. I. Title.
  TP577.S645 2005
  641.2'3'09493--dc22
                                    2005009055

Publisher: Ray Daniels
Technical Editor: Gordon Strong
Copy Editor: Daria Labinsky
Index: Daria Labinsky
Production & Design Management: Stephanie Johnson
Cover and Interior Design: Julie Korowotny
Cover Illustration: Alicia Buelow
Interior Photos by: Joe Preiser

Contents

Acknowledgements

To Chris, who once convinced me to spare a day and visit this tiny place called Beersel . . . and to walk up that blasted hill.

Special thanks to the Belgian and Dutch brewers and blenders who have shared with me the many secrets of their age-old art: Yves Benoit from Brouwerij Bavik; Marina and Marc Limet from Kerkom; Frank Boon from Brouwerij Boon; Jean and Jean-Pierre Van Roy and Yvan DeBaets from Cantillon; Lieven, Steven, and Pieter from Cnudde; Karel Goddeau from De Cam; Kris Herteleer from De Dolle Brouwers; Armand DeBelder from Drie Fonteinen; Paul Rutten from Gulpener Bierbrouwerij; John Matthys and Sidy Hanssens from Hanssens Artisanaal; Filip Devolder from Liefmans; Dirk Lindemans from the Brouwerij Lindemans; Tony Brown from Melbourn Brothers; Bruno Reinders from Mort Subite; Rudi Ghequire from Rodenbach; and Karl Verhaeghe from the Verhaeghe Brouwerij. Please support their art and buy their beers wherever you may find them.

Why do all of these breweries own a cat? To keep the *Brettanomyces* under control.

Thanks, also, to my friends in the U.S. beer industry whose creativity never ceases to amaze me: Sam Calagione from Dogfish Head Brewing, Mark Edelson from Iron Hill Brewery, Tomme Arthur from Pizza Port, Phil Markowski from Southampton Publick House, Vinnie Cilurzo from Russian River Brewing, Matthias Neidhart of B. United International, Keith Lemke and Lyn Kruger from the Siebel Institute, Chris White from Whitelabs, and Les Perkins and my "scientific adviser" Dave Logsdon from Wyeast Laboratories.

A special thanks to Peter Bouckaert from New Belgium Brewing, who teaches me something new every time we chat. Peter produces many truly unique beers.

To homebrewer Raj Apte, for his graphic approach to wild beers.

To Gordon Strong, whose eagle-eye editing saved me from a few technical blunders.

A pop of the cork to all of my friends in the Chicago Beer Society, whose friendship and passion are irreplaceable. A special toast to: Joe Preiser, my photographer, driver, and co-founder of the wild beer fraternity; Ray Daniels, who, if I told him how much he taught me, would be surprised I paid attention; Randy Mosher, who discovers the most radical brewing texts one could imagine.

And to *Brett*, without whom none of this would be possible.

Foreword

*I*t was somewhere in 1995 or so. I had shown two brewers, Daryl and David from Boston, around Brouwerij Rodenbach in Belgium. Somehow, we all ended up at my parents' home after that. My father had an old bottle of beer in his wine cellar. It was a bottle of *seizoens* (Flemish for *saison*), brewed in 1945 in Kuurne by Andries—the last year that brewery had brewed. Daryl somehow convinced my father to open it. Most of the CO_2 gas had escaped since the cork had dried and shrunk, but the beer had survived pretty well, flavorwise. My father decided to call the old brewer Ferdinant while we were drinking it, to ask how he made the beer.

Ferdinant was sick in bed and speaking with difficulty. His first reaction to the question of how he brewed the beer was, "Your son is brewer, he knows." After we insisted some more, he opened up to us. "After the coolship, the beer went in the barrels, where some sugar was added after a while." He also told us that we were crazy to drink this old stuff. "Is it any good?" He mentioned that his was one of the only breweries in the area that was able to keep its brewing equipment through the Second World War. You know, all the normal stuff. "Isn't your son the brewer at Rodenbach? Rodenbach was able to brew through the war. He knows." Since the brewer had a hard time speaking, we did not insist any further.

Was this old brewer talking about a lambic? No, a coolship and wood barrels were pretty standard in smaller breweries at that time in Belgium. Did he add yeast? Brewery Andries was also brewing year-round, different beers, so they might have used yeast from another brew. Maybe he got something from another brewery in the beginning of the winter season, maybe not. Were there other microorganisms added or present? For sure, but it was not really controlled. That was probably why he was referring to me and Rodenbach. In his time, Rodenbach was one of the larger local breweries that focused on wood aging with a mixed yeast culture.

Was this a "Wild Brew"? No, this was just a normal beer, according to Ferdinant.

Louis Pasteur wrote *Etudes Sur la Biere* (Studies on Beer) in 1876. Pasteur took a look under his primitive microscope to examine sick- or foul-smelling beer. He saw that, beside ellipsoid cells, many other tiny things were present in the sick beer. He and some other researchers and brewers around this time started to realize that those ellipsoid cells were crucial for the fermentation of beer.

Before 1876, what would a book with the title *Wild Brews* have meant? We used to have a zoo of microorganisms in brewing, but we did not even realize it. The effect of the other microorganisms was kept under control, with short shelf life, high hop rates, experience, sometimes more alcohol, and some other tricks.

What happened in those one hundred and forty years since Pasteur? We have learned tons about *Saccharomyces cerevisiae*. But we learned only limited amounts about *Brettanomyces, Pediococcus, Lactobacillus,* or you name it. We learned even less of the interaction between those critters. And what about the use of the wood vessels we keep them in?

After Pasteur, the use of single yeast cultures spread like wildfire. As in every technological development, there are also late adopters, such as the English ales and Berliner *weisse*. The brewer from the Andries brewery in Kuurne never adapted this seizoen. And then we have the hedgehogs, clinging furiously to the good old stuff, while the world keeps on turning.

This book talks about the hedgehogs in Chapter One. Jeff struggles to make sense of the information from the brewers he talked with. All of those brewers are like Ferdinant from brewery Andries to an extent. All those brewers are making their beer, in most cases, as their fathers did. What are you really asking for, Jeff? This is how you make beer, you know. All are relying on their experience of what went wrong and right. Those brewers are making their beer, not a style. As Jeff writes: "Guilds, imports, local tastes and *terroir* were all contributing factors to the individual character of Belgian beers."

Chapter Two in *Wild Brews* is digging up those fossilized beers that used to roam the world. I'm amazed at the amount of information in there. Belgian brewing history is not very well documented. In the following chapters Jeff tastes beer, looks more closely at the microbiology and the brewing process, and ends with suggestions on how to recreate those wild brews.

Wild Brews is an attempt to capture the wildest, and if you ask me, the most fun aspects of brewing. We do not make beer with barley malt, water, and hops! In the last one hundred and forty years, most brewers even started consciously using *Saccharomyces cerevisiae* or brewing yeast. It magically became the current workhorse of beer brewing, winemaking, and bread baking. Real fun only starts when we consider other things, like fruit and spices and, of course, other critters.

The use of different microorganisms is one of the least studied and (currently) least practiced fields of brewing. Jeff is trying to make sense of a limited amount of scientific publications and a larger amount of very opinionated brewers. The fact that those brewers have those opinions is based on their knowledge, experience, and creativity.

This is exactly what I love about brewing: Nothing is absolute. You will gain knowledge through reading this book. You will gain experience by trying out some of the recipes. Your creativity will lead you in new directions to your own piece of art.

I hope those three ingredients of brewing (knowledge, experience, and creativity) may become the ingredients of all your future brews. I hope they become an integral part of what you unconsciously know. So that you can say with a straight face as that old brewer from Kuurne said to my father: "Your son is a brewer, he knows."

Enjoy!
Peter Bouckaert
Brewmaster
New Belgium Brewing Company

Introduction

"It takes a few months to get a drinkable product and a few years to get a nice product and a lifetime to make the best product."

                                            –Frank Boon of Brouwerij Boon

In 1993, travel for me was still something of an extravagance. Two friends and I were on our "trip of a lifetime" to Europe. Given the well-known lore of German beer, as well as the dubious draw of a city like Amsterdam to three young men, convincing my fellow travelers to visit Belgium was not a simple task. Fortunately, Belgium proved only a short detour on the way from Frankfurt to the Netherlands. The number of beers served even in the smaller cafés dwarfed most anything I had seen in the United States. It wasn't really until we got to Brussels, however, that the light started to come on.

Armed with the first edition of *The Great Beers of Belgium*, we found our way to Chez Moder Lambic in Elsene (now closed). The concept of fifty beers on tap was staggering, and Moder Lambic did not disappoint. My eyes couldn't help but wander, however, to a beer cooler, where a number of colorful-looking bottles grabbed my attention. After much deliberation, I ordered a lambic, flavored with some odd tropical fruit. The bartender told me that if I wanted to try a very good beer, to drink this bottle, which he placed on the bar in front of me. The label featured a compelling drawing of a naked lady sitting on a fully clothed gentleman's lap. I was about to sample my first *Cantillon Rosé de Gambrinus*, and the complexity was beyond anything I had ever tasted.

A day or so later, we found ourselves in Antwerp at the famous café Kulminator. Here, someone told the three of us we could find vintages of different beers, or those from breweries nearly forgotten. One of my friends had been questing for a bottle of *Liefmans Goudenband* produced before the new owners of the brewery had changed the recipe (in 1992). The owner of the café brought a dusty bottle out of the cellar, lying on an angle in what could best be described as a narrow wicker basket. Expertly poured, we sampled the vintage brew. The aged *Goudenband* was at once malty and refreshingly tart with an unexpected sherrylike character. If Belgian ales tasted like these two examples, I thought, then I had certainly come to the right country. I would go on to discover that not all Belgian beers are tart, but those that would become my favorites made amazing use of that "obscure" characteristic.

A brewer at heart, I quite naturally had to learn how the indigenous beers were produced, and how I could make them at home. Several days later, Frank Boon received the three of us for a special brewery tour. I asked Boon how I could produce a lambic in the United States. His answer naturally came back, "You can't." Lambic may only be produced in a specific region of Belgium using centuries-old brewing methods. Of course, no

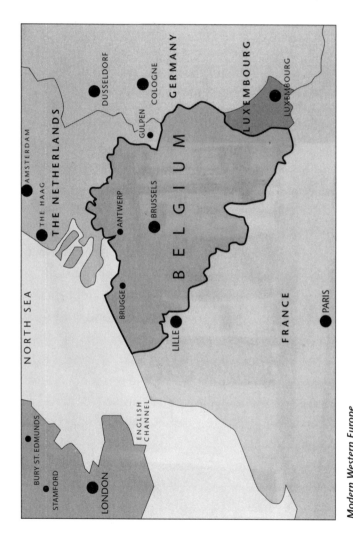

Modern Western Europe
Many wild beers are native to Belgium, but also the United Kingdom and the Netherlands.

American brewer of the past decade would ever accept that answer. I have since come to take the response of "you can't" as both a tribute to the magical properties of traditional Belgian sour ales and a challenge to see exactly what can be done both professionally and at home.

At one time, all beers exhibited some level of tart, sour, acidic character. Modern brewing methods helped to virtually eliminate these characteristics in beer. Only several traditional styles of wild beer exist, still brewed using traditional methods in Flanders, Brussels, and the surrounding countryside.

Lambic, the traditional beer of Brussels, is spontaneously fermented by the particular combination of microorganisms residing near the valley of the tiny Senne River and aged in wooden barrels. Once practiced the world over, Brussels and the Payottenland—the picturesque area of farmhouses to the west—remain the only regions where spontaneous fermentation will produce reasonably consistent results, time after time. The particular "wild" character makes the lambic utterly unique throughout the brewing world.

But don't despair; believe it or not, you can spontaneously ferment beer anywhere in the world. Jean-Pierre Van Roy of the Cantillon brewery in Brussels told me so on my first visit. I just didn't know what to make of the statement at the time. Since then, Van Roy's revelation has become a great deal clearer. Van Roy told me you must develop a taste for your own local lambic, although he never had to taste one result of his suggestion.

Upon returning from that trip to Belgium in 1993, one of my two fellow pilgrims decided to spontaneously ferment a beer, open, in his backyard in Hawaii. It's very clean in Hawaii, he mused. His wort fermented, sort of, and the taste was so indescribable that I will stop describing it right now. While possible through a number of methods to produce a reasonable facsimile of a lambic or even to actually spontaneously ferment a palatable beer, the process involves far more than a night under the stars, even in Belgium. If you aspire to produce a local lambic, by the time you finish this book, you will have the information necessary to approach that goal.

Other examples of wild beers include the red-brown acid beers of Flanders. Flanders red beers do not spontaneously ferment; they mature in oak casks with many of the same microorganisms present in lambic, albeit with different results. Both Flanders and lambic brewers blend beer to taste, a key step necessary to produce consistent results. Other newer, not-so-classic examples exist, and their production methods have roots in the traditional practices of Belgium.

Many beer drinkers often define lambic, Flanders red-brown ales, and other related beers with one primary descriptor: "sour." The term "sour," however, lends a misleading connotation. Pleasingly tart and/or quenchingly acidic, yes, but not overtly sour. A number of different beers may be described simply as "sour" as a convenient catchall, and because a little sourness— one of only four basic tastes—to most people goes a long way. The beers described in this book are not produced with sourness or acidity as a single dominant characteristic. Some wild beers are more sour than others, but to condense the flavors and aromas into the term "sour" disregards the complexity and balance so intensely sought after by the traditional brewers.

The title of this book, *Wild Brews*, describes the category of beers more definitively than simply "sour ales." Fermentation with numerous microorganisms not widely used by brewers in more than a century truly ties these Belgian and American inter-pretations together. A tart/acidic character results from the growth of microorganisms other than common strains of brewer's yeast (*Saccharomyces*) during fermentation, namely wild yeast and bacteria that produce a variety of different acids and esters. Most brewers scrupulously avoid these microorganisms and consider the result of their unwelcome intrusion an infection when they contribute their character to a lager or a pale ale.

The character of wild beers arises not so much from the ingredients but from the environment of the brewery: the air, the walls, the wood, and the casks. A unique combination of environmental conditions (winemakers call this *terroir*) present in every place where beer is produced determines the character of a wild beer. Lambic brewers will tell you "you can't" because of the *terroir* of the region and of the individual brewery. You will never exactly reproduce one of the classic examples of a lambic or Flanders red-brown beer. You can learn relevant brewing procedures and produce your own examples. Traditional brewing procedures retain their importance, as newer methods and products water down many of the tradi-tional beers of Belgium.

Traditional lambic producers lament that even in the Payottenland, people have forgotten the characteristics of a traditional gueuze. Beers seen on television and in the super-market often profess to be a traditional product. In reality, industrial, filtered *gueuze* may only contain a fraction of actual lambic, the remainder being top-fermented wheat beer. Saccharin and aspartame have both become popular additives, as they are sweeter than sugar and essentially unfermentable to wild yeast found in the air and in the barrels. This deluge of commercial products on the market obscures many traditional Belgian beers, including lambic and Flanders red-brown ales. The popularity in Belgium of continental-style Pilsener and high-alcohol beers is a postwar phenomenon. The remaining traditional beers of the Payottenland and Flanders point to what many beers were like until the latter half of the twentieth century. The sourish character desirable in beer for centuries throughout much of Belgium dwindled, as sugar became the dominant taste in food products throughout Europe and the United States. American craft beer drinkers rebelled and embraced the bitterness contributed by hops during the 1990s. At least a portion of American craft beer drinkers also have embraced the traditional Belgian beers. Many traditional Belgian brewers continue to produce their product to their own tastes, and many traditional Belgian wild beers still exist due to a boost from American sales.

The traditional producers of wild beers are artists, no less so than painters or poets. They create world-class beers. If you sketch a copy of the *Mona Lisa*, that doesn't mean you shouldn't visit the Louvre to see the original. I hope that many readers, if they already have not, will become pilgrims and take a journey to the last traditional refuge of wild beers. Learning to produce your own example is not a substitute for immersing yourself in the classics or meeting with the producers.

I feel a Payottenland pilgrimage or Flanders fling should be undertaken at least once (a year). Finding the brewers and blenders can be difficult; searching for the cafés that serve the products can make Belgium seem like a haystack. I remember once getting the strangest look from a Brussels native while searching for a colorfully named café when I asked him,

"Pardon me, can you please help me to find the Ultimate Hallucination?" To this end, I heartily recommend the book *Lambicland* (University Press, 2004) by Tim Webb, Chris Pollard, and Joris Pattyn as your tour guide, even for veteran travelers. For tours of Flanders and the rest of Belgium, Tim's ludicrously accurate *Good Beer Guide to Belgium* (CAMRA, 2004) is also an essential companion. Above all, "Don't Panic."

Imitation is often considered the sincerest form of flattery. Consider, then, the topic of wild fermentation from three vantage points: the history of the beers, the traditional methods, and how the methods can best be applied to produce beer in less-than-traditional circumstances. I begin this book with a description of the "classic styles" and delve into some history. I draw some similarities between these "styles" and treat them separately when appropriate. I also discuss the relationship to the wild beers produced in the United States using the application of traditional methods. Most importantly, I discuss how to produce wild beers, why they are still produced using traditional methods, and how you can produce your own examples. Some procedures require considerable effort, while others allow reasonable shortcuts, but "wild" yeast and bacteria offer a world of possibilities.

one

Classic Styles

"The sweet lambic, the sweet fruit beer, and the sweet gueuze don't exist. It's impossible. If it is very sweet there are three possibilities: It is not a lambic, it has aspartame added, or it is pasteurized. Lambic is a natural product."

–Jean-Paul Van Roy of the Brasserie-Brouwerij Cantillon

A BEER BY ANY OTHER NAME

Americans brewers enjoy categorizing beers into styles, particularly for the sake of competitions. Belgian brewers aren't terribly obsessed with the concept of style. The smaller producers create what they like to drink, and larger operations brew what they think they can sell, hopefully by the truckload. For the traditional producer, with an ever-diminishing market, producing a beer resembling that of one's own grandfather is still a matter of great pride.

Before the advent of planes, trains, and automobiles, transportation was more difficult (although some will say the auto has made getting around Brussels even more of an ordeal). Distances we might easily cover today took a longer period of time, especially with a few barrels of beer on the back of the wagon. Brewers from one area likely did not mix too often with those of another. For centuries, regional guilds controlled the production of beer in Western Europe and had great influence on the type of beer produced and imported. Like today, regional beers often grew and suffered based on the presence of imports. An imported beer, perhaps produced with inferior ingredients, would undercut the sales and popularity of the local brews, often based solely on cost.

People used to drink more of their regional beers in Belgium. People drank one type of beer for a lifetime (like my father, who has preferred the same brand of mass-produced American lager since he served in the Pacific during the War). Belgians now drink Pilsener, abbey beers, or the national style *du jour*. What has been a boon to American brewers has had the opposite effect in Belgium. The willingness of the American beer consumer to try new beer styles from new breweries has fueled the American craft beer movement. In Belgium, this same trait has enabled the decline of the traditional producer who brewed only his own unique style of beer. Historically, breweries in Belgium produced one basic type of beer, although today, those who remain so single-minded are a part of an exclusive community.

A Belgian brewer did not sit down and decide to produce a beer indicative of the region. Guilds, imports, local tastes, and *terroir* were all contributing factors to the individual character of Belgian beers. Today, beers that share similar content and characteristics are looked at as "styles," so potential drinkers can understand how they are likely to taste. Historically, beers of similar characteristics were brewed in the same region of Belgium, a designation that to some degree still holds true.

Flanders red-brown beers are produced in provincial Flanders and lambic in and to the west of Brussels, but a regional categorization is too broad for this book. For the purpose of this book, I categorize East Flanders brown, West Flanders red, and lambic based on similar taste, aroma, and production methods, wherever the origin. Belgian brewers consider this an English-language interpretation. A broad selection of flavors and aromas are possible within the styles of lambic and Flanders red-brown beers, broader than beer style guidelines might suggest. One lambic is more different from the next than most Pilseners or pale ales.

People often ask the question, "Does a lambic have to be brewed in or around Brussels?" The answer depends on the definition. A lambic is a spontaneously fermented beer produced with unmalted wheat and aged in wood. For most of the twentieth century, no one ever attempted to produce a lambic outside of the Senne Valley. Startup and production costs and uncertain results generally prohibit new traditional lambic breweries, even in Belgium.

That's not to say you can only spontaneously ferment and only achieve a beer resembling a lambic in the Senne Valley; you just won't achieve the exact same results, especially without some manual intervention. Consistent results from spontaneous fermentation along the Senne Valley likely occurred due to conditions fairly impossible to precisely reproduce. Even in the lambic-producing region, the changes in certain characteristics have caused some concern as to the long-term viability of consistent spontaneous fermentation.

Traditional lambic and Flanders red-brown beers have more in common than many people may realize (or admit).

Flavor and aroma characteristics develop due to the influence of a similar collection of microorganisms, including *Brettanomyces, Pediococcus, Lactobacillus,* and *Saccharomyces,* and the resulting by-products (acids, alcohol, and esters) of fermentation. Even though production methods of traditional Flanders beers have changed over time, they were once spontaneously fermented and are still traditionally aged in wood. The *terroir* of the brewery, plus the type of wort produced, and the reuse of yeast in succeeding batches, determine the differences in character between traditional lambic and Flanders red-brown beers. The *terroir* of a brewery must be favorable for fermenting wild beer, whether that includes the flora, air, roof, walls, and/or the barrels.

Brewers outside of the traditional regions of wild beer production already produce interesting interpretations. Pure cultures of wild yeast and bacteria have made it possible to produce a wild beer without waiting a generation for your brewery to become stably populated with the microorganisms necessary to produce a desirable and relatively consistent product. American and even some newer Belgian brewers may attempt to recreate a traditional "style" or be quite enthusiastic to develop a new wrinkle or two in this age-old tradition. Michael Jackson continues to espouse the creativity of the American brewer, and with good reason. Many step beyond the boundaries of traditional styles. The next sections detailing lambic, Flanders red-brown beers, and versions of both containing fruit tell us about possibilities, not limitations.

Overall, I feel you should not get too hung-up on style. If no brewer ever tried anything different, many world-class beers would not exist. I also believe brewers should let go of the concept of "cloning" regarding commercial wild beers, which has become prevalent when producing many beer styles. You cannot create your own precise replica of your favorite lambic any more than you could paint your living room to precisely resemble the Sistine Chapel.

West Flanders Red

Specifications:

Original Gravity: 12 to 14 °P (1.048 to 1.057 SG)

Apparent Final Gravity: 0.5 to 3 °P (1.002 to 1.012 SG)

Alcohol By Volume: 4.6 to 6.5% abv

Apparent Degree of Attenuation: Up to 98%

Malts: Vienna, Munich, light to medium cara-malts, Special "B," maize

Hops: Belgian, Czech, or German low alpha acid varieties, 10 to 25 IBUs

Organisms: Saccharomyces, Lactobacillus, Pediococcus, Acetobacter, Brettanomyces

Primary Fermentation: Up to 1 week at approx. 70° F (21° C)

Secondary Fermentation: Up to 3 years in oak at ambient temperature

Finish: Traditionally bottle-conditioned, now generally filtered, sweetened, and pasteurized

Traditional Flanders brewers generally produce red beers from moderately kilned malts and continental or British hops. Low alpha acid varieties are preferred but not essential. Alternately, some brewers will produce a wort solely from Pilsener malt and blend with a darker beer at bottling. The red ales may be originally fermented with a pure strain of *Saccharomyces* yeast or a mixed culture containing both yeast and bacteria. After

Characteristics of Flanders Red Ale

Medium reddish-brown to deep burgundy

Generally clear (any sediment should remain in the bottle)

Moderate carbonation, medium body

Fluffy, generally lasting white head

Fruity—plum, orange, black cherry, red currant

Vanilla, spices, chocolate (hints of Madeira)

Light perceived bitterness, sometimes a notable sweetness
(due to blending)

Sweetness decreases as acidity and alcoholic strength increase

Acidity moderate to high but never oppressive

Tart and often acidic in the finish

the primary fermentation is complete, resident yeasts and bacteria acidify the beer in oak barrels over a period of up to three years and it darkens a bit from exposure to oxygen and wood. Upon the completion of aging, different batches will be blended to taste, young and old beer, to produce the final product.

Flanders red ales are often called the "Burgundies of Belgium." Beyond the deep reddish-brown to burgundy color, resembling a red wine, the similarities are apparent but less obvious. Some of the typical, traditional flavors and aromas are akin to those commonly attributed to wine. Generally filtered, even when unfiltered the yeast should flocculate well, so the beers exhibit good clarity. Red beers possess average to good head retention in spite of long aging. As with fine red wines the spicy, vanilla character associated with oak may be present. Tannins add a crisp, tart astringency and full mouth-feel. An intense fruitiness is imperative, resembling the flavors of black cherries, plums, and red currants. A tart, acidic aroma and flavor ranges from complementary to deep and complex. This defining tartness, with both lactic and acetic notes, truly defines the style as reminiscent of red wine. Naturally highly attenuated, due to long aging with wild yeasts, some final products are pasteurized and blended with sugar or aspartame to add sweetness and body. Alcohol generally hovers around 6% abv in the final product but approaches 8% abv in some barrels before blending, unless an exceptional batch is devoted to a special release.

The character of Flanders red ales develops during long aging in old, uncoated oaken barrels whose resident microorganisms generally contribute more character than any derived from the actual wood. Wood is a porous environment, where yeast and bacteria with different oxygen requirements can thrive to meet their own specific needs. Blending beers of varying ages and colors balances the acidic character contributed by the microorganisms. Blending produces a complex and consistent beer generally not possible in a single batch. The palate of the producer, and also, to some extent, the preference of the customer determines the balance of the blend—ranging from sweet to acidic but never harsh.

Flanders red brewers freely admit that there is less aged beer going into the final product, as there appears to be less demand for the acidic character in their beer. Recently, a pale version or two has been released (without blending with a darker beer), just to reinforce the point of making a good beer and not a narrow style. Flanders aged pale, anyone?

East Flanders Brown
Specifications:
Original Gravity: 10 to 18 °P (1.040 to 1.074 SG)
Apparent Final Gravity: 2 to 3 °P (1.008 to 1.012 SG)
Alcohol By Volume: 4 to 8%
Apparent Degree of Attenuation: 80%
Malts: Pilsener malt, dark CaraVienna and CaraMunich, maize
Hops: Belgian, Czech, or German low alpha acid varieties, 25 IBUs
Organisms: Saccharomyces, Lactobacillus, Pediococcus
Primary Fermentation: Up to 1 week at ambient temperature
Secondary Fermentation: Up to 2 years in stainless steel at 90° F (32° C)
Finish: Traditionally bottle-conditioned, now generally filtered, sweetened, and pasteurized

Characteristics of East Flanders Brown Ale

Reddish-brown to brown

Generally clear (any sediment should remain in the bottle)

Moderate carbonation, medium to medium-full body

Fluffy, generally lasting white head

Fruity—raisins, plums, figs, dates, black cherries, prunes

Malty—caramel, toffee, orange, treacle, or chocolate

Light perceived bitterness, sometimes a notable sweetness (due to blending)

Sweetness fades, becomes more vinous and sherrylike with age

Often tart and sometimes warming in the finish

East Flanders' own red-brown beer, sometimes referred to as an *oud bruin*, exhibits different characteristics than the red beers of West Flanders. Made from pale malt and dark CaraMunich and CaraVienna malts with continental or British hops, East Flanders browns contain about twice as much bitterness as desired in a Flanders red, though mellowed by a malty sweetness. The Flanders browns may also be fermented with a mixed culture of yeast and bacteria and subsequently aged in stainless steel tanks at higher temperatures to allow lactic acid-producing bacteria to grow and acidify the beer. Similar to the red beers, brewers blend different batches of different ages, both for balance and consistency in the final product.

Oud bruin is not a precise term; some of the beers that use it are actually Flanders reds by character, and others exhibit little tartness. The term literally refers to a "traditional dark beer produced in Flanders" rather than a beer that meets a specific style. Simply put, dark, sourish beers were once the rage in Flanders. The distinction between the beers of East and West Flanders is a modern concept. Blending of young and aged beer defines both "styles," but West Flanders red beers are matured in oaken casks, while the brown beers mature in stainless steel tanks.

At one time, all of the Flanders beers were aged in wood, but this began to change around 1970. Aging in wooden barrels or stainless steel tanks became a fork in the road that resulted in beers of different production methods and characteristics. Stainless steel requires less care and maintenance than wood, but the end result differs. A wort aged in a warm steel tank will become acidified but never achieve the same flavors as in oak. The porous nature of the wood and the character of the wood contribute to the Flanders red but not the brown beer. The tradition of aging in wood has been lost by some Flanders brewers.

So what makes an oud bruin besides geography and warm aging in stainless steel tanks? The East Flanders brown is more solidly brown than its western cousin. Filtered, the brown beers exhibit good clarity. They possess average to good head retention in spite of long aging. An alelike fruitiness with an often-dominant malt character defines the East Flanders brown, balancing any hop bitterness. The acid-producing bacteria dominant during fermentation produce different by-products, largely due to the stainless steel vessels, so the brown becomes sour but never achieves the crisp, acidic character of the red beers. The tart, vinous character of aged beer is covered by the malty sweetness of young beer but grows in an East Flanders brown if aged.

Traditional Lambic
Specifications:
Original Gravity: 12.0 to 14.0 °P (1.048 to 1.057 SG)
Apparent Final Gravity: 0.1 to 2.5 °P (1.001 to 1.010 SG)

Liefmans, or 300 years of expertise.

Alcohol By Volume: 5 to 5.5% abv

Apparent Degree of Attenuation: Up to nearly 100%

Malts: 60 to 70% Pilsener malt, 30 to 40% unmalted wheat

Hops: Belgian, Czech, or German low alpha acid varieties aged 3 years

Organisms: Saccharomyces, Pediococcus, Brettanomyces, many others

Fermentation: 6 months to 2+ years, generally at ambient temperature

Finish: Unpasteurized, served from a cask or bottle, less commonly from a keg

The lambic bill consists of malted barley, unmalted wheat, and aged hops, traditionally mashed and boiled for a considerable period of time as compared to modern brewing methods. The wort cools overnight, open to the air, in a large shallow vessel know as a coolship. In the days before refrigeration, coolships

Characteristics of Lambic

Pale yellow to deep golden

Often cloudy, clearing with age

Uncarbonated unless long aged

Virtually no foam

Often bitter with a lactic sourness, mellowing with age

May exhibit small degrees of barnyard, earthy, goaty, hay, horsy, and horse blanket character

Developing characteristics of fruit, oak, honey, and white wine

Complexity increases with age

Bitter and yeasty, fading with age

Relatively full-bodied, drying with age

were far more common as the only method of cooling wort. After a night's rest in the coolship, the wort is transferred to wooden barrels, where fermentation may last up to three years. During this time, the organisms that inoculated the wort overnight, plus those resident in the barrel, produce a cornucopia of flavors and aromas. Traditionally brewed (and blended) beginning in the autumn and continuing into spring, the wild yeasts and bacteria that ferment and acidify lambic will be too aggressive during the warmer months.

Lambic presents a most unique sensory experience. I find a seemingly limitless number of descriptors to express the aroma and flavor, most of which do not apply to most other beer styles. Lambic is not, however, a free-for-all of strange attributes (i.e., barnyard, horsy, etc.). Acceptable in small amounts, more "funk" and more acid do not denote a better lambic. Contrary to some popular beliefs, lambic should not remind you of a diaper pail or Spot on a rainy day. Characteristics the brewer considers "offensive," including a large concentration of acid, provide clues that a batch of lambic might not be quite ready or may never be ready to blend or serve.

No traditional brewer intends for a lambic to be overtly sour or exceedingly acidic; balance is the key. Brewers search for characteristics considered "pleasant" within the realm of lambic.

The best lambics have some acidity, a bit like white wine, but not much more. According to Frank Boon, lambic brewers desire the character of Chardonnay. Many people speak only of acidity and sourness. A reasonable amount is essential to lambic; too much, and you have only vinegar or cleaning solution for the brew kettle. No single answer fits all the producers. The balance they strike depends upon their own preferences and traditions.

Lambic of less than two years old is "beer in progress"—still undergoing fermentation. Young lambic of five to six months old has a combination of the sweetness of the unfermented sugars and some bitterness from both hops and from yeast still in suspension. Young, cloudy lambic is a completely different beer than a mature lambic. After two years, a lambic can be quite dry and taste almost like a finished product (ready to blend as a gueuze). Just as you may keep some wines for several years, some lambics are good young, while others you must age.

Lambic is flat, since all carbon dioxide produced during lambic fermentation escapes from the barrel. Packaged young, lambic develops carbonation in a manner similar to a cask or bottle of real ale. Real ale is casked or bottled at the end of fermentation with just enough fermentable sugar left in solution to provide a gentle carbonation. The microorganisms responsible for lambic fermentation can consume virtually any type of sugar; therefore, the brewer never bottles young lambic. The fermentation of the remaining sugar in young lambic would

This café sign reads "A glass of gueuze lambic is more delicious."

produce enough carbon dioxide to shatter the bottle. Traditionally served on draft from a cask, young lambic must be consumed quickly, within about three days, or risk oxidization. Old lambic lacks virtually any fermentable sugars and may be bottled (or kegged) for later enjoyment.

Faro was once a blend of different strengths of lambic, produced with several different runnings (sparges) of the same mash and usually sweetened. Today, brewers blend dark sugar with lambic to produce faro. Unlike the pasteurized commercial bottles of faro seen on the shelves, traditional faro must also be served relatively quickly on draft, or the sugar will begin to ferment, destroying the desired sweetness.

Traditional Gueuze
Specifications:
Original Gravity: 12.0 to 14.0 °P (1.048 to 1.057 SG)
Apparent Final Gravity: Roughly 0.1 °P (1.001 SG)
Alcohol By Volume: 5 to 8% abv
Apparent Degree of Attenuation: 100%
Malts: 60 to 70% Pilsener malt, 30 to 40% unmalted wheat
Hops: Belgian, Czech, or German low alpha acid varieties aged
    3 years
Organisms: Saccharomyces, Lactobacillus, Pediococcus, Brettanomyces
    (and others)
Fermentation: Up to 3 years, generally at ambient temperature
Finish: Traditionally bottle-conditioned

Gueuze is a blend of one-, two-, and three-year-old lambic. Young lambic still has fermentable sugars and a higher concentration of viable yeasts than old lambic, which contains more

Gueuze Descriptors

Golden

Generally clear (any sediment should remain in the bottle)

Extremely carbonated and effervescent
(a cork should pop like Champagne)

Thick, lasting, moussey white head

Fruity—citrus, apples, and currants

Sometimes spicy or honeylike

May exhibit small degrees of barnyard, earthy, goaty, hay, horsy, and horse blanket character

May exhibit oaky, woody, or vanilla notes

Light to moderate bitterness

Light to moderate tannic, astringent character

Complementary to moderate acidity

Rounded, reasonably warming, and very dry in the finish

diverse and complex flavors and aromas. Lambic is flat, because the carbon dioxide produced during fermentation has escaped from the barrels. The effervescent character of gueuze results from the production of carbon dioxide in the bottle by fermentation of the sugars remaining in the young lambic. Generally aged before serving, the wild yeasts in a bottle of gueuze require time to finish "refermentation." The carbon dioxide and carbonic acid resulting from fermentation bring out even very subtle flavors and add to the perception of dryness, acidity, and tartness. A relatively unpredictable creation, lambic isn't necessarily ready to blend when the producer may be ready to blend. One of the many secrets of gueuze is blending with just the correct amount of young lambic to produce a forceful but not dangerous amount of carbon dioxide. Traditional lambic producers consider the difference between lambic and wine and between gueuze and Champagne very small. Naturally occurring yeasts traditionally ferment both wine and lambic in oak barrels. Champagne and gueuze are both blended and refermented in the bottle to produce a sparkling product. A superior vintage of Champagne or lambic may be bottled, unblended, as a "special *cuvée.*" A Champagne-like specialty wine can be found anywhere in the world, but the original product is native to a specific region of France. The original, traditional gueuze hails from breweries around the Senne Valley in Belgium. Natural fermentation, blending, and refermentation define the beermaking traditions of Brussels and the Payottenland.

FRUIT BEERS

Traditional Belgian brewers commonly add fruit to lambic, gueuze, and Flanders red-brown beers to impart the character of the fruit and produce a different beer. Fruit can be added to virtually any of the beers discussed in this book. Adding fruit to beer does not ultimately sweeten a beer (without pasteurization) but changes the flavor of a beer. Fruit contributes sugar to traditional beer as an additional fermentable. The acidity, flavor, aroma, and generally the color of a fruit beer will reflect to varying degrees that of the individual fruit. Wild fruit beers are generally not intended for aging, as the fruit flavor, aroma, and color will fade over time.

Fruit is sweet, fermented fruit is not. Wild yeasts ferment the sugar contained in the fruit. The fruit flavor and aroma and additional alcohol remain in the beer, but not any residual sweetness. A traditional wild fruit beer may often be more tart and acidic than the original beer due to the contributions of acids and tannins present in varying degrees in all types of fruit. The best fruits destined for fermentation by wild yeasts possess minimally a moderate level of acidity in balance with the sugar content.

Lambic and Gueuze Appellation Controleé

The most recent legal specifications for what may be commercially known as lambic came from the European Union in June 1998 at the request of the Confederation of Belgian Brewers, although the end result appears once again watered down by the influence of the large corporations. After 30 years of decrees and regulations, no real protection for 100% spontaneous fermentation exists.

I expect you may find the specifications somewhat vague; I do as well. What the following appellation does prescribe is that a lambic or gueuze labeled as "*Oude*" or "*Ville*" at least will have a certain flavor and aroma profile, even though the brewers who produce such beers use 100% spontaneous fermentation. The text of the appellation, loosely translated, reads as follows:

Beers that meet the following criteria may be called lambic and gueuze and use the EU symbol of "Spécial Traditional Guarantee":

An acid beer with a fragrant profile typical of a maturation in which the component decisive microflora is constituted from the species *Brettanomyces bruxellensis* and/or *Brettanomyces lambicus*.

• A minimum starting gravity of 12.7 Plato (1.051 S.G.)
• A maximum pH of 3.8
• A maximum color of 25 EBC (12.5 SRM)
• A maximum bitterness of 20 IBUs

Lambic and Gueuze Appellation Controlleé cont.

The gueuze or the gueuze-lambic is derived from a mixture of lambic in which the oldest component was ripened in wooden barrels for at least three years.

A fruit lambic is defined as no less than 10% and no greater than 30% of fruit (25% of cherries) or the equivalent juice or concentrate proportional to the final product produced in the above manner.

The beers that have, in addition to the above, the following characteristics are entitled to the indication of "*Oude*" or "*Ville*" (and are considered the most traditional examples of the style):

Beer that is the result of a blend of lambics that have been aged in wooden barrels, the average age being of at least one year and the oldest being of at least three years.

The mixture has undergone a refermentation and has been conditioned on yeast.

Contains a maximum 0.5 ppm isoamylacetate (after six months of maturation in the bottle) plus a minimum of 50 ppm of ethylacetate, a minimum volatile acidity of 10 milliequivalents NaOH (sodium hydroxide) per liter, and a minimum total acidity of 75 milliequivalents NaOH per liter.

Peter Bouckaert, the brewer at the New Belgium Brewing Company in Colorado, once conducted an enlightening taste test. Bouckaert blended his golden ale with a cherry lambic from Frank Boon in Belgium. The kriek was "bone" dry; all of the sugar had been fermented by wild yeast, while the flavor, aroma, and acidity of the cherries remained. The golden ale was full-bodied, with some residual sweetness from sugar unfermentable to the *Saccharomyces* used to ferment the beer. The blend had both the character of cherries and sweetness, the latter being the contribution of the sugar in the golden ale. This clearly demonstrated that you could have fruit flavor without sweetness in beer.

Brewers consider cherries the most popular fruit in the world to blend with traditional wild beer, and why not? Cherries have a tantalizing aroma, a quenching tart character, and a pleasing acidity in the best varieties. A wild beer blended with cherries is known as *kriek* or a kriek lambic, if lambic is used as the base beer. Other fruits added to wild beers within the past century are raspberries (*framboise*/framboise lambic), grapes (*druivenbier*/druiven lambic), apricots, strawberries, peaches, and black currants, the latter two prevalent in sweeter, filtered, pasteurized examples.

Popular Fruits in Wild Beers

Fruit	Time Frame
Cherries	For Hundreds of Years
Raspberries	Turn of the Twentieth Century
Grapes	Within the Twentieth Century
Black Currants	The 1980s
Peaches	The 1980s
Apricots	The 1990s
Strawberries	The 1990s

two

History

"All beer was once made by spontaneous fermentation, but those days are lost in the mists of history."

–Michael Jackson (the one with two gloves)

Philosopher George Santayana once said, "Those who cannot remember the past are condemned to repeat it." In the case of wild beer, we are not cursed at all, as science has yet to fully explain why many of the traditional brewing practices work, much less to improve upon them. The concepts for creating wild beer all have a historical basis. Examining even their spotty history can help to understand why certain things are or are not done today. I also hope that any student of beers fermented with wild yeast and bacteria will find their history quite interesting.

IN THE BEGINNING

Once was a time when all beers went sour and acidic relatively quickly. Yeast wasn't something maintained in a lab and pitched in a specific quantity, it simply existed wherever a fermentable source of food was found. Beer was fermented, over time, by wild yeasts that also produced acids that soured the beer. Wild yeast is still quite prevalent today, but this sort of fermentation is far too unreliable, haphazard, and probably distasteful for most brewers to consider. One goal of brewers throughout the long, largely forgotten history of beer has been to minimize and even eliminate the pungent sour character possible with spontaneous fermentation. Only then did we find that spontaneous fermentation could be pleasant and desirable if done correctly.

One theory suggests the invention of beer was an accident. A hapless gatherer of the Middle Stone Age accidentally left a bowl of grain uncovered in a hot damp or rainy place. The grain sprouted, and the mixture was inoculated by *Lactobacillus* on the grain and wild yeast in the air. This method may not have produced a complete fermentation but likely would have produced an infected alcoholic "soup."

Canadian homebrewer and paleontologist Ed Hitchcock put this theory to the test in 1993, going so far as to pound newly sprouted barley into gruel, mash the paste in the sun, and leave it out overnight to attract wild yeasts. This result of this prehistoric method of both mashing and fermentation was indeed filled with bacterial activity, insects, mold, and a noxious odor that even the hungriest caveman probably would not taste.

Another theory suggests early brewers actually produced bread from sprouted grain, then mashed it in a sort of "bread soup." The resident enzymes converted starches into sugar, which were ready for fermentation. Fermentation most likely originated due to airborne microorganisms, possibly aided by the addition of fruit, raw grains, or other ingredients bearing surface yeast and bacteria.

Hitchcock went to lengths to find conditions favorable for the development of an ancient malted grain-fermented beverage. He made "biscuits" from sprouted grains, mashed them in hot water with ground-sprouted barley, and fermented the mixture with yeast cultured from unpasteurized apple cider. Hitchcock described the eventual beer as cloudy, yeasty, bready, and cidery, and said that it "was good enough to warrant a second glass." Spontaneous fermentation was never, therefore, a simple matter. Steps had to be taken to promote a pleasant outcome.

One of the earliest occurrences of a specific wild beer was known as *sikaru* and is related to lambic beers. *Sikaru* was produced about 5,000 years ago in Mesopotamia. A cuneiform writing reveals the composition of the wort to be virtually identical with that of lambic—about 60% malt[1] and 40% raw grain. Author and microbiologist Jean-Xavier Guinard notes the spontaneous fermentation of the *sikaru* wort was attributed both to wild *Saccharomyces* and *Schizosaccharomyces*, a yeast that reproduces by fission as opposed to budding and is resistant to high levels of acetic acid, similar to *Brettanomyces*.

Another contribution to the lore of wild beer is heather ale, which comes to us from the Picts, inhabitants of northern Scotland during pre-Roman times. Wild yeasts inhabited many places, including heather blossoms, and these would have contributed fermentative capabilities as well as sugar from the nectar. This wild variation of beer is sometimes known today simply as Pictish ale. Like many lambic brewers, the Picts were known to guard their secrets carefully. Legend often has a father and his

---

[1] History professor Richard Unger notes the Mesopotamians malted barley by soaking it and drying it in the sun for several weeks and would have been prevented from doing this during the summer months, when the temperatures were too hot. Brewing was traditionally a seasonal practice. Summer temperatures still affect traditional lambic brewers, albeit for different reasons.

sons, the last survivors of their race, being captured and coerced, unsuccessfully, into revealing the secret of their ancient drink. (I thank the lambic brewers and blenders for not forcing me to go to such lengths to learn about their trade.)

The warrior-driven Celts were originally meadmakers, although their culture was already firmly rooted in ale around 3,000 years ago, when they occupied Europe north of the Alps as well as the British Isles. The Celts are credited with introducing brewing technology to Western Europe. Hops had not yet found their way into the kettle, so one major way of flavoring the ale was with a marsh and woodland plant called meadowsweet. Similar to the use of hops for certain antibacterial properties, research has shown this plant would have had a preservative effect on the beers of the day.

The Romans evicted the Celts around 57 B.C., and some historians suspect they brought with them an already ancient

The text in the second panel of these illustrations, found on the grounds of the Liefmans brewery, says, "Beer through the centuries."

brewing process, perhaps practiced by the Egyptians, involving spontaneous fermentation. Archeologists discovered a Roman villa dating from the third or fourth century with additional buildings they believed were used to produce beer in the Belgian province of Namur. Among the relics uncovered were an assortment of pots and beer glasses that include inscriptions that clearly refer to beer. Another advancement contributed by the Romans was the use of wooden casks, first mentioned in A.D. 21.

Author and exhaustive researcher Martyn Cornell speaks of the occasional problem with fermentation of beer in the first few centuries and the reliance on God for fermentation. One account has a fragment of the cross of Saint Aed being dropped into an apparently impious brew to jump-start fermentation. Of course, you have to watch what you ask for. Another account has the brewer in Cloman Elo's monastic brewing company asking the patron saint to help with a failed fermentation only to have a "gushing nonstop fountain of beer as a result." Coincidentally, the first (unpasteurized) version of *Lindemans Gueuze* shipped to the States met with the same result in transit. (Faced with the problem of a batch fermenting too slowly, traditional lambic brewers simply wait another year.)

Across parts of Western Europe, early records of towns in the Hanseatic League during the Middle Ages documented powerful guilds based around white and red beers that were important for trade. Little is known about this broad tradition of fresh, cloudy, low alcohol, sourish beers—the *weissbrau* (white beer) being principally of wheat, and the *rothbrau* (red beer) being of barley. We do know that beer was made in Brussels as early as the twelfth century, as supplied by its municipal charter made official in 1229. The use of raw wheat also dates back quite far; in 1137, the dukes of Brabant granted special water privileges to the brewing class for the crushing of wheat as well as malt. In thirteenth century Flanders, brewers still produced local beer with a spice mix known as *gruit*, while Hanse merchants were able to ship their beer to Flanders since they brewed with hops, already known by the brewers of the day for their ability to retard infection of the wort by various bacteria. It wasn't until the end of the fourteenth century that beer production in Brabant and Flanders changed from a domestic industry to one producing hopped beer for locals.

The brewers of the fourteenth and fifteenth centuries had much in common with twentieth century producers of spontaneously fermented ales. According to Unger, "Brewers usually started work early, even before dawn, so they could get the wort into the fermentation troughs in the cool of the evening and night. Those troughs would be in a place open to breezes. Later brewers even had hand-driven fans to push cool air across the top of the troughs. Brewers had to give careful attention to the rate of cooling so the yeast would grow." It was not uncommon to restrict brewing and malting to the cooler months, as they felt both processes needed the cool and even temperatures.

Centuries ago, beer was produced throughout Flanders and Brabant in tiny farmhouse breweries (*kam*). The farmers grew wheat and barley to brew the beer and feed the animals. Brewing did not happen during the summer months, because the land demanded the farmers' attention. The goal of the farm was not to produce beer to sell but to survive. Beer was produced for consumption by the family and farmhands and likely used only in trade for necessities the farm could not produce.

It wasn't until the mid-fourteenth century that a Flemish recipe book made mention of adding yeast to beer, although brewers may have been skimming foam off the top of a fermenting brew to start the next one during the early 1300s. By the fifteenth century, brewers had an understanding of naturally occurring top- and bottom-fermenting yeasts. By using the former, the brewer was able to conduct fermentation in a single cask. The brewer could skim the yeast as it rose to the top of the cask, through a hole in the barrel. If the brewer wished to speed the process of fermentation, the beer was put into smaller barrels, which "put more yeast surfaces in contact with vegetable matter." The bungholes were covered before tapping to keep the air out of the casks.

During the fifteenth century around Brussels there were beers known as *walgbaert* and *hoppe*, white beers made with a blend of raw wheat and oats; *roetbier*, red beers made from barley; and

A classic contrivance once used to trade lambic with other farms, now parked outside of Frank Boon's brewery in Lembeek.

zwartzbier, which was black. "All of these, however, with others, were gradually displaced by the lambic, or strong beer, the *mais*, or small beer, and faro, a mixture of each," notes an early twentieth century text. Ghent, in northern Flanders, was known for a beer called *uitzet* or *uytzet*, brewed to various strengths using a combination of multiple mashes. Typical was to remove a part of the wort after five- to six-hour boils and ferment it with an "old yeast." (According to authors Perrier-Robert and Fontaine, thirty- to forty-hour boils were perfectly acceptable at the time. In hindsight, this may have actually been a "rolling simmer," due to inefficient heat sources under large brewing kettles.) In 1549, Plactomus called beer produced with wheat "white beer" and beer produced with barley "red beer." In broadest terms, lambic and *wit* may be remnants of the paler wheat beers, while the Flanders red-brown beers are the descendants of the red barley beers.

From the very creation of beer, brewers sought to understand the mystery of fermentation and exert control over the process whenever possible. Far more than a haphazard process, spontaneous fermentation requires a source of wild yeast and favorable circumstances. Brewing was seldom carried out during the summer when the hot weather promoted the extreme growth of organisms whose by-products made the beer undrinkable. Prior to the dominance of the hop, other plants were sought for their antibacterial properties in wort. Intensely sour, acidic beverages were never desirable. A truly good beer, at most points throughout history, was no accident.

A key point in the history of fermentation occurred when medieval brewers learned to skim the foam from a fermenting batch of wort as the start of the next fermentation, rather than rely on airborne yeast to ferment each and every batch of beer. This early fork in the road of fermentation led more and more brewers down a different path, until only the lambic brewers of Brussels still practiced spontaneous fermentation.

THE BEERS OF BRUSSELS
Brussels and the surrounding countryside remain famous for their lambic beers, the first written documentation dating to around 1320. From this, lambic can lay claim to being the oldest existing beer style in the world. Farmers surrounding Brussels once commonly had their own breweries. While other brewers slowly went with newer methods of brewing and fermentation, eventually leading to the use of pure cultures of yeast, the many brewers in and around Brussels kept the traditional methods, including spontaneous fermentation.

Up until the time of the French Revolution, lambic was simply "old beer," but lambic was the beer that kept the best. According to Frank Boon, most of the other white and dark top-fermenting beers of that day kept only a week or two and then became unpleasantly acidic. The methods employed in the brewing and blending of lambic, however, produced a beer with a more palatable tart character. Lambic was a beer that would keep for years without turning to vinegar. The concept of "good" and "bad" sour may be foreign to many drinkers, but lambic was a beer whose unique acidic character was embraced by the local people of Brussels as well as current aficionados of the style.

The oldest existing beer style, traditional producers consider lambic "the mother of all beers." It is the only purely spontaneously fermented beer style left in the world, and its history is deeply rooted in Belgian culture. The consumption of rough

The mash tun at the Cantillon brewery reflects the shallow versions popular during the 1800s.

ale was at the center of rustic country life in sixteenth-century Belgium. Pieter Bruegel the Elder's famous paintings depict the lifestyle (and religion and death) of the Flemish people. Bruegel depicts peasants enjoying beverages out of stoneware jugs. Identical jugs are still used to serve lambic, then called "yellow beer."

Bruegel lived to the west of Brussels and often wandered through the villages of the Payottenland, inspired by the people and the landscapes. A collection of signposts mark the Bruegel Route, designed to lead the traveler through the villages and countryside that once served as his muse. Still brewed in a number of villages along the route, the thirsty traveler can enjoy lambic from a dwindling number of classic cafés or even directly from the brewers and blenders.

The origin of the lambic name lies, at least in part, in the village of Lembeek. At one point in this tiny village of roughly 600 lucky inhabitants there were about 43 different breweries, all banded together into a brewers guild. (Currently, the Boon brewery is the only one for around 4,000 still reasonably fortunate residents). Up until about 1800, there were no taxes paid. It was a tax-free zone—a free town between Brabant and Hainaut. The breweries generally used to both brew beer and distill *genever* (gin) in the same plant.

Duke Jean IV of Brabant, in search of a new brew, purportedly had the thought of macerating and boiling barley and hops in a still. In French, a still is known as *alambic*. To the French, both the town and the beer it was known for was Alambic, or "beer from stills." The name lambic may have evolved from this term. Considered very harsh to the palate, people also may have believed that a lambic was actually a distilled beverage.

The typical lambic grist consisting of wheat and barley has apparently been around for at least 400 years. Jean IV decreed in 1420 that all brewers in Brabant were required to use wheat in order to improve the quality of their beers. Remi le Mercier of Halle told the brewers of Brabant in 1559 that everyone should use at least 16 "razieren" of grain, including six "razieren" of wheat and ten "razieren" of barley.

The typical lambic mash traces its origins to a Dutch law introduced in 1822, and subsequently kept by an independent Belgium, that fixed a duty upon the capacity of the mash tun. This tax led to each brewery installing as small a mash tun as possible and filling it to the limit for each brew. Only a small amount of cold liquor could fit into a mash tun already over-flowing with a mixture of raw grain and malted barley. The well-respected English brewing scientist George Maw Johnson wrote that any attempt at approaching what is commonly considered a strike heat would result in a set mash. The temperature during the early stages of mashing was not sufficient enough to gelatinize any significant proportion of starch contained in the raw grains. Portions of the liquid had to periodically be removed and heated in a separate copper. The mashes of early Belgian brewers were, therefore, turbid. This type of mash, full of starches and dextrins, is still common in the production of lambic. Brewer G. Lacambre described the traditional turbid mash of a lambic in his *Complete Treaty of the Manufacture of Beers and Distillation of the Grains* (Brussels, 1851).

The size of the mash tun made lower gravity beers more profitable. *Mais* or *mars,* at about 2% abv, was less than half the gravity of lambic and often considered a product of the second runnings of water through the mash. Other people believe lambic may have simply been liquored (watered) down in the cask. Mars did follow the tradition of having a low-cost and low-alcohol beer, consumed in large quantities, to refresh the body during a time when manual labor was more prevalent. Also, diluting the beer was one way by which brewers could pass on rising costs to their consumers.

If the drinker found lambic too acidic, he or she commonly added a bit of sugar, crushed into the glass with a device known as a *stoemper* (a sort of mortar). Faro, on the other hand, often came presweetened. Candi sugar, caramel, molasses, and perhaps even some spice were used, so faro was commonly darker than lambic or mars. Faro was an everyday beer, just like the lambic, so it may have been served rather quickly, before the sugar was completely fermented. Near the end of the nineteenth century the popularity of faro dropped, so casks often went sour before they were emptied. Café owners remedied this situation by hanging strings of candi sugar crystals in the cask to "resweeten" the beer.

The faro drinker was often pictured as off balance or out of control.

Essentially a blend of lambic and mars, lambic brewers seldom blended faro for themselves, They sold lambic and mars to the *gereedmaker*—perhaps an early version of a blender—who carried out the task. According to Perrier-Robert and Fontaine, faro spent up to two years in the barrel. When faro was served, it had "a moderately sweet flavor and beautiful bright appearance."

Lambic was stronger than the low-alcohol beers of the day. Johnson wrote in 1895, "The spontaneous beer of which I spoke just now weighs generally about 1063, or as much as *Bass's Pale Ale* for export." Some evidence also points to faro once being a stronger beer than even records may show. A twentieth-century brewing text discussing faro stated, "Belgian beers are like those of France, rather vinous in nature, and are often known as a barley wine." Not surprisingly, then, faro became a rowdies' drink as well as the target of abuse, when beers brewed with Senne River water, where people discharged their waste, were blamed for several cholera epidemics. Faro was known as "the beer which is drunk twice."

The origin of gueuze dates back to the early nineteenth century, when the brewers of Brussels found a way to keep gas in casks and bottles of lambic by applying the *Méthode Champenoise*, the classic French method of Champagne production applied to many sparkling wines. After primary fermentation is complete, a sugar solution (*liquor de tirage*) is added to the unfiltered wine. The bottles are then stacked and allowed to referment (aging *sur lie*). After a period of at least one year, the bottles are put through an extensive series of tilts and turns, by which gravity conveys the sediment to the neck of the bottle (*remuage* or *riddling*). The wine is then chilled to around 38° F

(4° C) to minimize loss of carbon dioxide as the bottles are opened and the sediment removed (*disgorgement*).

Gueuze was very simply the blend of one- , two- , and three-year-old lambic. The fermentation of the sugars remaining in the young lambic over a period of roughly one year produced the high level of carbonation in a bottle or cask similar to that in Champagne. Gueuze differed from the traditional method of conditioning Champagne, as the yeast was left in the bottle or cask. Also, nothing other than 100% lambic—no sugar—went into a gueuze. There are a number of theories as to the origin of the term, but the most popular refers to the gas or carbonation in the cask (and eventually the bottle), which is why it obtained the term, "The Champagne of Brussels."

Documents attest to the import of gueuze to Constantinople in 1844. One of the first published mentions of gueuze was in A. Laurent's *Dictionnaire de la Brasserie* (Brussels, 1875). The people of Brussels happily consumed large quantities of gueuze at the Brussels International Exhibition in 1897. One hundred years ago, 90 to 95% of all lambic was sold straight, and gueuze was only a very small volume. It was quite customary in Brussels in the late 1800s to meet with friends after work over a glass of lambic or faro. Today, most people choose gueuze over a simple lambic.

Numerous cafés or pubs in Belgium and the United States routinely offer hundreds of beers to their customers. Historically, this was not the case. Many years ago, only the local products were available, and the beer selection was quite limited. Local fruits were sometimes added to local beers in order to make the beer lists a bit longer. Adding cherries was quite the rage to the north and west of Brussels at the end of the nineteenth century. Lambic fermented with whole cherries or raspberries, known as kriek lambic or framboise lambic, were still traditionally dry, as most of the sugars would have been fermented. To the south and east of Brussels, where lambic brewers of the day were still firmly entrenched in the valley of the Yssche River, they didn't add cherries or raspberries to their beer but rather grapes, which had been cultivated in the greenhouses of Hoeilaart, Huldenberg, and Overijse.

Fruit was commonly blended with lambic by the café owner, not the brewer, to create a different beer at each different café; a tradition that has sadly disappeared. Café keepers traditionally produced fruit beers, such as kriek, during the summer by adding cherries from their own gardens to a cask of lambic in their cellar. The resulting kriek was served for one to three weeks in October until the cask was empty. A kriek was traditionally produced in a very small volume, for variety, when the selection of beers was limited.

The concentration of fruit around Brussels was likely one key contributor to the success of spontaneous fermentation in that area. Wild yeast likes to inhabit the skins of fruit. (This is the reason the unpasteurized juice of apples or grapes will ferment without the addition of any yeast). The famous British brewery Marstons—which also once fermented in wooden casks—claimed its original yeast strain was found on the skin of an apple. While Brussels' famous Schaarbeek cherries are all but extinct, the buildings to the west of Brussels' historic center retain at least some of the age-old characteristics ideal for spontaneous fermentation.

Lambic producers occasionally brewed or purchased lagers or blonde ales for the purpose of diluting their lambics, perhaps to stretch a batch. Ale makers, likewise, used to buy lambic to blend with their ales to make a beer more tart, a desirable characteristic one hundred years ago. A blend of lambic and ale was meant to be something very balanced and consumed relatively quickly. Any longer than roughly three months, and the lambic would overpower the other beer. The blend was poured straight from a barrel; a bottle could become dangerous. Adding traditional lambic to a top- or bottom-fermented beer may result in enormous pressure once the wild yeasts of the lambic ferment the sugars in the ale.

THE BEERS OF FLANDERS

Blending was a common thread among wild brewers. Practitioners of spontaneous fermentation for centuries, the brewers of Flanders required new ways to cheaply produce beer with a popular tangy character. Blending provided the key, but opinions differ on the origin of the Flemish practice. As far back as the early 1700s, the British were blending old and new, mild and stale beer. The *London Chronicle's* Obadiah Poundage observed that Londoners could choose from heavy and sweet ale and more highly hopped beer. London's brown beers were becoming hoppier to compete with the burgeoning pale ale brewers of the day. The tradition grew of allowing beer to age to develop a tart, vinous quality commonly associated with a traditional Flemish oud bruin. This character was correctly attributed to *Brettanomyces*, commonly found in fully matured examples of both English and Flemish beers. Customers often preferred a blend of ale and beer.

The brewers of Flanders also blended young and aged beer. It is difficult to determine exactly on which side of the English Channel this tradition began. The people at the classic West Flanders brewery Rodenbach cite the similarity with the practice of blending in the United Kingdom, and ancestor Eugene Rodenbach was known to have studied brewing in England. Some people credit Rodenbach with bringing the method of tall wooden cask construction and accompanying fermentation process to Belgium around 1860. Says Michael Jackson, "Some people believe that Rodenbach's techniques of aging and blending were taken from the porter and stout brewers of Britain and Ireland. I think it was initially the Flemish who taught the islanders about such matters, although knowledge did begin to flow the other way after the Industrial Revolution." Wherever the tradition began, the English and Flemish traditions are inexorably linked.

Just as the British taste in ale for many centuries was for low-carbonated, cask-conditioned ales served directly from the barrel, so the typical beer for much of Flanders was for centuries a dark, sourish ale that had been aged in casks at the brewery. (Around Brussels, this same dry, tangy flavor came from lambic-based beers.) The problem was, fresh ale was cheap and commonplace, while aged beer was elusive and expensive. It is reasonable to assume, therefore, that a respectable use for aged beer was to mix it with new beer to reach a popular taste in a less cost-prohibitive manner.

During the time Rodenbach was in England, a pub owner could purchase fresh beer directly from the brewery. Traders commonly purchased beer, aged it for several years, and

Patron St. George has guarded the Rodenbach brewery for nearly two hundred years.

eventually sold it to a pub for about twice the price. The customer could ask the publican for a drink of cheap young ale, expensive old ale, or a blend of young and old. In Flanders, enterprising third parties also matured beer to sell to the publicans for blending with their own young beer.

In the early 1800s, London porter was commonly matured in large, oaken vats. Only about 10% was aged for two years and, according to Cornell, was "helped on its way to maturity with the addition of everything from returns to pubs of unsold brown stout to ullage from the bottom of the brewery vessels." (There are, coincidentally, some hints that the founder of the Belle-Vue lambic brewery-pub in Brussels was not well respected and produced his lambic with help from beer discarded from other breweries and returned from cafés.) The trend in

England toward larger and larger vats, each brewer attempting to outdo his competitors, swiftly ended in 1814, as a vat belonging to Henry Meux's brewery, filled with 3,550 barrels of aged porter, gave way, releasing a torrent of sour beer onto Tottenham Court Road.

The tradition of conserving (aging) beer to blend with young beer was common in Flanders in the 1800s. Beer may only have been stable for about two to three weeks before it went sour, so it had to blended and consumed quickly. This caused the limited supply of aged ale to be quite expensive. If a brewer could not age his own beer, he may have purchased it from another producer, such as Rodenbach, for blending with his own beer. The advent of modern brewery sanitation helped to produce beer of greater stability. While "cleaner" beer became more available, the people of Flanders still enjoyed the sourish taste, because it was more refreshing.

Adjuncts, primarily maize, were commonly used to produce traditional Flanders beers. The adjuncts were boiled in a separate kettle and added to the main mash as it reached saccharification temperature. A tax advantage promoted the use of adjunct grain. The Dutch law of 1822 that fixed a duty upon the capacity of the mash tun had one loophole. This law made a provision for raw grains not directly mashed with the malt in the tun, thus giving a financial advantage to the use of corn, oats, or wheat in a separate cereal cooker.

Attributing a separate style of beer to the provinces of East and West Flanders is a twentieth-century phenomenon. Once, the distinction between the red beers of West Flanders and the brown beers of East Flanders was not so well recognized. The river Schelde bisects the important East Flanders brewing town of Oudenaarde, a division of historic demarcation. Prior to the establishment of modern Belgium, the Germans and the French each had ownership of a part of the Flanders fields, with the Schelde being an early version of an uncrossable line. As modern fermentation practices became more prevalent, breweries on the west side of the river produced sourish ales, while those on the east side did not. Both by brewing culture and by geography, it should be obvious which country occupied which bank. This geographic division of beer production still holds true. The distinction between the beer of West and East Flanders truly diverged when brewers in the east began fermenting in stainless steel, while those in the west continued to age in wood.

TWENTIETH-CENTURY BLUES

Evidence indicates that spontaneous fermentation survived as far east of Brussels as Düsseldorf, Germany, until the early 1900s. Between Belgium and Germany lies the Dutch province of Limburg. The principal city of the province, Maastricht, was once known for a beer called *Mestreechs Aajt*. A relative of the Flanders red-brown, Mestreechs Aajt hit its height of popularity around 1900.

There was no artificial refrigeration during the late 1800s and early 1900s, so beer did not keep terribly well. Beer that was too old and could not be sold was put into open wooden vessels and experienced spontaneous fermentation for three and often up to twelve months. The aged beer was blended with newer beer, just as brewers and blenders were doing over the border in Belgium, and was becoming less popular across the channel in the United Kingdom.

In Holland, women and children commonly drank Mestreechs Aajt. A beer for the people, it was not so strong, perhaps 3% abv. Limburg once boasted about 1,600 breweries, although certainly not all produced this remnant of spontaneously fermented beers. The last brewery that made Mestreechs Aajt, the Marres brewery, stopped in 1940 during the early days of World War II.

Breweries in eastern Brabant (east of Brussels) once produced traditional white or wit beers by spontaneous fermentation. The wit beers could be quite sour, so fruit and herbs were often used in their production. The Peeterman beers of Louvain, similar to a wit, were produced from raw wheat, malted barley, and old hops (just like lambic), "yearlings or older." At the beginning of the twentieth century, the Peeterman and Louvain white beer, the latter produced with oats, both used a "special yeast" and had a method of reintroducing yeast to start

Mestreechs Aajt was the classic beer of Dutch Limburg at the turn of the twentieth century.

fermentation. They smelled strongly of ethyl butyrate (like pineapples), and that hydrogen gas escaping from the cask would flash blue if a flame was brought into contact.

The region east of Brussels appeared indicative of wild fermentation. Belgian brewers of the day knew that special yeasts could be obtained from "frontier towns" such as Maastricht, one of which fermented free maltose in twenty-four to forty-eight hours, and the second finished the attenuation in six to eight days and adhered to the sides of the barrels. A variety of solutions, including fruit, spice, and different yeasts, were sought to mask the sour character of many local beers.

The lambic of Brussels exhibited a different character than the top-fermented beer of the region, which went sour due to the contributions of uncontrolled bacteria that produced unpleasant amounts of acid. With the ability to age gracefully, lambic was highly sought after for more balanced and mellow

Cantillon is the only operating lambic brewery within the Brussels city limits.

flavors. The aging and blending of the darker Flanders beers, too, sought to balance the acidic character to more pleasant levels. Too much acid was never entirely desirable, though more so than it is today. Consider the sour character exhibited by many of the top-fermented beers if the lambic and Flanders beers of the day were more acidic than today's traditional descendants.

In spite of the emergence of German lager in Belgium during the 1860s, the brewers of Flanders and Brabant flourished at the onset of the twentieth century. Nearly every village had its own brewery, usually owned by the *major* of the village. The political opposition often set up a brewery to compete with that of the *major*. Some villages contained two competing breweries producing as many as ten different types of beer for a population often less than 500 people. In Flanders, the people drank dark, somewhat sour, blended top-fermented beers. Around Brussels, the people drank lambic and gueuze produced at roughly 3,000 breweries. Imports, however, had found their way into the Belgian cafés and were slowly eroding the market of the traditional products.

The two World Wars were not kind to the Belgian brewing industry. Many brewers were not allowed to brew, and equipment, particularly those articles made of copper, were taken for the German war effort. After the war, Brussels alone still had more than 50 lambic brewers and blenders, although the stock of gueuze on hand was depleted. Guinard describes the 1950s as "glorious times," for the lambic brewers, fathers and sons, often produced more than fifty batches a year.

From 1950 to 1980 roughly 70% of all breweries in Belgium closed. The increasing popularity of Pilsener beers, a lingering effect of the war, reduced demand for the traditional products of Flanders and Brussels. Producers that survived felt they must export their beers out of the region, and that meant sweetening the beer to meet a more generic taste and pasteurizing to aid in consistency when shipping. Lambic also was blended with mediocre Pilsener to lower production time and cost.

The 1960s saw the beginning of sweet lambic, gueuze, and fruit beers, not surprisingly preceded by the introduction of soft drinks into Europe in the 1950s. The top of the sugar run was in the 1970s and 1980s. Saccharin quickly became a popular alternative to sugar, as it is essentially unfermentable, even to wild yeast. Beginning with the 1970s, still spurred on by the postwar popularity of Pilsener, many of the remaining traditional brewers and blenders continued to disappear. Lambic was found only in and to the west of Brussels.

The memorial to many lambic brewers and blenders that closed during the 1980s and 1990s, outside the Oud Beersel brewery, also closed.

Flanders, too, felt the sting of the sweet tooth. Breweries closed, fewer and fewer examples of the traditional products were being produced, and less and less aged beer was being blended with young beer to make those that remained. There seemed little market for the traditional tangy, refreshing, even acidic character once found so desirable in Flanders and Brussels.

Since the end of the 1980s and beginning of the 1990s, however, some people have begun to come back to the traditional beers. Many producers in Flanders and the Payottenland create at least one and often more traditional beers of the region. There just needs to be a sizeable enough minority to support the traditional product. Traditional breweries continue to close, unfortunately, due to financial and personal difficulties. Producing traditional beers in the traditional manner requires time and money, although the resulting product is well worth the effort.

ACROSS THE POND

The United States had no wild beer culture for most of its history, the beer roots being English, German, and Czech. Much of America's beer culture was seriously compromised both during and after "The Great Experiment" of the total prohibition of alcoholic beverages from 1920 to 1933. U.S. craftbrewers gained a knack for adapting the beer styles of other countries and, in the process, rediscovered parts of their own beer culture that had been lost. Americans have come a long way in wild beer production since the first homebrewer took a beer that got infected and entered it in a competition as a lambic . . . and won!

American homebrewers first began working with cultures of wild yeast and bacteria sometime in the late 1980s. Beers of a lambic profile were the goal, and examples got progressively better—though far from perfect—as yeast suppliers became better versed in the handling of the appropriate microorganisms. Professional brewers eventually followed suit once brewers got over the phobia of allowing "that stuff" into the brewery.

Among the early commercial adopters of wild beer were the Cottonwood Brewery of Boone, North Carolina, and Joe's Brewery of Champaign, Illinois. Brewer John Isenhour gained a "cult status" for his production of beers with a lambic profile in the mid-1990s using wild yeast and bacteria that he kept active at various stages of the lambic fermentation cycle. John quite successfully marketed the "lambic" to his rather conservative clientele in this central Illinois college town as "Belgian lemonade."

The twenty-first century has brought everything from a growing selection of one-off brewery versions of a lambic to nearly full-scale Rodenbach-inspired wood-aged beers. A few adventurous brewers take wild yeast, bacteria, and fruit to create their own unique beers inspired only by the Belgian tradition.

Much of the history of wild beer has gone to the grave with our ancestral brewers. The Belgians did not start the tradition, but theirs is the richest and most firmly rooted in culture. While we can only hope the traditional producers in Belgium cease to dwindle in number, Americans are doing their best to continue the broad tradition of wild beers abroad.

three

Drinking Wild Beer

"If you do not enjoy my beer, then I say it is a pity for you!"
    –Armand DeBelder of the Brouwerij Drie Fonteinen

The traditional beers of Flanders and the Payottenland are unlike any on the planet. Each beer is more a product of the *terroir* of the brewery than simply the actual ingredients. Curiously enough, while most producers would share the details of their process, few would contribute specifics regarding the ingredients. While the nature of fermentation with wild yeast and bacteria, particularly spontaneous fermentation, remains much a "magical" process, the brewer directly controls (and guards) malt, hops, the gravity of the beer, and other related factors. I go into detail regarding potential ingredients and production methods and try to demystify fermentation in later chapters. In this chapter, I explore a number of interpretations of traditional and not-so-traditional styles.

The traditional styles mentioned in the first chapter are generalizations, while each product is a unique interpretation. You don't set out to reproduce a *Cantillon Gueuze* or a *Rodenbach*

Grand Cru as you would attempt to clone a popular India pale ale. You can attempt to slant the variables toward the profile of a particular beer and possibly produce something reminiscent, but in the end your beer will taste unique. *Vive la difference!* When New Belgium Brewing of Fort Collins, Colorado, began its program of barrel aging, it respected the Flanders tradition, but the goal was always to make a good, acidic beer pleasant to the brewer's palate. The result is something unique. The traditional beers of Flanders and the Senne Valley set standards to which other brewers can aspire, especially in the beginning. Producing a quality product out of style is difficult until you can produce one in style. American producers have followed this path, and several now produce very unique wild beers.

Belgium is filled with both small country pubs and trendy city center cafés that offer dozens of different beers. Small, local breweries once owned their own cafés or sold beer to those in the area. Today, many independent cafés have an exclusive arrangement with one of a few larger brewery groups. Those cafés carry that group's overall line, including a Pilsener, an abbey beer, etc. This tie makes local beers difficult to find even a moderate distance from the brewery. Surprisingly enough, a

LA FOLIE
Wood Aged Beer

1 PINT 9.4 FL. OZ. (750 ML)
6% ALC/VOL   4.8 ALC/WT
BREWED, AGED AND BOTTLED BY NEW BELGIUM BREWING COMPANY, INC. FORT COLLINS, COLORADO USA

number of wild Belgian beers are more readily available in parts of the United States than in their native land. One thing the Belgian and American examples have in common is that usually the best way to find them is to visit the respective brewery. First, I discuss some of the traditional Belgian brewers and their products, and then I move on to some new American interpretations. The path to understanding wild beers runs through the breweries of the people who create them. Their history covers several hundred years of brewing traditions within Flanders and around Brussels. The wild beers brewed in the United States illustrate just how much is possible with at least a little knowledge and a lot of enthusiasm. All of the wild beers produced in Belgium cannot possibly be covered. I mention the beers I find most representative of traditional characteristics and production methods. I feel all of the following beers are worth seeking out; many are world class and worth drinking again and again.

DRINKING IN FLANDERS

Part of the ancient kingdom of Flanders encompasses much of the northern portion of modern Belgium. Modern Flanders is divided into two provinces. East Flanders shares a border with the Netherlands to the north and meanders lazily eastward nearly to Brussels in the center of Belgium. West Flanders shares a common border with France to the south and contains the 65 kilometers of Belgian coastline along the English Channel to the northwest. The proximity of the United Kingdom to the west, across the Channel, speaks volumes about the similarities of drinking traditions between Flanders and eastern portions of England.

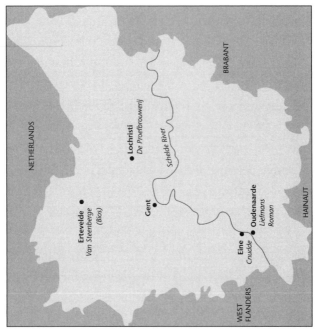

Wild Beer Producers of Belgian East Flanders
Brewery names in italic.

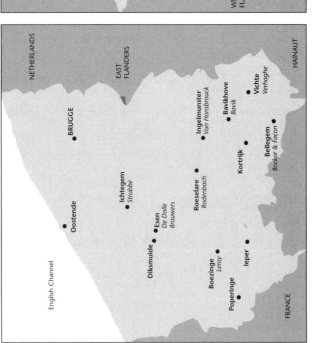

Wild Beer Producers of Belgian West Flanders
Brewery names in italic.

Just as the British taste in ale for many centuries was low-carbonated, cask-conditioned ales served directly from the barrel, the traditional beer of Flanders for centuries was a dark, sourish ale that had been aged in casks at the brewery. Brewers in both England and Flanders aged some of their beer for up to several years in barrels where resident microorganisms produced an acidic character. The taste for aged ale was both popular and expensive. Brewers discovered that this desirable taste could be achieved sufficiently by blending aged with newer beer. There are some breweries in Flanders (and in the United Kingdom) that still follow this tradition.

The most widely recognized example of the West Flanders red style comes from the **Brouwerij Rodenbach** in Roeselare, located almost in the center of the province, near many famous World War I battlefields. Alexander Rodenbach purchased what was in 1820 the St. George Brewery, the namesake of the patron saint of England. Successor Eugene Rodenbach studied brewing in England, and while no records suggest exactly where, only Suffolk's Greene King (not far from the Channel) still produces a beer in England by blending oak-aged and young beer (known as *Strong Suffolk*). The famous red beer is not one of many styles of beer produced at Rodenbach, it is the only type of beer they produce.

The legend of Rodenbach rises from room after room of ceiling-high oaken tuns, produced and maintained from wood of a specific forest by in-house coopers. The brewers at Rodenbach age a wort of 1.052 (13 °P) for eighteen to twenty-four months, until the brewers feel the contents of a particular barrel has achieved the proper character. A portion of the wood-aged beer is sold unblended (with a touch of sugar) as

Rodenbach Grand Cru (6% abv). A second wort of 1.044 (11 °P) is warm aged for four to eight months in stainless steel tanks to promote development of lactic acid. This will be blended with the aged beer and sold as *Rodenbach Klassiek* (4.6% abv). Rodenbach once used 33% of the aged beer to produce *Rodenbach Klassiek* (formerly *Rodenbach*), but this percentage has been lowered to 25%, resulting in a sweeter beer. The traditional kriek, *Rodenbach Alexander*, sadly was discontinued after the Palm Brewery Group purchased Rodenbach in 1998.

Moving southeast out of Roeselare, we head for the town of Bavikhove. You can't miss the turn; an old brew kettle sits in the middle of the roundabout, marking the exit. Adolphe De Brabandere, a farmer, started the **Brouwerij Bavik** in 1894, while his son, Josef, created the first brews. Until this time, the De Brabandere family concentrated on farming and, like many other families, brewed beer for their personal consumption. After World War II, Bavik expanded to produce a number of mainstream products, although it still dedicates a portion of the production to traditional methods.

Until the 1970s, Bavik purchased aged beer from Rodenbach to blend with its very sweet *Oud Bruin* to match the classic Flemish taste in beer. As the number of producers of the aged, acidic beers of Flanders dried up, Rodenbach was able to sell less and less beer in order to meet its own production demands. Finally, Bavik saw the need to purchase several oak tuns to age beer for itself. The brewers added "live" beer, such as gueuze, to "condition" the wood. The microorganisms in the gueuze took up residence in the new barrels and, over time, the barrels became quite suitable for the aging of beer in the Flanders tradition. Since the barrels are relatively new, beer may take up to three years to properly acidify.

Bavik actually ages a pale, relatively highly hopped wort (about 33 IBUs) brewed entirely of Pilsener malt in its barrels. The aged pale beer is blended with its sweet, top-fermented *Oud Bruin* to produce *Petrus Oud Bruin* (5.5% abv). Even blended, *Petrus Oud Bruin* is still more bitter than other Flanders beers while still displaying notes of oak and acidity associated with Flanders acid beers. The aged pale beer has seen only a limited release (in the United States) as *Petrus Aged Pale* (7.3% abv), with a more pronounced bitterness, oaky character, and a sharp, acidic bite in the finish. *Petrus Aged Pale* may have unintentionally begun a new "style," if there was such a thing in Flanders.

Proceeding even farther southeast, nearly to the East Flanders border, we search for a tiny place called Vichte. Down what resembles an alley, off of a side road, the most recent **Brouwerij Verhaeghe** has been in this location since 1880. The Verhaeghes have been farmhouse brewers since the 1500s, likely brewing for their personal consumption. The old brewhouse, coolship, and open fermenters stand as a testament to the history of Flemish brewing, although the accessibility is not for the faint of heart. The new brewhouse dates from the 1960s, although roughly a dozen oak tuns, standing in whatever space the buildings can spare, appear much older. The brewery remains a family-run operation; Karl Verhaeghe handles the business, while his brother takes care of the brewing chores.

Verhaeghe produces three products from wort aged in oak barrels, which appears lighter in the wood than the final burgundy color of the beers would suggest. *Duchesse De Bourgogne* (6.2% abv), a blend of young and aged wort, has a pleasant, acidic character balanced by a sweetness from the young beer and pasteurization. *Vichtenaar* (5% abv), essentially unblended though still reddish and fruity with a sharper lactic and acetic character, better exemplifies the traditional Flanders taste in beer. *Echte Kriek* (6.8% abv), the same base beer as *Vichtenaar* but fermented with cherries, has won numerous awards.

Two other breweries in this part of West Flanders producing wood-aged, soured, blended beers are **Brouwerij Bockor** of Bellegem and the rather commercial **Brouwerij-Brasserie Van Honsebrouck** of Ingelmunster. These two breweries both produce a form of lambic in West Flanders. Bockor and Van Honsebrouck each keep their production methods rather secretive, although rumor has it one brewery uses an oaken coolship that was "inoculated" with lambic beer and both use wooden barrels for aging and souring. The resulting beer from the barrels is almost exclusively released as sweetened, pasteurized fruit beers by each brewery. The exception, Van Honsebrouck's dominantly lactic *St. Louis Gueuze Fond Tradition*, does not use the traditional appellation. These two breweries also make a beer in the Flanders tradition, Van Honsebrouck the caramelly, tart *Bacchus* (4.5% abv), Bockor the tart, fruity, *Bellegems Bruin* (5.5% abv). Both breweries use a portion of wood-aged "lambic" beer to produce the final blends.

Heading back northwest, in the direction of the English Channel, one remaining West Flanders brewer deserves attention. The brewery of **De Dolle Brouwers** (The Mad Brewers), in Esen, dates back to 1835 and looks at least that old. Artist and historian Kris Herteleer purchased the antique brewhouse around 1980 rather than see it decay and be demolished. Kris' beers were never what would be popularly considered the current "Flanders style." He has a number of completely different beers that all developed sourness and acidity over time due to a mixed culture of yeast obtained from Rodenbach. Shortly after Palm purchased the famous Roeselare brewery, the supply of yeast was discontinued, resulting in "cleaner" beers from De Dolle. A new yeast culture that would return the wild character is rumored to be in the works.

Following in the Flanders tradition, Kris purchased a number of Bordeaux and Calvados barrels to mature his beers. The first was the amber, massively fruity, and oaky, *Stille Nacht Reserva* (12% abv)—the highest in alcohol of the wild beers in Belgium. The second, *Oerbier Special Reserva* (12% abv), is darker, more vinous, cidery, and dry in the finish. The beers aging in the barrels all taste very different, even if from an identical wort, and often have one dominant characteristic. The taste of a beer from one barrel may be predominately oaky, while another

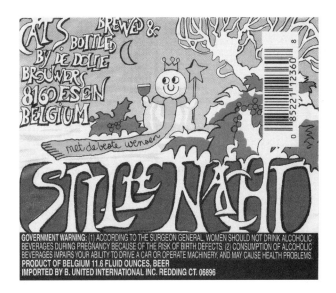

may be fruity. New releases continue to reflect the depth resulting from blending beers with differing characteristics.

According to Filip Devolder, brewery manager at **Brouwerij Liefmans**, in 1939 there were reportedly eight breweries in East Flanders making the "style" of beer called oud bruin. Today, the last brewery commonly associated with the East Flanders tradition is Liefmans of Oudenaarde, not quite half the distance from Roeselare to Brussels. The Liefmans brewery is on the former German-controlled side, when the Schelde divided German territory from that of France, but started in the center of Oudenaarde in 1679 and moved to a new home on the east bank in 1930. The more easterly and more stoic **Brouwerij Roman** also follows the French/German geographic tradition and never produced sourish, aged, blended ales.

When Riva purchased the Liefmans brewery in the early nineties it moved production to its plant in Dentergem. If you took one look at the old Liefmans brewhouse, you would understand exactly why. In addition to a kettle that required five to six hours to achieve the effect of a standard boil, the mash tuns are characteristic of the smaller vessels of the 1800s. (It's a shame Riva doesn't see fit to hold an open house, perhaps once a year, with the old system being fired up.) Riva did decide that the Liefmans beers would not achieve the same character in Dentergem—although contamination of the primary yeast was also a concern—so it still open ferments and ages the beers in Oudenaarde.

The example best associated with an East Flanders brown is *Liefmans Goudenband* (8% abv) (pronounced who-den-bond), billed as a provision beer for "lying down" in the cellar. The depth of *Goudenband* lies in the complex layers of malt, fruitiness, and alcohol, derived from the blending of different ages of a single dark wort matured in stainless steel tanks. Aged in stainless steel, *Goudenband* exhibits a predominantly lactic tartness. Riva raised the alcohol of *Goudenband* from the traditional 5.2% abv after purchasing Liefmans in 1992. The lower alcohol content once put *Goudenband* more in line with its West Flanders counterparts and a role as an everyday "session" beer.

The old brewhouse at Liefmans of Oudenaarde once caused many brewers to be late for dinner.

Riva maintains a proprietary yeast culture that originally came from Rodenbach (my, that yeast got around!). *Goudenband* was formerly the base of the *Liefmans Kreik, Liefmans Framboise*, and other fruit beers, but not any longer, as the refermentation of the fruit in the tanks produced a beer too high in alcohol.

Liefmans makes a product that never leaves the town—and might not leave the brewery—called *Odnar* (4.2% abv). Unblended, only minimally sweetened, drier, and more lactic than *Goudenband*, *Odnar* better reflects the traditional oud bruin as a session beer. An obscure beer, if you ask a local where to find *Odnar* he may look at you with amazement, especially if you are standing in the Oudenaarde town square. The local pronunciation of *Odnar* falls close to that of its traditional home. The beer actually called *Liefmans Oud Bruin* (5% abv)— the new base for *Liefmans Kreik* and *Liefmans Framboise*—is slightly stronger and much sweeter. Well, what's in a name?

The beer truly exemplifying the traditionally local nature of all Flanders beers hails from the **Brouwerij Cnudde** (pronounced "ka-nude-eh"), a short hop north of Oudenaarde in Eine (pronounced "a-nay"), and run by three brothers. Their one beer, only available at pubs (and a barber shop) within the town, simply goes by the name of the brewery. *Cnudde* is aged in large, uncoated metal tanks and has a claret color, a faint tart character, and a refreshing dryness. Made with 100% pale malt, Cnudde derives color from two shades of syrupy brewers' sugar. *Cnudde* really doesn't fit a style; it just is. Once a year, the family blends beer with cherries from their own trees and ages it in the brewery cellar in small, plastic vessels. The resulting kriek ages from tart and fruity to near portlike. Intended only for family and friends, the kriek is not for sale.

Three beers produced in West Flanders appear to typify the current characteristics and production methods of the eastern beers: *Facon Ouden Bruin*, *Paulus*, and *Ichtegem's Oud Bruin*.

The family-owned **Brouwerij Facon** has been in Bellegem since 1874. *Facon Ouden Bruin* (4.8% abv), a blend of young and aged beers not matured in wood, tastes somewhat sweet with a pleasant acidity. The **Brouwerij Leroy** of Boezinge produces a fruity, sourish example—the color resembling *Cnudde—*

Pieter Cnudde adds dark sugar to the kettle on one of six yearly brew days at his brewery in Eine.

known as *Paulus* (6% abv). Fermented with a proprietary yeast culture, *Paulus* is aged "for years" in metal tanks. A very odd version comes from the **Brouwerij Strubbe** in Ichtegem, founded in 1830. *Ichtegem's Oud Bruin* (5.5% abv), open-aged in metal vessels for eighteen months, is brewed with licorice root and aged hops.

Brouwerij Van Steenberge (also know as Bios) north of Ghent, in Ertevelde, produces the sweet and somewhat lactic *Vlaamse Bourgogne*, a blend of young and aged beers, the latter from uncoated iron tanks. The grandfather of owner/biologist Paul von Steenberge, a microbiologist, isolated a culture still in use today at this 200-year-old brewery.

The brewery that ties Belgium together, or perhaps rewrites the story, is **De Proefbrouwerij**, east of Ghent in Lochristi. Often cited as being responsible for many familiar beers produced in Belgium both prior to and after the founding of his own brewery in 1996, brewmaster Dirk Naudts formerly brewed at the Roman brewery in Oudenaarde. De Proef may best be described as a Flemish "pilot plant." Naudts creates, brews, and analyzes different beers for many Belgian and international brewers. Naudts' willingness to experiment with cultures of wild yeast, a subject almost taboo throughout Belgium, further separates De Proef from other Belgian breweries.

Naudts' first wild yeast brew was *Reinaert Flemish Wild Ale* (9% abv), a spicy, fruity ale with a mild *Brettanomyces* character and the light malt of a *tripel*. That release spawned an entirely new series of beers known as *Flemish Primitive*, all fermented with strains of *Brettanomyces* and different varieties of hops. Another taste of delicious sacrilege, *Zoetzuur Flemish Reserve*, is Naudts' take on a Flanders red beer. Produced without the benefit of blending beer aged in wizened wooden tuns, *Zoetzuur Flemish Reserve* develops a tart, fruity character in stainless steel tanks. Naudt uses wild yeast and bacteria, American Tomahawk hops, and a bit of sour black cherry juice to produce the brew.

DRINKING IN THE PAYOTTENLAND AND BRUSSELS

Prior to the official founding of the city in 1229 by Henri I, Duke of Brabant, beer was already being produced in Brussels. For centuries, Brussels maintained a tradition of high fashion, good food . . . and good beer. To the west, in Flemish Brabant, lies the Payottenland—flat farmland with a few gently rolling

The author relaxes for a moment near the river Senne, southwest of Brussels.

hills that historically provided food and drink for the citizens of Brussels. Formerly the main waterway in and out of Brussels, today the Senne River meanders through the occasional farm and alongside busy highways in the Payottenland, only to be forced underground as it reaches its ancient destination. Only within a roughly five-hundred-square-kilometer radius in the "valley" of this tiny river, from Lembeek in the south to Brussels in the east to Kobbegem in the north, is lambic still consistently produced, as it has been for centuries. The traditions of lambic and gueuze are still lovingly practiced in the Senne Valley region by eleven producers and an equally small number of classic cafés.

Lambic occasionally may be found on draft, and less frequently in bottles throughout the region. Gueuze is far more common, although some traditional products can be difficult to find, even in the ancestral homeland. Lambic seldom travels far from the point of origin around the Senne. To sample this most ancient beverage, young and old, in the most idyllic of settings, you must journey to the source.

Lambic was once an economic decision. Many people preferred beer on draft. Serving lambic straight from the cask was far simpler and more cost-effective than blending gueuze. Today, local tastes drive the availability of draft lambic. Do the people prefer young or old lambic or simply gueuze? Some people enjoy the slight sweetness of very young (*goenk*) lambic, others the mature character of old (*vieux*) lambic without the filling carbonation of gueuze.

Only when the brewing season starts will there be young lambic. Old lambic may be available after blending: perhaps one barrel hasn't been totally emptied. Young lambic is often served

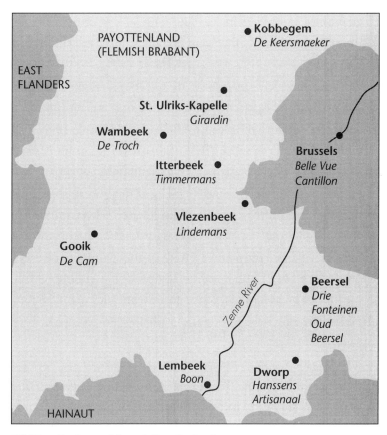

Wild Beer Producers of Brussels/Payottenland
Brewery names in italic.

on the English system (handpump) and must be consumed quickly once prepared for serving, or it will become oxidized. Generally bottled, old lambic may be aged further. Some brewers serve young lambic using a "bag in a box product" or old lambic in stainless steel with an inert gas to reduce the risk of oxidization.

Unlike lambic, some form of traditional gueuze can be found all over the world. I've had a bottle of *Cantillon Gueuze* as far away as Tokyo, while dining in an indoor scale replica of Brussels' famous Grand Place. Historically, independent blenders—often café owners—purchased lambic of one to two days old from different brewers and aged the beer in their own barrels for the purpose of blending gueuze. The lambic of a number of different brewers was sought to provide the greatest variety of flavors. Given the scarcity of independent blenders, only three brewers still provide lambic for blending: Boon, Girardin, and Lindemans. Since so few lambics are available, the blenders purchase and blend with the lambic of all three breweries.

Today, the original producers of the lambic blend most of the gueuze in Belgium. The brewer ages, blends, packages, and sells his own gueuze to cafés, wholesalers, and importers. While several blenders still exist, they no longer blend gueuze to sell in their own cafés. Nine brewers and two blenders can be found during a journey that crosses the length and breadth of the Payottenland and finishes close to the historic center of Brussels.

In Lembeek, the southerly cradle of lambic production, is the **Brouwerij Boon**. Evidence of a brewery at this site can be traced back to 1680, when J. B. Claes bought a farm to double as a brewery. Frank Boon began blending in 1975 and in 1978 took over for blender Rene De Vits, who had blended in nearby Halle since 1927. Boon opened the current brewery on this historic site in Lembeek in 1986, and it has grown into a large operation that still produces a number of traditional products now distributed by the Palm Brewery Group.

One of only three still available to gueuze blenders, the Boon lambic generally exhibits more bitterness than other lambics. Most of the Boon lambic eventually becomes gueuze but, primarily as a gesture to the local area, is available on draft in a couple of cafés. The gueuze, *Oude Geuze Boon* (6.5% abv) exhibits a spicy character with a dry, bitter finish. *Oude Kriek Boon* (6.5% abv) combines the characteristic dryness with an intense fruity character. *Oude Geuze Boon Mariage Parfait* (8% abv) displays the considerable depth of old lambic, but perhaps due to the higher gravity, could benefit from additional aging.

Northeast of Lembeek lies the town of Dworp, home to one of two remaining lambic blenders, **Hanssens Artisanaal**. The

Bottles of gueuze and kriek and traditional stone pitchers at Hanssens Artisanaal in Dworp.

Mayor of Dworp, Bartholome Hanssens, originally founded Hanssens Artisanaal in 1896 as the St. Antonius Brewery. During World War I, German soldiers stole the brewing copper, so the site became used instead for the blending of gueuze. Jean Hanssens retired in 1997, leaving the duties to his daughter, Sidy, and her husband, John Matthys, with the stipulation that they keep their primary jobs and only blend as a hobby. John and Sidy blend gueuze with the lambic of Boon, Girardin, and Lindemans, aged in their own barrels. *Hanssens Artisanaal Oude Gueuze* (6% abv) maintains an aggressive acidic character through a dry, tart finish. *Hanssens Artisanaal Oude Kriek* (6% abv) develops additional acidity from blending with cherries. John and Sidy also blend a strawberry lambic called *Oudbeitje* (6% abv); not a blend steeped in history but, nonetheless, one that uses the traditional methods. A blend of young lambic and whole strawberries matures for one year before being bottled. A delayed secondary fermentation occurs in the bottle due to absence of fermentable sugars from young lambic, so *Oudbeitje* is virtually uncarbonated unless further aged. Unlike cherries or raspberries, the strawberry lends a very subtle character and no color. You will be hard-pressed to find the horsy, modestly acidic straight lambic, even locally.

Henri Vandervelden was part of a third generation of lambic brewers from the town of Beersel, due north of Dworp. Vandervelden's **Brouwerij Oud Beersel** dated from 1882 until its unfortunate closure in 2003. Economics played a role, as well as family issues; Vandervelden and nephew Danny Draps brewed only two or three times a year. Gone with the brewery is an adjoining lambic café of historic proportions where a tannic, bitter, refreshing eight-month-old lambic was served on draft. A memorial to some of the most recent brewers and blenders to close, not including Oud Beersel, remains in front of the former café. Hops aged from only one to two years, along with the English infusion mashing system, were used to produce the Oud Beersel lambic. Still available commercially, *Oud Beersel Oude Geuze* contains layers of fruits with a modest hop character; likewise, fruitiness rather than acidity contributes to the profile of *Oud Beersel Oude Kriek*.

Gaston DeBelder took over the **Drie Fonteinen** café of Beersel in 1953 from Jean-Baptiste Denaeyer, the mayor and considered the best gueuze blender of the town. Founded in 1887, the café was seat to famous Flemish writers such as Herman Teirlinck and the literary and artistic group *de Mizjol*. Drie Fonteinen, originally located around the corner at the now shuttered Drie Bonnen café, moved to the Beersel town square

The Oud Beersel lambic brewery in Beersel, now closed.

in 1961. DeBelder's sons, Armand and Guido, took over operation of the café in 1982. Armand and his father blended together until the late 1990s, and in 1999, Armand opened on the site the first new lambic brewery in eighty years. While Armand still blends gueuze with lambics other than his own, Drie Fonteinen is slowly becoming a larger portion of each blend. The brewery is now run as a separate business with the products still prominently featured at the Drie Fonteinen café, where Armand developed a number of the sumptuous traditional Flemish dishes.

The *Drie Fonteinen Lambic*, served in the café from English handpumps, is generally refined and fairly mature, while the kriek lambic may exhibit some touches of sweetness. Faro may be found on draft with sugar added to old lambic of indeterminate age. The *Drie Fonteinen Oude Gueuze* (6.5% abv) bursts with flavors of citrus and oak, Armand's favorite characteristics in a gueuze. The rare *Schaarbeekse Kriek* (6% abv), produced with the near-extinct Schaarbeek cherries, lends an unequalled explosion of cherry flavor; surpassing the dry, tart *Drie Fonteinen Oude Kriek* (6% abv).

Armand's approach to gueuze is best summed up as uncompromising. He has gone to great lengths and outlays of cash to produce what he considers a superior gueuze. Peer into Armand's barrel stores, and you will find them spotless and temperature controlled, conditions once considered impractical and cost-prohibitive to lambic brewers or blenders. Absent is an acetic or "barnyard" character many people associate with gueuze, replaced by the oak and citrus Armand relates to a fine wine. All gueuze drinkers do not favor this subtlety among gueuze, but if you do not like it, I refer you to the quote at the beginning of this chapter.

Armand and brewer Marc Limet of the **Brouwerij Kerkom** in Kerkom-St. Truiden revisited the tradition of blending top-fermented ale with lambic in 2003. Limet produced a blend called *Reuss*, part Drie Fonteinen lambic and part *Bink Blond*. If you are near St. Truiden in August, you may be fortunate enough to catch *Reuss*, produced for consumption during an annual summer festival. Quite volatile, the blend of lambic and top-fermented beer will not last very long, three months at the longest.

Traveling west, one passes through St. Pieters-Leeuw, home to the café of former gueuze blender Herberg Moriau. (The café of a blender often simply went by the name of the blender.) On the outskirts of town is the industrial Belle-Vue brewery, owned by InBev, where the production of its commercial gueuze and kriek has been consolidated. A destination of far more consequence to the traditional lambic and gueuze drinker lies farther west, in the town of Gooik.

The first new gueuze blender in forty years opened shop in Gooik in 1997. **De Cam** was the realization of a dream for Willem van Herreweghen, the brewing director of Palm, whose father Hubert was a respected writer/lecturer on gueuze. Van Herreweghen, however, eventually found his position at Palm quite demanding and sought out a successor, which he found in brewing student Karel Goddeau. Goddeau fulfilled his final student project—to brew lambic and top-fermented beers in the same brewery—at Drie Fonteinen. In turn, Armand DeBelder taught Goddeau something of blending before he agreed to blend the gueuze and kriek at De Cam. The similarities between DeBelder and Goddeau include the use of Pilsner Urquell barrels and the production of a characteristically soft gueuze. Goddeau also brews top-fermented beers up the road at **Slaghmuylder**. Blending gueuze for a living sadly does not pay the bills.

Goddeau, like Hanssens, blends with lambic primarily from Boon, Girardin, and Lindemans. Once a year he brews lambic at Drie Fonteinen to age in his barrels. One of only two blenders or brewers to regularly bottle an old lambic (the other being Cantillon), the five-year-old *De Cam Oude*

The doors to De Cam, the newest gueuze blender.

Lambiek (5% abv) is intensely dry and woody. *De Cam Oude Geuze* (6.5% abv) displays a spicy character with a dry woody finish. Past vintages of *De Cam Oude Kriek* (6.5% abv) were comparatively sweet, while later releases have become pleasantly tart and dry. A kriek produced with Schaarbeek cherries, grown in the backyard of Goddeau's parents, should be released in 2005.

Having strayed far enough from the mighty Senne, we venture northeast to the town of Vlezenbeek, where brewing was first documented at the **Lindemans** farmhouse in 1809. In 1890, the family brewed only to keep everyone working during the winter months, but by 1930, brewing was so successful the Lindemanses gave up farming wheat and barley to concentrate on the production of lambic beers. Lindemans is another of the three lambics sold to blenders and generally considered quite fruity. If fortunate, you may find the draft lambic at a neighboring café or two. The sweetened gueuze and fruit lambics are found all over the world. Patriarch René Lindemans first blended the current traditional gueuze, *Lindemans Gueuze Cuvée René* (5% abv), in the early 1990s, reportedly under pressure from the U.S. importer. *Cuvée René* has a powerful citrus character with an expressive bitterness and dry finish.

Continuing north, pay respects to two lambic breweries whose doors were closed in the 1990s: De Neve in Dilbeek and the beautiful "brewery on the hill," Eylenbosch in Schepdaal. Very near is the **Timmermans** brewery, purchased by Franz Timmermans from Paul Walravens in 1911, though founded as early as 1781. The John Smith beverage distribution group bought the Timmermans brewery in 1993. Timmermans produces many sweetened products; the one close to traditional is

The famous brewery on the hill, now a vacant warehouse in Schepdaal.

Timmermans Gueuze Caveau (5.5% abv), a filtered gueuze with some tart character. *Timmermans* draft lambic may occasionally be available at a local café.

De Troch, in nearby Wambeek, is often considered the oldest of the surviving lambic breweries. Pieter De Troch first owned a brewery on the site sometime in the eighteenth century, and a land use plan from the nineteenth century mentions a brewery owned by Petronnella De Troch. Jos Raes, youngest of the four sons of Raymond and Magdalena De Troch, took over the family tradition in 1974 and ran the brewery until 2003, when son Pauwel took over the reins. De Troch produces a wide range of sweetened products often blended with some very odd fruits under the *Chapeau* label. The mellow, fruity, faintly sour *Cuvée Chapeau Oude Gueuze* (5.5% abv) is the one traditional product, making appearances only in the local market.

The **Girardin** farmhouse brewery may be one of the most splendid sites in the Payottenland, the copper kettles rising across the fields, animals grazing nearby, as you make your approach on a small side road. The brewery and farm in St. Ulriks-Kapelle has been family owned and operated since 1882 when founded by Francis Alexis Girardin. A classic farmhouse of the day, the Girardins grew wheat and barley, used both to brew and feed the animals. Francis and son Jean Baptiste both served as mayor of St. Ulriks-Kapelle.

Louis Girardin took over the brewery in 1962. In deference to the commercialization of the industry, he was quoted as saying, "The goal is not to expand, but just to stay alive." Beer was sold in the true farmhouse manner—just enough to support the family. Louis produced the beer, while his sons, Paul and Jan, would make deliveries each weekend to local cafés. As a small concession to modern technology, Louis installed a second-hand German brew kettle and Italian bottling line. Paul, Jan, and mother Jacqueline continue the family tradition.

Armand DeBelder called the Girardin brewery, "The *Château d'Yquem* of lambic breweries in Belgium." The Girardin lambic is highly sought after by gueuze blenders, who consider it to have the greatest "lasting properties" of the three available. Available on draft both "jong" and "oud," Girardin also blends a rare kriek lambic, in season. Blending their own gueuze is still a fairly recent undertaking for the Girardin family but necessary with the decline in the number of blenders. *Girardin*

Gueuze 1882 (5% abv) simply bursts with traditional character but is rumored to leave the brewery comparatively young so may benefit from additional aging. The gueuze may be exported to the United States on occasions when Paul Girardin believes he has enough to share.

The farthest north of the lambic breweries, **Mort Subite**, formerly known as De Keersmaeker, lies in the largely inaccessible village of Kobbegem. Written records place a brewery on this site as early as 1686 and in the hands of Jean-Baptist De Keersmaeker in 1869, although it was not solely a lambic brewery until André De Keersmaeker went in this direction beginning in 1965. In 1970, De Keersmaeker made an arrangement with the famous café La Cour Royale in Brussels, owned by the gueuze blender Theophile Vossen. That café would eventually become the famous Mort Subite, named after the "sudden death" finish of a local dice game (*Pitjesbak*). Since the year 2000, the brewery

Gueuze and kriek have only been exclusively produced at Mort Subite in Kobbegem since 1965.

has been owned by Alken-Maes, Belgium's second-largest brewer. Paul De Keersmaeker still brewed until his departure in 2001, turning over full responsibility to longtime brewer Bruno Reinders.

One trip to the cellar, and you will know Reinders' heart lies with the traditional products. You will not find the unblended lambic in any cafés, although Reinders sells to locals who show up with a "can"—"five liters, ten liters, no problem." The *Mort Subite Oude Gueuze* (7.2% abv)—soft, balanced, acidic, and bitter with notes of wood—finally uses the *"oude"* appellation. Mort Subite has a wonderfully dry, tart kriek in the tanks that sadly never sees the Belgian sun in "natural" form; every drop is sweetened prior to release.

Only two remain of more than fifty lambic brewers and blenders operating in Brussels after World War II: the **Cantillon Brasserie** and **Brasserie Belle-Vue**. Philémon Vanden Stock began blending gueuze in Brussels in 1913. He acquired the brewery-pub Belle-Vue in Mollenbeek-St. Jean in 1927. The brewery overlooks the Brussels-Charleroi Canal, which I once mistook for the Senne, thinking someone had forgot to brick it over this far from the center of Brussels.

The Belle-Vue brewery, now owned by InBev (formerly InterBrew), was responsible for successfully marketing gueuze beyond the region, and in the process made it a filtered, sweetened, mass-market product. The barrels are chestnut, as opposed to oak, and they yield some excellent lambic, but all of the Belle-Vue products are now produced at the plant in St. Pieters-Leeuw. The one traditional product from the historic home of the largest producer of beer called lambic in the world, *Belle-Vue Selection Lambic* (5.2% abv), is an aggressive yet balanced gueuze with a very dry finish. Sadly, the most recent vintage of this product appeared in 1999.

Near to the historic center of Brussels lies the Cantillon brewery, founded in 1900 by gueuze blender Paul Cantillon. Traditional lambic has been produced on this site since 1937, with a detour in the 1970s when it temporarily fell victim to the trend toward sweeter gueuze. Since that time, Jean-Pierre and son Jean Van Roy have religiously guided the brewery down the path of tradition. They produce a wide variety of traditional products and promote the brewery as a living museum to the glory of gueuze.

Cantillon produces a bottled lambic—the only other brewery besides De Cam—called *Grand Cru.* Produced from an exemplary batch of three-year-old lambic, *Broucsella* (5% abv) is fruity, sharp, dry, and characteristically uncarbonated, although I have

seen it develop carbonation if aged for a period of time. *Cantillon Lambic* and *Faro*, usually made from one-and-a-half-year-old lambic, are available on draft at the brewery and often at a select few Brussels cafés.

Cantillon Gueuze (5% abv) has long been the most acidic of gueuzes, intensely tart and refreshing with a dry, tannic finish. *Cantillon Kriek* (5% abv) and *Rosé de Gambrinus* (5% abv) gain additional flavors from the fruit, the kriek sharp and horsy, the framboise vibrant and acetic. All three products have mellowed somewhat in recent years. Cantillon produces other special gueuzes, including *Loerik* (5% abv)—literally "Lazy Boy"—that refermented more slowly in the bottle, producing a soft, well-rounded character, and *Cuvée des Champions* (5% abv), a gueuze dry-hopped in the cask!

Cantillon produces a number of other lambic beers, including *St. Lamvinus* (5% abv) and *Vigneronne* (6% abv), blended with varieties of grapes, *Foú Fovne* (5% abv), blended with apricots, and the *Lou Pepe* (5% abv) series consisting of a gueuze, kriek, and framboise. Blends of the same two-year-old batches of lambic from different casks, Jean considers his special beers gueuzes because they are refermented in the bottle. Candi sugar provides a source of refermentation that still produces natural carbonation. Young lambic has not diluted the concentration of fruit and old lambic in the blend. Carbonation may be low in young vintages, so it is best to heed the brewer and age the bottles before drinking.

Cantillon produces the one spontaneously fermented beer in Belgium that is not a lambic. *Iris* (5% abv) is a beer produced with only malted barley—no wheat—50% old hops and 50% fresh hops at the end of the boil. Dry-hopped with fresh Styrian Goldings after two years, *Iris* contains two distinct tastes, the acidic and the bitter in this "special *cuvée.*" More than any other, *Iris* begins to bridge the gap between the Belgian and American interpretations. Instead of being bound by tradition, the Van Roys strive to produce new products with traditional character.

DRINKING IN EUROPE AND THE UNITED KINGDOM

Much of the rest of Europe shuns wild beers.[1] Three places where the Belgian traditions do shine, however, are secretly tucked away within the Netherlands, United Kingdom, and Italy.

The **Gulpener Bierbrouwerij** in the Dutch city of Gulpen, nestled between Belgium and Germany, brought back the style of beer known as *Mestreechs Aajt* in the 1980s. Popular at the turn of the nineteenth century, *Mestreechs Aajt* finally died out during World War Two. Inspired by the reds and gueuzes of Belgium, Gulpener sought assistance from the people who operated Rodenbach. A moderately dark wort is spontaneously fermented in wooden barrels in a closed room in the nearby De Zwarte Ruiter pub—well away from the brewhouse—for between eleven and thirteen months.

To produce *Mestreechs Aajt* (3.5% abv), the spontaneously fermented beer is blended with two other beers: a sweet, low-alcohol brown beer called *Oud Bruin*, and a lightly hopped pale beer called *Dort* (6.5% abv). The spontaneously fermented beer, referred to generically as *oerbier*, tastes quite tart in its raw form, while the principal blending beer, the *Oud Bruin*, tastes very full-bodied and sweet. The *Oud Bruin* gets an almost cloying sweetness from the addition of saccharin. *Oerbier* from multiple barrels constitutes 25% of the final product. *Mestreechs Aajt* has a sour-sweet,

---

[1] I have not forgotten Berliner weisse and *gose*, produced in the eastern part of Germany, but those styles are beyond the scope of this Belgian-inspired book.

slightly acidic character typical of some West Flanders beers. "The taste is so strange that there is very little market in Holland," says brewery director Paul Rutten. "It is for tradition and promotion."

Mestreechs Aajt (5% abv) was first shipped to the United States in 2004. America, however, has a negative view of saccharin not shared by Europe. We also tend to expect our specialty beers to be reasonably high in alcohol. To remedy these issues, the U.S. version of *Mestreechs Aajt* was blended without artificially sweetening the *Oud Bruin*, leaving a higher alcohol content. This lightened the body, brought the acidic character more to the forefront, and left a drier finish. Sadly, Gulpener stopped producing *Mestreechs Aajt* in 2005, due to problems with the barrels.

Snuggled comfortably in the center of England, the present **Melbourn Brothers Brewery** in Lincolnshire dates back to 1825, when it began life as the All Saints Brewery. Herbert Wells

The author and friends in the courtyard of the Melbourn Brothers Brewery in England. Note the room near the smokestack, where the coolship is located.

Melbourn purchased the brewery in 1869, and in the next one hundred and fifty years it suffered two fires and two resulting closures. The old brewing equipment was restored in the late 1990s, when Samuel Smith's Old Brewery purchased the venerable tower brewery. The new owner decided the old tower brewery would be used to make spontaneously fermented fruit beers. Lincolnshire has a moderate climate that is favorable for growing fruit. The wild yeast present on the skins of fruit may have been one factor that made it attractive to practice spontaneous fermentation at this location.

Melbourn Brothers Brewery has a coolship surrounded by louvered panels, like many of the lambic breweries in Belgium, that allows the wort to be exposed to wild yeast and bacteria in the air. Lambic was, and is, periodically splashed onto the exposed wood surrounding the coolship to encourage beer-souring microorganisms to become resident in the coolship room. The wort is fermented for one-and-a-half to three years in fiberglass tanks previously used to ferment port or in plastic-lined wooden barrels. Oak chips soaked in beer and exposed to the air to promote inoculation by wild yeast and bacteria may be added to a tank, if the brewer believes fermentation is not progressing in a satisfactory manner.

Melbourn Brothers produces an apricot, a strawberry, and a cherry beer (3.4% abv). Two- to three-year-old hops are added to wort composed of roughly 85% malted barley and 15% torrefied wheat. Whole fruit is also added to the kettle and boiled with the wort. At bottling time, fruit juice increases the appropriate fruit character and color. All three beers are pasteurized and fairly sweet, with the appropriate fruit character and an acidic background lending a fairly dry finish.

Spontaneous fermentation outside of Belgium makes the Melbourn Brothers beers intriguing.

Closer to the English Channel, in historic Bury St. Edmunds, lies the **Greene King** brewery. The Greene and King families founded this brewery in 1887, although records show a brewery on that site since at least 1700. The Greene King of the late twentieth and twenty-first centuries is a regional brewer and pub company. In the mid-1800s it was one of many small breweries practicing the methods of aging and blending beer in tall wooden tuns. *Strong Suffolk Vintage Ale* remains the only example of that practice still produced in England.

Strong Suffolk Vintage Ale is a blend of two ales: *Old 5X* and *BPA*. *Old 5X* matures in 100-barrel oak barrels for at least two years, where it reaches an alcohol content of around 12% abv. Reddish, vinous, and acidic, *Old 5X* (12% abv) is reminiscent of an unblended Flemish beer. Sadly, it is seldom seen in that form. *Old 5X* is almost exclusively blended with *BPA*, a dark, sweet, freshly brewed beer. Dark ruby in color and fruity, *Strong Suffolk Vintage Ale* (6% abv) has more tannic and oaky character than most Flanders red beers.

The **Panil** brewery in Torrechiara (Parma), Italy, founded by Doctor Renzo Losi, first brewed in 2000. Given the Italian love of wine, perhaps a wood-aged red beer makes perfect sense. Not surprisingly, Losi also feels an appreciation for Belgian beers. *Panil Barriquée* (8% abv) experiences three fermentations: fifteen days in a stainless steel tank, ninety days in cognac and Bordeaux barrels, and thirty days in the bottle. *Panil Barriquée* is fruity, vinous, and intensely woody.

DRINKING IN THE STATES

While Belgium is a small country, the United States is not. Breweries making types of wild beers stretch from sea to shining sea. Lest you get the impression of a secret underground society of wild beer producers hundreds of members strong, let me qualify that last statement by saying that the United States has fewer producers than Belgium has within its considerably tighter borders.

Many unique beers are produced in Belgium by some very obscure breweries. At first glance, some breweries in the United States may appear unlikely producers of wild ales, but many secrets often lie within both fashionable metropolitan brewpubs and colorful rural microbreweries. You won't find any of these products available far from the brewery of origin. They are almost always available in bottles and often only at the brewery.

On the East Coast, and receiving many accolades, is **Dogfish Head Brewing** of Milton, Delaware. This brewery began life as a brewpub in the Atlantic oceanside town of Rehoboth Beach in June 1995, before opening as a microbrewery in nearby Lewes and moving to the current location in 2002. Founder Sam Calagione has always ventured more than a branch off the mainstream and has attributed Dogfish Head's propensity for unusual beers to the desire to drink something interesting during the rigorous brewing schedule on the original 12-gallon system.

Dogfish Head's *Festina Lente* (7% abv) can be loosely described as "a peach neo-lambic." A pale beer fermented an additional three months on oak chips with *Brettanomyces* and whole, stoned, unsterilized Delaware peaches containing an indeterminate amount of wild yeast, *Festina Lente* has a spritzy acidity, distinct peach flavor, and late tartness.

Nestled in the vacationland of New York City dwellers, the **Southampton Publick House** lies near the tip of Long Island.

Brewer and author Phil Markowski has consistently experimented with producing unique beers since the brewpub's inception in 1996. Markowski has produced characteristically tart and acidic Flanders red ales, oud bruins, and lambics using both stainless steel and wooden barrels and finds, quite naturally, the best results come when using wood. Phil feels the typical characteristics of *Brettanomyces* better develop with the use of wood.

The **Iron Hill Restaurant and Brewery** was founded in Newark, Delaware, in 1996 and quickly expanded into two additional locations in Pennsylvania. Brewing director Mark Edelson, having a homebrewer's background, has always enjoyed producing unique beers. Mark periodically creates lambics both with and without fruit. The lambics begin life in a stainless steel tank with a blend of yeast and bacteria, just to make certain they are active, before finishing in wooden barrels.

New Glarus Brewing Company is located in a small, picturesque Swiss village near Madison, Wisconsin. From the inception of the brewery in 1993, Dan Carey stated he would brew some type of sourish Belgian-style beer. He did not disappoint with the production of *Wisconsin Belgian Red* (5.1% abv), produced with Door County cherries and a portion of beer aged in oaken barrels. This ruby red beer offers an intense cherry character but only modest acidity. *Raspberry Tart* (4% abv) matures for one year in oak vats with fresh Oregon raspberries, where wild yeast on the skins is allowed to referment the sugars from the fruit. A more recent brew is *New Glarus Brown Ale*, aged in wood, including used port barrels.

At the foothills of the Rocky Mountains, about an hour north of Denver, is Fort Collins, Colorado, home to **New Belgium Brewing Company**. The brewery was opened by

husband and wife Jeff Lebesch and Kim Jordan in their base-
ment in June 1991. Two brewhouses later, their monument to
the mix of American and Belgian culture, including hand-painted,
ceramic cartoon tiles surrounding each brew kettle, and a brewery
powered largely by wind, is a mecca for beer lovers both here and
abroad. Lebesch and Jordan were already quite successful when
they hired former Rodenbach brewer Peter Bouckaert to oversee
the brewing operations.

Among Bouckaert's numerous contributions was the inception of Flanders-style aging for beer in large, wooden barrels. *La
Folie* (6% abv), which means "a folly" or more loosely "a business

*In Colorado fields, between the bicycles, New Belgium marks its place in the brew-
ing world.*

endeavor on which you will lose money," is a blend of several barrels. *La Folie* features a balanced acidity and lactic dryness missing from many of the sweetened, pasteurized examples currently produced in Belgium. *La Folie* may be pale or dark, depending on Bouckaert's current projects (or moods). One of them is *Biere de Mars* (6.2% abv), an ever-changing light, fruity ale that gradually includes more and more *Brettanomyces*. Another is *Transatlantique Kriek* (6.2% abv), blended from *New Belgium Golden Ale* and kriek lambic from Frank Boon. *Transatlantique Kriek* has a tart character filled with cherry flavor followed by a sweet finish.

The **Bristol Brewing Company** in Colorado Springs opened in June 1994 in the shadow of Pikes Peak. Brewer Jason Yester and microbiologist Ken Andrews have taken the concept of lambic one step closer to its roots. They have isolated three strains of wild yeast and three strains of lactic acid bacteria from the local sources, including North Cheyenne Canyon, found on the skin of raspberries. Andrews produced a "local cocktail" of yeast and bacteria to inoculate both used wine and whiskey barrels.

Bristol produces six to eight different beers best described as a "skull and bones series of local lambic styles," including an oud bruin, Flanders red, aged pale, strong ale, grand cru, sour wheat, aged IPA, and special *cuvée*. Wort fermented with *Saccharomyces* is added to oak barrels, which originally took two to three years to produce excellent beers. One long-term wish is to open a new brewhouse and dedicate the current one to the production of aged, wild beers.

A bistro in Austin, Texas, known as the **Bitter End**, has been an unexpected bastion of wild ales for many years. The Bitter

End has produced the dry and acidic *Lip Burner Lamb-Beak* as well as the equally acidic and fruity *Sour Prick*, both roughly in the lambic-style and both Great American Beer Festival winners.

Russian River Brewing Company was originally a part of the Korbel Champagne Cellars in the historic Russian River valley in Guerneville, California. Korbel lost interest in producing beer and in 2002 sold the name to head brewer Vinnie Cilurzo. He moved the brewery to the current location in Santa Rosa, which opened in the spring of 2004. Cilurzo's close ties to the wine industry drove him to the use of wine barrels for aging beer and fermentation with the wild yeast *Brettanomyces*. The aging cellar is proudly visible from the bar, much to the chagrin of local winemakers, who seem to live in fear of spreading *Brettanomyces* in their wineries. To reduce this risk, Vinnie has offered to allow visiting vintners to burn their clothes upon leaving the brew-pub.[2]

The line of Belgian-inspired beers available from Russian River Brewing includes *Temptation, Supplication, Depuration,* and *Sanctification,* at least for starters. *Temptation* (8.5% abv)—a Belgian golden ale aged in French oak white wine barrels—was inoculated with *Brettanomyces* after primary fermentation and added to barrels that had previously been used to ferment Chardonnay. *Supplication* (6% abv) is amber beer aged in Pinot Noir barrels with cherries and a number of wort-souring microorganisms, while *Depuration* is a similar beer aged with Muscat grapes. *Sanctification* (6.5% abv) Belgian blonde ale was fermented entirely with three different strains of *Brettanomyces* in stainless steel. As you would expect, all four beers exhibit

[2]*Brettanomyces* is important to the wine industry. Some winemakers appreciate the character that subtle amounts can impart, while others live in fear of infection.

unique characteristics dependent both upon the relevant microorganisms and upon the barrels in which they were aged.

The Pacific oceanside town of Solana Beach, California, just north of San Diego, might remind you more of the north shore of Oahu than of Belgium. **Pizza Port** was established here in 1987 as a simple pizza parlor, but a 7-barrel brewhouse was installed in 1992 and head brewer Tomme Arthur hired a few years later. Rather than be constrained by style—or anything, for that matter—Arthur chooses to develop entirely new tastes in beer.

Perhaps Arthur's greatest triumph is *Cuvée de Tomme*. The base wort is the dark and chewy *Mother of All Beers* (11% abv), a Belgian *"quadrupel"* aged in used bourbon barrels with cherries and wild yeast and bacteria. Vintages vary in tartness, acidity, cherry flavor, oak, and bourbon character.

Arthur's newest creation, produced in collaboration with Peter Bouckaert of New Belgium Brewing, is *Mo Betta Bretta* (6.5% abv)– a beer of 100% Pilsener malt fermented entirely with one species of *Brettanomyces*. *Mo Betta Bretta* exhibits few of the traditional esters or acidity commonly expected from *Brettanomyces*. Instead, this pale, modestly hopped beer projects an extremely fruity, pineapple character.

Along with Brian Hunt of Moonlight Brewing Company in Windsor, California, Arthur's latest project delves into the world of spontaneous fermentation. Literally a "farmhouse brewery," north of San Francisco, Arthur and Hunt hope to discover firsthand the results of spontaneous fermentation in the United States.

four

Beer-Souring Microorganisms

"Nothing essentially Belgian about it—Brettanomyces *occurs naturally around the world."*

—Tomme Arthur of Pizza Port, Solana Beach

Four dominant types of microorganisms commonly ferment and acidify wild beers: *Brettanomyces, Lactobacillus, Pediococcus,* and *Saccharomyces.* Several other important players also merit a mention, including *Acetobacter, Enterobacter,* and various oxidative yeasts. A wide variety of different strains of *Saccharomyces cerevisiae* ferment beer, and they all have different requirements and characteristics. This same fact applies to wild yeast and bacteria.

Different strains of wild yeast have different environmental and nutritional requirements and produce different by-products. There are not one or two varieties of beer-souring microorganisms but dozens and sometime hundreds of different strains. Scientists have isolated more than two hundred different organisms at work in the fermentation of lambic. Many of the same microorganisms are responsible for the fermentation of Flanders red-brown beers.

Only a few strains have been readily available to the brewer as pure cultures, but additional strains now exist in the United States (see Appendix). Let's be perfectly clear—beer-souring microorganisms are feared contaminants in most places that carry out alcoholic fermentation. Once they take up residence in a brewery or cellar, they can be virtually impossible to eliminate. But don't fear, spontaneous fermentation and top fermentation can successfully be carried out in the same brewhouse. Foresight, care, and common sense must be exercised to avoid contamination. Isolate equipment used with beer-souring microorganisms from your other brewing equipment. Thoroughly clean and disinfect everything with which they come into contact. Just to be safe, anything porous should be reused only to produce wild beer or discarded. Once bacteria infect a porous item, such as a gasket, they cannot effectively be removed.

I will take a closer look at the lead roles and some of the supporting cast responsible for wild fermentation before delving into some specifics about differing methods of wort production and fermentation, and how they affect these microorganisms, in the next chapters. First, some background on the by-products of beer-souring microorganisms that contribute the bulk of wild beer character.

ACIDS AND ESTERS

The characteristics of many beers primarily originate from hops and malt. By contrast, fermentation products, primarily acids, define the flavor and aroma of wild beers. This is true both due to the attributes of the acids and to the esters derived from the acids and alcohol. Sour flavors and tart, pungent aromas come from acids, while fruity aromas and flavors originate from esters.

The microorganisms found in wild beer produce both acids and alcohol.[1] The acids most important to wild beers include lactic and acetic acid. Acetic acid, present in copious amounts in vinegar, is sharp, pungent, and greatly increases the perception of sourness. Lactic acid, found in spoiled milk, is less objectionable and contributes a "tangy" character, sometime perceived as "sweet" by brewers in contrast to the other acids.

Wild beer commonly contains a number of other acids, desirable only in modest amounts, as their characteristics can be quite dominant. Three of these acids, from a class called fatty acids, include caproic (hexanoic), capric (decanoic), and caprylic (octanoic) and share a characteristic described as "goaty" or "zoolike." Still other fatty acids are objectionable in all but trace amounts, including butyric and isobutyric acids, lending a "rancid" or "sweaty" character. The human palate can recognize lactic acid at 400 parts per million and acetic acid at 175 ppm, while butyric acid requires only 4 ppm to be noticeable in a beer.

The character of a wild beer will be determined both by the blend of acids and by the total acidity. The total acidity, determined by either pH or TA[2], represents the "amount" of acid present in the beer. Acid increases the perceived sourness of a beer and is objectionable in higher quantities. The ratio of the

---

[1] Bacteria excrete by-products during growth and reproduction; yeasts generate by-products during alcoholic fermentation.

[2] The acidity of a beer is often measured using two methods. The pH (potential hydrogen) level indicates the "concentration of the acidity" or "relative acidity"; the TA (titratable acidity) measures the quantity of the acids. The pH is expressed in numeric values of 1 to 14—a pH of 7 is neutral (the value of pure water at 77° F (25° C); lower values are more acidic, higher values are considered base. TA (titratable acidity) identifies what amount of a base solution to add to arrive at the neutral pH of 7.

different types of acids present, distinguished by the human palate, also determines the character of the beer. Lactic acid, considered desirable when dominant in a reasonable concentration, lends a balancing character to other, sharper acids. Alcohol (ethanol) will commonly add a pleasant warming sensation, as well as enhance flavor and add to the perception of sweetness, smoothness, and body of a beer. Additionally, beers of a higher alcohol content have a longer shelf life. Ester production requires the presence of both an acid and alcohol. Esterification only occurs when yeast provide enzymes (esterases) to act as a catalyst in the presence of acids and alcohol.

The esters ethyl lactate and ethyl acetate largely contribute the aroma of wild beers, derived from the respective acids. Ethyl acetate becomes less fruity and more solventlike—resembling nail polish remover—as the concentration increases. Ethyl lactate provides a softer, balancing, tart, fruity character. The esters ethyl caproate (hexanoate), ethyl caprate (decanoate), ethyl caprylate (octanoate), ethyl butyrate, and ethyl isobutyrate also derive from alcohol and the respective acid, and may contribute a distinctive, overpowering fruity character in all but modest quantities. The human palate can detect ethyl butyrate at the minuscule level of 0.2 ppm; conversely, ethyl lactate requires a concentration of roughly 60 ppm.

A concise description of common characteristics of the acids and esters important to wild beers, plus a comparison of the alcohol and total acidity of selected alcoholic beverages, can be found in the following tables.

Characteristics of Acids and Esters Commonly Found in Wild Beers

Acid	Character	Ester	Character
Acetic	Sour, Pungent	Ethyl Acetate	Sharp, Musty, Fruity, Pineapple, Black Currant, Apple, Solvent, Nail Polish
Lactic	Tart, Tangy, Sour	Ethyl Lactate	Soft, Tart, Fruity, Buttery, Butterscotch
Caproic	Goaty, Sweaty, Fatty, Zoolike	Ethyl Caproate	Waxy, Fatty, Fruity, Pineapple, Green Banana
Capric	Soapy	Ethyl Caprate	Waxy, Oily, Fruity, Apple, Grape, Brandy
Caprylic	Goaty, Fatty, Zoolike	Ethyl Caprylate	Waxy, Wine, Floral, Fruity, Pineapple, Apricot, Banana, Pear, Brandy
Butyric	Rubber, Rancid,	Ethyl Butyrate	Fruity, Juicy Fruit®, Pineapple, Cognac
		Cheesy, Fatty	
Isobutyric	Rancid, Sweaty, Cheesy, Fatty	Ethyl Isobutyrate	Citrus, Fruity
Isovaleric Acid	Rancid, Cheesy, Horsy	Ethyl Isovalerate	Fruity, Sweet, Apple, Pineapple, Tutti Frutti
N/A		4-ethyl-phenol*	Band-Aid®, Antiseptic, Stable, Barnyard
N/A		4-ethyl-guaiacol*	Smoky, Spicy, Clove

*Actually a volatile phenol

Comparison of Alcohol and Acidity of Selected Alcoholic Beverages

Beverage	% abv	pH	Total Acid (as Tartaric, % weight)
Leinenkugel Original	4.7	4.1	-
Mort Subite Pêche	4.3	3.6	0.7
Kriek de Ranke	7.0	3.5	0.7
Preston Merlot, 2000	13.5	3.5	0.6
Cantillon Iris	5.0	3.4	1.4
Petrus Aged Pale	7.3	3.4	1.0
Lindemans Cuvée René 1993	5.0	3.3	1.0
Drie Fonteinen Gueuze (2002)	6.5	3.3	0.9
Verhaeghe Duchesse de Bourgogne	6.2	3.1	1.5
Rodenbach Grand Cru	6.5	3.1	1.1
New Belgium La Folie	6.0	3.1	-
Landskroon Chardonnay, 2003	13.0	3.0	0.7
Hanssens Oudbeitje	6.0	2.8	1.5

Reprinted by permission of Raj B. Apte

ACETOBACTER

Acetobacter species, including *A. aceti* and *Gluconobacter oxydans* (formerly *A. suboxydans*), are responsible for the production of vinegar, oxidizing ethanol to acetic acid. *Acetobacter* sp. can destroy beer or wine they infect by producing excessive amounts of acetic acid or the derived ester, ethyl acetate, both of which can render a beverage unpalatable. A sharp, sour acid (some acids are softer), acetic acid is palatable only in low to moderate quantities in wild beers. *Acetobacter* sp. largely contribute the acidic bite to the flavor profile of Flanders red beers, play a smaller role in the lambic profile, and are generally not evident in Flanders browns.

Many beer-souring microorganisms find the introduction of oxygen or the production of alcohol during fermentation detrimental to their viability. *Acetobacter* sp. require oxygen to convert alcohol to acetic acid. Commonly airborne, *Acetobacter* sp. will infect alcoholic beverages anywhere in the world. A good example is the common smell of an unclean bar. *Acetobacter* sp. may produce a type of viscosity resembling an oily or moldy film (pellicle) on the top of wort. *Acetobacter* sp. can reproduce at alarming rates in fermenting beer exposed to oxygen for a lengthy period of time; conversely, the bacteria cannot grow without oxygen.

BRETTANOMYCES

Around 1904, N. Hjelte Claussen, laboratory director for the Carlsberg brewery in Denmark, discovered a microorganism that caused a slow, secondary fermenta-

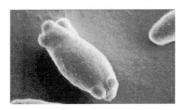

Brettanomyces

tion in English stock ales. Claussen named it *Brettanomyces*, literally meaning "British brewing industry fungus."

Extremely important to wild beer production, *Brettanomyces* contribute to the character of lambic, Flanders red ales, and beers that defy style, including newer American beer varieties fermented with only *Brettanomyces*. Winemakers differ on whether *Brettanomyces* are friend or foe. Some winemakers consider *Brettanomyces* an important part of their wine, while others consider it a spoilage organism, contributing only off-flavors. *Brettanomyces* are, nevertheless, virtually unavoidable and considered very typical in some older wineries. For example, *Brettanomyces* largely contribute the well-known character of *Château de Beaucastel*, a Chateâuneuf-du-Pape.

The five currently recognized species of *Brettanomyces* include (with several synonyms): *B. anomalus* (*B. claussenii*), *B. bruxellensis* (*B. abstinens, B. custersii, B. intermedius, B. lambicus*), *B. custersianus, B. naardensis*, and *B. nanus*. Many different strains of each species exist within the genus *Brettanomyces*. The strains available from yeast suppliers such as Wyeast Laboratories or White Labs often use a synonym to distinguish each individual product, like a nickname.

The name *Dekkera* is often used interchangeably with *Brettanomyces*. Actually of the same genus, *Dekkera* refers to the spore-forming (sporogenous) type of the yeast, which exhibits moldlike characteristics, while *Brettanomyces* produce no spores, a characteristic of yeast. The importance of this designation lies in the speed of reproduction. If it grows fast, it isn't *Dekkera*. Unfortunately, the identification between *Brettanomyces/Dekkera* is seldom clear when obtaining a particular strain.

The species of primary importance to the wild brewer is *B. bruxellensis*. Strains of this species produce much of the "wild" character found in lambic, including the classic "horsy" and "pie cherry" character. *B. bruxellensis* often refers to a strain obtained within Brussels, *B. lambicus* to strains cultured in the Payottenland. Individual strains all exhibit different characteristics. Lambic brewers consider strains of *Brettanomyces* to be unique to each brewery, just as the different *Saccharomyces* available today were once isolated from their brewery of origin.

A much lesser-known species, strains of *B. anomalus* have been isolated from several different types of beer. Strains labeled *B. claussenii* have been attributed to the "winelike" character often found in British old ales. Strains labeled simply *B. anomalus* have found favor with brewers in the United States for rapid fermentation and ester production. The practice of identifying different strains with common synonyms often makes it difficult for the layperson to identify a particular beastie. Base the choice of *Brettanomyces* on fermentation characteristics. How will the strain be used, how does it behave, and what will it produce in wort? The complexity of traditional wild beers will benefit from the use of multiple strains.

Brettanomyces are superattenuating yeasts. They will continue to slowly consume sugars—even dextrins that are unfermentable to *Saccharomyces*—for many years. The behavior of superattenuation is attributed to, in part, the ability of beta-Glucosidase inherent in *Brettanomyces* to break down starch and dextrins and liberate glucose. Many scientists consider the presence of *Pediococcus* important to achieve the high level of attenuation of Flanders red ales and the nearly 100% attenuation found in lambic. Most but not quite all of the sugars in a beer containing *Brettanomyces* can be fermented, given the proper time and conditions. *Brettanomyces* require a minimal concentration of sugar to survive so will never consume absolutely all of the available wort sugars.

Brettanomyces classically ferment best in worts with a lower pH (after primary fermentation has begun) with or without the presence of oxygen but, unlike *Saccharomyces*, prefer aerobic conditions. *Brettanomyces* will cease to reproduce below a pH of about 3.4. Important by-products of *Brettanomyces* fermentation include esterases, acids, esters, volatile phenols, and tetrahydropyridines. *Brettanomyces* produce both lactic and acetic acid, the latter only under aerobic conditions. *Brettanomyces* esterases will synthesize the esters ethyl acetate and ethyl lactate from alcohol and acetic and lactic acid, and hydrolyze any isoamyl acetate produced by *Saccharomyces* during fermentation into an acid and alcohol. *Brettanomyces* may produce, in various quantities, any of the acids and esters mentioned in the table found earlier in this chapter. In particular, winemakers consider the volatile phenols 4-ethyl phenol and 4-ethyl guaiacol indicative of *Brettanomyces* growth.

A particular off-character known as "mousy," "mouse taint," or "horsy" may appear in wine and beer "infected" with *Brettanomyces* (although this character may also be attributed to certain species of heterofermentative *Lactobacilli*). Tetrahydropyridines produced by *Brettanomyces* (and *Lactobacillus*) in the presence of lysine and ethanol[3] contribute a character described in smaller concentrations as "bready, popcorn, or cracker" but in larger concentrations as "a most disgusting smell reminiscent of mouse urine or acetamide" or sometimes "wet horse." Some brewers feel production of enough of the compounds leading to this "mousiness" may be strain dependent.

---

[3] Both lysine and ethanol are commonly found in wort once fermentation is under way.

Brettanomyces exhibit the odd propensity to form a pellicle—an often thick, lumpy white coating—on the top of liquid during fermentation.[4] The yeast cells form chains that can float on the top of wort, making use of atmospheric oxygen, characterizing *Brettanomyces* as an oxidative yeast. The pellicle will form in the fermenting vessel or even in a bottle if the *Brettanomyces* sp. still have a source of sugar to ferment. The pellicle helps to guard against oxidation during a long fermentation process, as well as against unwanted mold and *Acetobacteria*, so should be left intact.

Experts continue to debate exactly how *Brettanomyces* become established; none are precisely certain. *Brettanomyces* commonly reside on the skins of fruit. The cherry orchards surrounding Brussels served as a home to *Brettanomyces,* until the orchards' demise in the latter portion of the twentieth century. Commonly found in the grape orchards and soil of long-established French wineries, *Brettanomyces* are spread by equipment, barrels, and personnel. *Brettanomyces* may become airborne, and there have been suggestions that the fruit fly may be able to promote the spread. Once in the brewery, exposed wood, including floors, beams, tiles, and especially barrels provide an ideal environment for growth.

Brettanomyces favor cellobiose, a carbohydrate that occurs as a result of the firing process that cooperages use to toast barrels. *Brettanomyces* produce the enzyme beta-Glucosidase, which allows them to feed and grow by breaking down glucose from cellobiose. In a study conducted by a number of California wineries in the early 1990s, new barrels that came into contact with only sterile wine still experienced growth of *Brettanomyces,* thus

---

[4]*Brettanomyces* and the pellicle are known collectively to winemakers as a Flor—"Flower"— "a type of yeast that is able to float on the surface of a wine, while growing and fermenting.

demonstrating favorable conditions without exposure to infected wine or barrels. No such growth occurred in stainless steel tanks. A tour of the Lindemans brewery provided a firsthand experience with this wild yeast. Customary jars of ingredients found during most brewery tours, including jars of malt and hops, were supplemented by one marked *Brettanomyces.* I joked the jar was empty and was subsequently urged to refill the jar . . . by opening it and scooping some out of the air!

ENTEROBACTER

Enterobacter (sometimes called Proteolytic bacteria), including the genera *Citrobacter, Enterobacter, Escherichia, Klebsiella,* and *Hafnia,* produce the flavor compounds traditionally present in young (one- to two-month-old) lambic. Most species of *Enterobacter* ferment glucose into acetic and lactic acid and produce ethyl acetate and other by-products such as dimethyl sulfide. Some will ferment lactose, produce carbon dioxide, and grow in the presence of oxygen. *Enterobacter* produce many of the flavor and aroma compounds often considered unfavorable in lambic, including vegetal, smoky, moldy, and the ever-popular baby diaper. (One lambic producer asked me, "In America, do you really drink something that smells that way?") In a successful fermentation, these by-products will hopefully not be so evident, and some lambic producers seek to arrest this phase altogether.

Enterobacter can pose health risks to humans (*E. coli, Salmonella*), but no pathogenic bacteria affect lambic or survive to see the final product. Susceptible to both rising levels of acidity and alcohol, *Enterobacter* survive for a relatively short time during lambic fermentation, ceasing to reproduce at a pH of 4.3. While many of the contributions of these bacteria to the final product are considered undesirable, *Enterobacter* are quite natural and were historically accepted by many practitioners of spontaneous fermentation.

LACTOBACILLUS

Lactobacillus plays a major role in the fermentation of Flanders beers and a minimal one (at best) in lambic. A facultative anaerobe, *Lactobacillus* can ferment both in the presence or

absence of oxygen but prefers reduced levels. By the name it should be easy to determine that *Lactobacillus* sp. produce lactic acid, a less objectionable acid than acetic responsible for some of the pleasant tang found in most wild beers. Pure

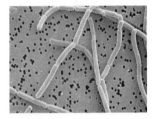

Lactobacillus

lactic acid has little aroma of its own, although accompanying by-products of fermentation help to contribute a tart, tangy character. The ester ethyl lactate, catalyzed from lactic acid, contributes additional tart, fruity aromas.

Lactobacillus delbrueckii, one of the most common species available to U.S. brewers, was discovered by one of the founding fathers of microbiology, Max Delbrück. Homofermentative, *L. delbrueckii* produces one product (lactic acid) from one substrate (glucose). *L. delbrueckii* produces only lactic acid (as well as carbon dioxide) as a by-product of fermentation.

Different heterofermentative species, such as *Lactobacillus brevis*,[5] will produce several compounds from one substrate.

[5] "*L. brevis* is an obligate heterofermentative bacterium. It is one of the best-studied beer spoilage bacterium and grows optimally at 30 °C and pH 4 to 6 and is generally resistant to hop compounds. It is physiologically versatile and can cause various problems in beer such as superattenuation, due to the ability to ferment dextrins and starch." *Professor Kanta Sakamoto from his work on L. brevis.*

Heterofermentative species may "bacteriologically" produce acids such as acetic, isovaleric, and isobutyric commonly attributed to *Brettanomyces*, plus diacetyl, sometimes above the palate threshold of humans. Tetrahydropyridines, contributing a "mousy" character, also may be synthesized by heterofermentative *Lactobacilli* in the presence of lysine and ethanol.

Like most bacteria, *Lactobacillus* prefers higher temperatures, much higher than normally employed for beer fermentation and aging. *Lactobacillus* finds 98° F (37° C), the temperature of the human intestines, ideal for growth. With enough of a food source and heat, *Lactobacillus* sp. will grow quite rapidly. In the presence of other organisms, or after primary fermentation is complete, growth occurs considerably more slowly. High levels of alcohol and lactic acid can destroy *Lactobacillus*. Even though the microorganism produces lactic acid, *Lactobacillus* will cease to reproduce at a ph of around 3.8.

Like most gram-positive[6] bacteria, the presence of certain hop acids retards the growth of most *Lactobacillus* sp., although this character is strain dependent. Many strains of *L. delbrueckii* shiver at the site of a hop cone, while those of *L. brevis* may be favored or feared for their resistance to hop acids. Sensitive to alcohol formation, as the concentration increases *Lactobacillus* will die. Alcohol and hop acids help to keep lactic acid production in check in lambic and Flanders beers.

OXIDATIVE YEAST

Yeast of the genera *Candida*, *Cryptococcus*, *Hansenula*, *Kloeckera*, and *Pichia* can produce copious amounts of acetic acid when

---

[6]Gram-positive bacteria are characterized by a blue-violet color reaction to the gram-staining procedure, because most cell walls contain peptidoglycan. Gram-negative bacteria reflect the counterstain, because the cell wall is low in peptidoglycan (and high in lipid content), so the primary blue-violet color escapes from the cell.

exposed to oxygen. Oxidative yeasts will float on the surface of beer, along with *Brettanomyces* (also an oxidative yeast), having formed a similar series of chains. Considered spoilage organisms to wine, many species of oxidative yeast grow naturally on the skins of fruits such as grapes. Naturally, therefore, these oxidative yeasts commonly occur in lambic, given the use of old wine barrels in lambic fermentation and the former growth of grapes to the east of Brussels. *Kloeckera apiculata* is of particular interest to the lambic brewer. It will ferment glucose but not maltose, impart some highly volatile fruity, floral esters, and secrete proteases into the wort that can break down proteins. Generally, oxidative yeasts have minimal contributions to the flavor and aroma of lambic unless the wort becomes exposed to oxygen.

PEDIOCOCCUS

Responsible for the bulk of lactic acid production in lambic, *Pediococcus* shares that responsibility with *Lactobacillus* in Flanders beers. *Pediococcus* ferments glucose into lactic acid but, unlike *Lactobacillus*, produces no carbon dioxide. A homofermentative bacterium, *Pediococcus* does not produce tetrahydropyridines or

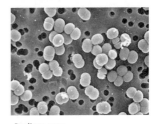

Pediococcus

other acids during fermentation but produces diacetyl at levels well above the palate threshold of most humans. Any diacetyl produced generally (and hopefully!) breaks down during the fermentation of wild beers. A somewhat hop-resilient gram-positive bacterium, *Pediococcus* still adversely reacts to rising levels of alcohol.

Pediococcus is microaerophilic—it ferments poorly if at all in the presence of oxygen. Frequently called a fastidious organism,

Pediococcus grows rather slowly, if at all. It grows to low concentrations, even in lambic. Higher concentrations of *Pediococcus* can easily produce such high amounts of lactic acid as to make a beer unpalatable. *Pediococcus* produces a layer on the top of wort resembling long elastic threads best described as ropy and a hazy viscosity, a bit like oil. This harmless yet unappealing slime, composed of carbohydrates, acids, and proteins, plays an important part in the fermentation cycle of the lambic. The esterase of growing cells of *Brettanomyces* may break down (hydrolyze) this slime.

Pediococcus damnosus, sometimes known as *Pediococcus cerevisiae,* is a specific lactic acid-producing organism found in the fermentation of lambic and Flanders beers. A particular species identified in Rodenbach, *P. parvulus,* can begin to reproduce at a higher pH and function at a lower temperature than *P. damnosus. Pediococcus* cease to reproduce at around 3.4. Aggressive lactic acid producers with somewhat greater tolerance to hops than many *Lactobacillus* sp., *Pediococcus* can be employed in any beer where high levels of lactic acid are desired.

SACCHAROMYCES

Literally "sugar fungus," species of the yeast used to ferment beer still play a role in wild beer production. Despite all of the different microorganisms present in wild beers, *Saccharomyces cerevisiae* still ferment most of the available wort sugars, including maltose, glucose, and maltotriose, into alcohol. In addition to *Saccharomyces cerevisiae,* another member of the species, *Saccharomyces bayanus* (sometimes

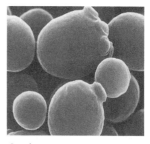

Saccharomyces

called *Saccharomyces globosus*), occur naturally in lambic fermentation. Often used by vintners to make sparkling wines, *S. bayanus* can tolerate alcohol concentrations of up to 18% abv and will restart stuck fermentations. Also a *Saccharomyces* sp., sherry yeast exhibit very high alcohol tolerance and, similar to *Brettanomyces*, may survive in the walls of a barrel.

A number of factors influence the growth of beer-souring microorganisms, including alcohol, acid production, hop acids, oxygen, the presence of starch in the wort, and temperature. Different microorganisms produce different levels of acid and require different periods for optimal growth. The following table illustrates a number of important factors.

Characteristics of Common Beer-Souring/ Fermenting Microorganisms

	Alcohol Tolerance	pH *	Lactic Acid	Acetic Acid	Starch	Time**	Oxygen	Temp, °F (°C)
Acetobacter	18%			8% P	+	30	++	70 (21) 110 (43)
Brettanomyces	18%, P	3.4	P	P		100	+	40 (4)- 95 (35)
Enterobacter	2%, P	4.3	P	0.5% P		2	+	50 (10)- 122 (50)
Lactobacillus	8%	3.8	1% P	-	+	4	-	60 (16)- 140 (60)
Pediococcus	8%	3.4	2% P	+	+	100	—	45 (7)- 140 (60)
Saccharomyces	25%, P	4.5	-	0.5%—	-	2	+	40 (7)- 95 (35)

Reprinted by permission of Raj B. Apte, With additional data by author
P produces   ++ required   — toxic   -, + moderate effect
* Approximate level at which microorganism ceases to reproduce
** Days for optimal growth during traditional fermentation

Production Methods

"It depends on what you want, if you want to brew it with respect to tradition. We respect the tradition with the equipment of the twenty-first century."

—Karl Verhaeghe of the Brouwerij Verhaeghe

Having examined the variety of acid beers available and the microorganisms that sour them, I turn our attention to their production methods. Lambic beers retain the most traditional, labor-intensive, and time-consuming procedures of any beer in the world. Some shortcuts have been developed, but the traditional methods still produce the finest beers. Traditional lambic production includes the use of unmalted wheat, a lengthy, multiple step mash known as "turbid," a high-temperature sparge, and a very long boil.

Flanders beers and new American examples of wild beer require simpler procedures, but the type of wort produced is no less important. The wort plays an important role in how the microorganisms behave and their contributions to the flavor profile of the eventual beer. Ingredients and production methods are one of the few areas over which the brewer has direct control.

GRAINS

Malted barley makes up at least 60% of the grist of all modern examples of wild beers. The larger and even some of the smaller producers would have malted their own barley, as Rodenbach did until 1974. Like many breweries, the larger wild beer producers now have malt produced to their exact specifications, while the smaller breweries make use of similar commercially available malt.

Many lambic brewers use Pilsener malt for its availability, price, neutral flavor, and low resulting color. Pale two-row malted barley may compose 60 to 70% of the grist for modern lambic beers, although some brewers substitute varying amounts of six-row malted barley. Six-row contains a greater amount of diastatic enzymes and thicker husk than two-row. Some brewers consider this advantageous, as unmalted wheat comprises the remainder of the lambic grist, which is both more difficult to

lauter and contains no enzymes of its own. A higher protein content and the potential for a phenolic taste due to polyphenols in the husk make six-row malted barley problematic in high concentrations.

Many breweries often favor malted spring barley. A portion of winter barley—up to 75%—was once commonly used when malted barley made up as little as 50% of the lambic grist. Winter barley reportedly contained more "straw" and served as an aid to lautering. Winter barley matures more quickly than spring, so it can have cost advantages, particularly in large quantities, although I can see no others. Some lambic producers state their preference for spring barley.

The grist of Flanders red and brown beers are composed of 80 to 100% malted barley. The malt does not contribute to the body of a lambic, while the Flanders beers may exhibit a smooth, malty palate. Flanders brewers may use medium-kilned malts such as Vienna and, to a lesser extent, Munich. For color and fruit, Special "B" is also commonly used in moderate quantities. Aromatic malt will add both color and malt aroma. A specific moderately kilned malt from Weyerman Specialty Malts known as Carahell will contribute to both body and head retention. The exact grain bill a "secret," the specific malts used are tuned to the specifications of each brewery. We must attempt to mimic the grain bill with what is commercially available.

By all accounts, Rodenbach does not use any Pilsener malt in its classic red beer. The brewers desire the reduction capacity of the "darker" malts over the life of the secondary fermentation of the beer in the wood. Bavik, on the other hand, ages a beer made entirely of Pilsener malt (sometimes released as *Petrus Aged Pale*) and blends with a sweet, brown beer to arrive at

Petrus Oud Bruin. A common West Flanders practice involves brewing one beer for the purpose of aging and a different one for the purpose of blending as a young beer. In East Flanders, however, *Liefmans* produces *Goudenband* from a single grist of 70% Pilsener malt and 20% of the darkest CaraVienna and CaraMunich available (plus 10% maize).

Once a common ingredient in all beer, today, unmalted wheat only composes a portion of the grist of traditional lambic and wit. Brewers following traditional lambic production techniques use 30 to 40% unmalted wheat, although at the end of the nineteenth century, it accounted for as much as 50% of the grist. Flanders red producers do not traditionally use unmalted wheat, though a few U.S. brewers have found as much as 25% to be appropriate in reproducing this classic style of beer.

While quite commonplace today, malted wheat was once a bit more dear, as the complex chemical composition made it more difficult to germinate. Simply put, unmalted grains are less expensive than malted. This was especially true during the early 1800s, when tax advantages made it profitable for brewers to use unmalted wheat. Wheat proves more difficult to lauter because, unlike barley, it has no husk. The quantity of wheat in the grist was reduced as a tradeoff to easier lautering.

Brewers consider the soft variety of wheat suitable for brewing, usually white rather than the red durum variety commonly used today to make certain types of pasta. More difficult to lauter than red wheat, the softness of the white wheat kernel significantly contributes to the "gummy" nature of the traditional lambic mash. Wheat chaff, the part of the plant wrapped around the kernel while on the stalk, was sometimes used as a lautering aid. Lambic brewers decided the yellow color and strawlike odor contributed by the chaff when exposed to near boiling liquid during the mash and sparge was undesirable, so it is no longer used.

Wheat contains a higher starch and total nitrogen (protein) content than barley. While being more difficult to lauter, the soft, white varieties generally have a lower total nitrogen content than red wheat. Brewers consider a high nitrogen content an undesirable characteristic for a grain used in brewing. The high starch content remains a key factor in the suitability of unmalted wheat for use in brewing lambic.

According to Frank Boon, unmalted wheat—to some extent wheat, in general—has many special qualities that help a beer to keep well. Beers brewed with unmalted wheat will keep longer than those without and may be a contributing factor to the long aging potential of a gueuze. The starches found in unmalted wheat give the beer more complex material that will break down more slowly than that of malted grains and will nurture the yeast and bacteria over a long period of fermentation, particularly those active during the later phases. This starch is evident by the haze unmalted wheat contributes to beer. A beer brewed with unmalted wheat takes a very long time to become bright. A lambic takes at least eight months; more often twelve is the norm.

Brewers who have never crushed unmalted wheat are certainly in for a treat. The small kernels fall right through the gap in most mills intended for grinding malted grain. Wheat kernels are also very hard and can cause a mill to seize up. A good, professional mill should suffice. Attempting to grind unmalted wheat using homebrew equipment, such as a hand-turned adjustable roller mill, will be an arduous task. Purchase or find a friend who has already adapted a motor, set the mill to as fine a grind as possible, and run the wheat through several times. Since wheat does not have a husk, it can be ground a bit finer than barley; just don't grind the wheat to powder.

If working with raw wheat appears too cumbersome, there are several other options. Good old malted wheat behaves much like malted barley, except it has no husk. Essentially "puffed" like a breakfast cereal, torrefied wheat lends more solid consistency within the mash. Flaked wheat is gelatinized (cooked) raw wheat, pressed through rollers for ease of use. All three forms of wheat may be mashed using a simple infusion mash with a protein rest. Unmalted wheat requires special consideration, detailed in the next section.

Maize (a.k.a. corn) can comfortably make up around 10% of the grist of a wild beer and can go as high as 20%, although that amount can cause the lauter to seize up. Generally used for both economical and flavor considerations, maize will add starch,

considered beneficial to lactic acid bacteria over the course of fermentation. According to Peter Bouckaert, beer brewed with a starch adjunct such as corn is lighter and more digestible.

Two types of maize exist: corn grits and refined corn grits. The former is cheaper, dry milled, and requires cooking times of up to forty-five minutes, while the latter is wet milled, nearly pure starch (very desirable to bacteria), and requires only about fifteen minutes. As a substitute, flaked maize comes already gelatinized and can be ordered from your brewing supplier, although it will not add as much starch as raw grain with an adjunct mash. Large breweries generally chose corn grits; the cheaper of the three forms of maize. Rodenbach uses up to 20% maize for the red beer, while Liefmans uses 10% in its brown, and Mort Subite adds 10% to its traditional lambic.

EXTRACT

First, the bad news; Wyeast Laboratories tested every extract on the market with all of the commonly available strains of yeast and bacteria used to produce lambic. Beers made with extract were identified every time when tasted next to those made with an all-grain wort. Your decision depends on your capabilities and what you wish to achieve, but if you are trying to make a beer that will age for two to three years, why take a shortcut of a couple hours on the wort? But don't be discouraged (really!) if you are an extract brewer. I have some suggestions, probably not considered by the folks at Wyeast, to help overcome certain limitations.

Even a pale liquid extract will produce a resulting wort darker than the desired color for a lambic, although with generally more dextrins than dry extract. Choose a wheat-based extract of about 30% wheat or an even proportion of barley- and wheat-based extracts. Use dry extract for lambic to approach the proper color. The traditional lambic mash produces a high amount of dextrins. One way to account for the fermentability of dry extract may be the addition of maltodextrin powder to the kettle or the use of a less fermentable dry malt extract such as Laaglander. A mini-mash of a pound or so of wheat and/or dextrin malt also will add some helpful compounds to your lambic wort.

Unfortunately, no extract will effectively produce a wort resembling the final color of a Flanders red ale, although dark extract will approximate a Flanders brown. One issue with extract—darker extract in particular—is you don't actually know the content. Many brewers find pale, wheat-based extract beneficial in producing Flanders beers. A mini-mash of Vienna or Munich malt and flaked maize will help with the color, add malt character, and add needed starch and melanoidins to extract wort.

HOPS

In most beers, hops add bitterness to balance the sweetness of the malt. Flanders beers do not require much bitterness from hops, and lambic requires essentially none at all. In addition to contributing bitterness, hops also have an antibacterial quality towards certain microorganisms whose by-products, in higher concentration, can spoil a perfectly good wild beer. Hops provide specific antibacterial properties and preservative qualities to lambic wort.

Hop fields were formerly a more common site in Belgium, although they are now restricted to the area around the city of

Poperinge, in the southwest of Flanders, where you may visit a museum to the glory of the Belgian hop. One hop variety used in the production of lambic until the late 1950s was Coigneau, sometimes sold as Alost, after the name of the region in which it was grown. Three different varieties of hops grew in this region, but 85% of the crop was Coigneau, notable for its low bitterness.

The most commonly known component of hops adds bitterness to beer: alpha acids. Alpha acids and iso-alpha acids (produced in the boil) also retard the growth of gram-positive bacteria such as *Lactobacillus,* and, to a somewhat lesser degree, *Pediococcus.* Some traditional Flanders beers are hopped at a low level (10 IBUs) to allow *Lactobacillus* (and *Pediococcus*) to reproduce more freely. Other Flanders beers

may be hopped to a much higher degree yet still exhibit a characteristic acidity. Remember, resistance to hop acids depends on the particular species, and sometimes even strain, of gram-positive bacteria.

The brewers at Rodenbach use hops to achieve a low bitterness of about 8 to 10 IBUs (and have been known to use hop extract to obtain a consistent IBU level). The pale wort aged at Bavik begins life significantly more bitter at 33 IBUs but loses about 7 IBUs over the long period of aging. Unlike Rodenbach, Bavik uses a significantly sweeter and completely unsoured beer for blending with aged beer, so the final product contains even less overall bitterness. *Liefmans Goudenband* begins life at 25 IBUs but has quite a bit more residual sweetness in the final blend than the West Flanders beers.

Brewers use a large amount of aged hops to brew lambic, to maximize the antibacterial effect while not contributing any noticeable bitterness. A reasonable rule of thumb for lambic: 0.8 ounces of hops per gallon (6 g/l) of wort or 1.55 pounds per U.S. barrel (580 g/hl) of two- and often three-year-old hops. As hops age (without vacuum sealing), they oxidize. When they oxidize, alpha acids lose their bittering potential. Four of the factors that determine the condition of hops during storage include time, temperature, damage, and exposure to oxygen.

Most lambic producers purchase and store hops by the bale. Packing into bales may crush the lupulin glands of the hops, which contain the relevant bittering compounds, decreasing stability during storage. After six months at ambient temperatures without vacuum sealing, hops can lose 25% or more of their alpha acids. After three years at ambient temperature, hops have lost virtually all of their bittering power.

Lambic brewers realize that, while aged hops have lost their ability to contribute bitterness to wort, they have not lost their preservative capabilities. Two other compounds—beta acids and polyphenols—do not suffer any notable affects (in context) from aging and oxidation. The beta acids contained in hops also have a powerful antibacterial effect against the growth of thermophilic gram-positive lactic acid-producing bacteria, namely those in the genus *Lactobacillus*. (*Lactobacillus*, therefore, plays virtually no role in lambic fermentation. *Pediococcus damnosus* produces most of the lactic acid.)

Similar to alpha acids, beta acids (lupulones) are insoluble in cold water and beer. Unlike alpha acids, beta acids cannot be isomerized during the boil. The oxidation products of the beta acids that form as the hops age (hulupones), are quite water-soluble. Oxidation both virtually eliminates the bitter potential of alpha acids and solubilizes the beneficial components of beta acids, which are much less bitter than iso-alpha acids.

As hop resins oxidize, they can produce a cheesy aroma and flavor. Some people believe this character represents an important contribution to the flavor of lambic. The hops I've seen used in lambic production are old and oxidized but not stinking to the point of hop-cheddar. Aged hops actually may retain a bit of their natural aroma. Any aromatic compounds transferred to lambic wort should dissipate during the requisite long boil.

Some lambic brewers purchase new hops and age them in the brewery, while others purchase hops already aged, largely depending on availability and, therefore, price. Most Belgian wild brewers prefer Belgian hops, partly due to cost, but English, Czech, or German hops may be used due to limited supply. Many of the traditional producers prefer hops that begin with a low amount of alpha acids. One hop farmer I spoke with in Washington claims hops with a low level of alpha acids at harvest serve as a better "holding hop"—one intended for aging. Also, while I am aware of no conclusive studies, hop scientists generally believe that low-alpha acid (aroma) hops grown in a temperate climate have a higher content of low-molecular polyphenols than higher alpha acid (bittering) hops or hops from zones with artificial irrigation.

The polyphenols contained in hops—including antho-cyanogens, catechins, and tannins—contribute another positive characteristic. Most brewers consider polyphenols an undesirable substance in beer, as they can contribute color, haze, and astringency. Aged hops lose some but not all of their polyphenols, limiting the puckering mouthfeel contributed to lambic. Polyphenols act as natural antioxidants, protecting beer against oxidation and improving stability, a very desirable characteristic for a beer that will take years to go from kettle to glass. Some experts even believe polyphenols help to retard certain health problems.

Traditionally, lambic brewers use whole hop flowers. The Mort Subite brewery uses pellet hops aged five to seven years. The reason? Like most breweries, the choice of pellet over whole hops is a matter of equipment. Mort Subite found pellets were easier to clean, once the brewers began using a whirlpool after the boil was complete. Plant manager Bruno Reinders says he finds no difference in the taste. (Now you have a potential use for any old pellet hops lying around.) The alpha acids in pellets break down more slowly than those of whole hops, so they must be aged longer before use. Grinding them up a bit will help to help accelerate the reaction.

If you choose to age your own hops, increasing surface area can help achieve consistency. By spreading the hops over a long, shallow container, more air comes in contact with each cone. The process may also be accelerated, in a pinch, by baking the hops at a low heat—no greater than 200° F (93° C)—until they begin to turn brown. These methods may be practical to the homebrewer, although commercial brewers will probably not be able to age a large enough quantity of hops using either technique to suit their batch size.

FRUIT

Brewers add fruit to many types of wild beer to produce a completely new beer. The fruits most commonly used to flavor traditional wild beers include cherries and raspberries. Traditional lambics also may ferment grapes, strawberries, and

Characteristics of Fruit Commonly Added to Wild Beer

Fruit	Sugar	Acidity	Acid Type	Tannins
Apricot	Medium	High	Malic	High
Black Currant	Medium	Very High	Citric	High
Cherry (Tart)	High	High	Malic	Medium
Grape (Wine)	High	Medium	Malic	Medium/High
Peach	Medium	Medium	Malic	High
Raspberry	Low	High	Citric	Medium
Strawberry	Low	High	Citric	Low

Data from Ben Rotter

apricots, while some commercial products use peaches and black currants. Rather than being bound by these selections, use them as a guide, although not all fruits lend themselves well to wild beer.

Choosing the proper type of fruit is important. Four factors to consider when choosing fruit include sugar content, acidity, the type of acid, and the level of tannins in the fruit. Without pasteurization, wild yeast will ferment all of the sugars within the fruit, so brewers consider those with some inherent acidity generally as best suited for use in wild beer. Fruit with a content of malic acid will undergo a type of secondary fermentation known as malolactic (covered in a later chapter). Tannins can be pleasant in wild beer. As tannins increase, so does the perceived dryness of the beer. Sometimes when one characteristic of a fruit is high, the others are a bit lower, adding balance to the character contributed to beer. Fruit with high characteristics across the board will naturally produce a very aggressive beer.

Traditional wild brewers prefer fresh fruit for its quality, taste and perhaps wild yeast on the skins. Use of fresh fruit will bind the wild brewer to the cultivating season. Often picked prematurely, grocery store fruit rarely offers a flavorful option for brewing. Better sources include farmers markets and purchasing directly from orchards. Some fresh fruit may be packaged with sugar to help prevent oxidization, so be aware: You may be getting quite an unexpected source of fermentable sugar. Purchase quality fruit and freeze it rather than settle for an inferior product at a convenient time.

Winemakers practically obsess over the best time to pick and use fruit. Why, then, do many brewers often dump fruit from the first available source into their fermenters? Selecting quality fruit is essential to the quality of your wild beer. The sugar content of a fruit increases as it matures on the plant, while the acidity decreases. The earlier the harvest, the lower the amount of sugar, and the higher the amount of acid the fruit will possess. Too much acid in fruit without enough sugar can lead to unpleasant acidic characteristics. When fruit is full of sugar, it exhibits a wonderful balance between acidity and sweetness. According to Jean Van Roy of Cantillon, if June is cool and rainy, you get a fruit with a high water concentration and more acid. If June is full of sun and no rain, the fruit will have a high sugar concentration.

If fresh fruit simply isn't an option, then frozen fruit may be a necessary tradeoff. Brewers consider fruit puree preferable to juice or syrup. Fruit juice and syrup will add a sweetened flavor without much complexity. Pasteurized, filtered, sweetened beers are often made with juice, both for ease of use and because the beer better retains the color of the fruit.

The cell walls of fruit must be broken down to allow the flavor and aroma components to mix with the beer. Strains of *Saccharomyces cerevisiae* used in standard fermentation cannot do this on their own, so the fruit may be macerated or frozen before being added to the fermenter in order to break down the skins. The wild yeasts and bacteria used to ferment wild beers do not face this limitation and will thoroughly attack and ferment fruit in a native state. You probably won't even recognize the fruit after an extended period of time undergoing a wild fermentation.

Cherries remain the most popular fruit to add to wild beer, be it Flanders red, Flanders brown, or lambic. For practical reasons, local cherries were used whenever possible to produce traditional

Belgian beer—a contributing factor to the popularity of Schaarbeek cherries among lambic producers. The classic cherry used to produce kriek lambic, and even some krieks from Flanders, the mighty Schaarbeek cherry is native to "suburban" Brussels. Twenty to thirty years ago, the Schaarbeek cherry trees were quite plentiful, but the orchards succumbed to both blight and urban sprawl. The Schaarbeek cherries were very much a part of Brussels, the trees a common sight in the yards, the wild yeast on the skins an important part of the *terroir* of the region.

The Schaarbeek contributes more color to beer than many other types of cherries. The Schaarbeek cherry does not have much skin, does have a large pit, and when they are black they are ripe and ready to pick. The flavor contributed is often described as vanilla and almond when the pits are included

(and they should be) in the fermentation. Traditional lambic producers still consider the Schaarbeek the best cherry in the world and the best with which to produce kriek lambic. Today, many of the cherries for kriek lambic come from a region in the south of Poland known as Galicia, although the area surrounding St. Truiden is also popular and still has some of Belgium's finest cherry orchards.

Cherries generally come in two types: tart (also called sour) and sweet. The former variety produces better kriek. According to mead guru Ken Schramm, the quality of tart cherries cultivated in the United States is not currently on par with those of Europe. A brewer must determine the tradeoff between fresh, relatively inexpensive local cherries and more expensive imported varieties that will likely be frozen. The amount of whole cherries added by the traditional producers of wild beers varies from brewery to brewery. The amount of cherries used to produce kriek is generally 2 to 2.5 pounds per gallon (240 to 300 grams per liter), although some brewers claim to use as much as 400 to 600 grams per liter or roughly 3.3 to 5 pounds per gallon. The pulp-to-pit ratio is generally lower on cherries used to produce kriek lambic than on most commercial cherries, which could account for a high ratio of fruit to liquid.

More finicky and expensive than cherries, brewers have still used raspberries in wild beer for around a hundred years. Some producers lament the effort, because the raspberries completely decompose during secondary fermentation, leading to filtration problems. When added to an unpasteurized wild beer, raspberries will increase the perception of dryness and add noticeable acidity and even some astringency, although not an unpleasant amount.

A number of other fruits, including strawberries, apricots, grapes, peaches, and black currants, are not as steeped in history as the cherry or even the raspberry but will produce a pleasant wild beer. Lower in acid content than many other fruits, strawberries lend little or no color and a very soft, subtle flavor and aroma that ages surprisingly well. Apricots will add a turbidity, golden color, and notable acidic character. Muscat grapes will produce a pleasing astringency and acidity. Purple grapes, such as the Merlot and Cabernet Franc varieties, result in a lambic with a reddish-burgundy color and rich, fruity aroma and flavor reminiscent of a fine red wine.

Juices made from peaches and black currants are used to create sweetened, pasteurized lambic. One American producer used whole peaches to add both flavor and an acidic quality to his lambic, although peaches do not easily contribute flavor and can often "morph" into other flavors. The highly acidic black currant can give a drying character to a beer. One American producer who flavors his lambic with whole black currants says they can lend a (no fooling) "cat pee" aroma.

Many commercial wild fruit beers contain a ratio of around two pounds of fruit per gallon of wort. This ratio represents a good starting point until you determine how much fruit character is suited to your taste as well as the nature of the specific fruit you select.

WATER

Many popular brewing styles developed because of the suitability of the local water to a particular characteristic possible in a beer. Pilsener, for instance, developed largely due to the amazingly clean, soft character of water in the city of Pilsen in the Czech

Republic and its suitability for producing pale, bitter beers. Many breweries in Belgium traditionally produced only one type of beer, perhaps suited to the character of the local water.

The water sources in the provinces in Belgium commonly associated with wild beer production all have a fairly high level of temporary hardness (HCO_3), which lends itself to the production of dark, malty beers. West Flanders has a very high level of sodium (Na), and East Flanders and Brabant are still relatively high, compared to other famous brewing cities. Sodium can contribute a sour, salty taste to beer. A reasonable assumption might be that before brewers were knowledgeable about altering the chemistry of their water, Flanders brewers naturally produced dark, sourish ale. This assumption does not hold true for Brussels and the Payottenland (Brabant), where the beers were sourish but not dark and malty.

Traditional wild beer producers often brew using water from their own wells, so each source may be a bit different but should not deviate to a great extent from the profiles listed in the chart below, which were taken from a sampling of pumping stations throughout the regions. Lambic and Flanders breweries alike

Water Analysis for the Provinces of Belgium Known for Wild Beer (1999)

Province	Ca	Mg	Na	SO$_4$	Cl	HCO$_3$	Hardness
Brabant	111	12	14	74	40	315	328
East Flanders	134	22	52	76	47	306	424
West Flanders	114	10	125	145	139	370	328

Data from Jacques Bertens and Ronald Baert. All data in mg/L (ppm)

treat their water to remove temporary hardness. Rodenbach uses calcium hydroxide to remove temporary hardness as the final step in its water treatment. This process may be too cumbersome for homebrewers and probably most craftbrewers. Simpler methods to reduce temporary hardness include precipitation and dilution with water from a softer source. Conversely, if water exhibits too much softness, particularly when brewing a lambic (a problem encountered at Wyeast Laboratories), add some calcium sulfate (gypsum) to the mash to aid with conversion and keep the pH from dropping too quickly.

BREWING SEASONS

Traditionally crafted between the beginning of October and the end of April, spontaneously fermented beers still follow the seasons. During the summer, brewers consider the wild yeast and bacteria "too wild" for proper fermentation. Several lambic brewers specifically warn of high risk of "thermo-bacteria" when the temperatures are elevated, particularly at night.

"Thermo-bacteria" refers to thermophilic gram-positive bacteria, the best known being *Lactobacillus* sp., including *L.*

Brewing Seasons

"Hence the urgent reason for brewing in the spring season; because, at this time, both air and water are stored with exhalations from growing vegetables, which unite with others, especially with those of the same kind; and thus it is that the particles which float in the air, are, as it were, inhaled by those of the water, malt, wort, and hops . . . "

–W. Brande from *The Town and Country Brewery Book* (London, 1830) *delbrueckii* and *L. brevis.* These particular species of bacteria play a major role in the fermentation of Flanders beers. Very small amounts of thermo-bacteria are quite natural, but larger counts can be quite detrimental to lambic, producing a pungent sourness. Isomerized alpha acids and hulupones contributed by the oxidized beta acids of hops inhibit gram-positive thermophilic bacteria. The use of a high volume of aged hops by lambic brewers demonstrates just how undesirable they find the by-products of *Lactobacillus* sp. The contribution of the aged hops may not be enough to successfully inhibit certain strains of the heat-seeking "thermo-bacteria" during the summer months.

Lactobacillus sp. generally do not pose a problem to aged beer, since *Saccharomyces cerevisiae* will have metabolized many of the amino acids in the wort necessary for cell growth. A problem arises when aging beer has not been separated from autolyzing yeast sediment, a condition present in traditional lambic fermentation. This sediment combined with the hot temperatures of summer will provide the "thermo-bacteria" with enough amino acids to reproduce.

Temperature has long been an important variable no lambic brewer or blender could control. Even today, that sort of control is beyond the budget of many producers. Armand DeBelder of Drie Fonteinen has gone to great lengths to fix the temperature in his rooms of fermenting barrels at 61° F (16° C). "It makes the brewing seasons a bit less meaningful. At 16° C you don't get that much acidity." Without reliable temperature control, however, lambic brewing takes a summer holiday.

High concentrations of "thermo-bacteria" present during spontaneous fermentation can lead to bad beer. Often considered simply "sour" or "lactic," Frank Boon describes the character as "a celery juice and parsnip taste." Lambic production also fares better during dry weather. Wild yeast and bacteria do not like too much rain any more than humans. Damp conditions can cause the growth of mold detrimental to the flavor and aroma of the beer.

THE MASH

Lambic brewers traditionally use a turbid mash, while other styles, including Flanders red and brown, are produced with some simpler form of infusion mash. Both tradition and the components contributed to the wort for use by the wild yeast and bacteria determine the choice of mash type. The type of mash and subsequent wort will influence the behavior of the microorganisms in fermentation.

The beginnings of the turbid mash can be traced back to the Dutch law of 1822 that fixed a duty upon the capacity of the mash tun. Given this financial limitation, brewers constructed

The old mash tun at the Lindemans brewery in Vlezenbeek

small mash tuns and filled them as full as possible with grain. This left little room remaining for mash liquor. The liquor was said to be, of necessity, relatively cold, as a high strike heat would result in a set mash. A small amount of cold liquor used with raw grains produced a mash liquor with a large amount of ungelatinized starches and other matter.

The mash, sometimes containing raw grain as well as malted barley, resembled "a sponge out of which you had to coax some wort." This was accomplished by pushing a "brewer's basket" into the top of the mash. The resulting impression filled with turbid mash liquor, which was hand-pumped through a tube into a separate kettle. This liquid portion was boiled and then sprinkled back over the top of the mash. The process was repeated until the mash liquor clarified, after which the liquor was pumped into a second kettle. This method left a sizeable amount of dextrins in the low-alcohol beers of the day.

A shift to the English system of infusion mashing became economical by the repeal of the mash tun tax in 1885. The problem arose that the low-gravity beers of the day now tasted thin and lifeless, owing to the higher attenuation possible with the single, high-temperature English mashing system. The Belgian turbid mashing system, widely in use in Belgium and northern France by 1915, came about as the result of a refusal to continue using the English mashing system. The traditional lambic producers have retained the turbid mash method, as the highly attenuative wild yeasts find the resulting dextrins quite desirable.

The infusion system of mashing involves doughing-in with the total amount of liquor at high temperatures and washing out the desired compounds from the grain relatively quickly to arrive at a clear wort. The turbid system begins with a small volume of colder liquor, only enough to thoroughly wet all of the grain. Boiling liquor is added to the mash to raise the temperature to the next rest. A portion of the mash liquor is removed, heated almost to a boil, and held at that temperature throughout most of the mash, effectively denaturing any enzymatic activity. These two steps are repeated to reach the next temperature rest. The mash goes from thick and dry to thin and soupy, as the additional boiling liquor is added to the tun. Add more boiling liquor to reach the third rest, then run off the mash liquor into the primary kettle for heating. Finally add the original starchy liquid back to the mash for a mash-out rest. The temperature rests vary somewhat from brewery to brewery. The contents of the mash tun are recirculated to clear the run-off of husks and chunks before sparging.

The wheat starches in the liquor removed from the tun, boiled, then reintroduced to reach the final temperature rest have not been modified by the mash. This results in a turbid, starchy, milky wort at the beginning of the boil. The turbid mashing procedure breaks down the long-chain proteins of the raw wheat and malted barley into free amino acids. The resulting low-protein wort will provide less suitable nutrients for the microorganisms predominantly active during the early stages of fermentation, and a greater amount of dextrins and starches to nourish those that grow during the latter stages (even during bottle-conditioning). Without the complex sugar/starch profile needed for the growth of the microorganisms through the course of fermentation, the finished beer can appear thin and lifeless. In judging lambic beers produced in the United States, I find this one of the most common flaws.

Every traditional lambic brewer has an idea about which mash technique he should use. A certain technique may have been chosen due largely to economic reasons. Some brewers have designed their own specific combination of the two mash systems. The English-style infusion mash will take fewer resources and less time to produce the wort, although in the

Turbid Mash Schedule

This mash schedule represents an approximation of the traditional turbid mash, suitable for small producers.

Assume 2 quarts of H_2O/pound of grain (1.9 liters/450 grams).

1. Dough-in wheat, and malt with 20% of H_2O to achieve 113° F (45° C), rest for 15 minutes.

2. Add 20% H_2O at 212° F (100° C) to raise mash to 126° F (52° C), rest for 15 minutes.

3. Remove 33% of the liquid, heat in kettle to 190° F (88° C), and hold.

4. Add 30% H_2O at 212° F (100° C) to raise mash to 149° F (65° C), rest for 45 minutes.

5. Remove 50% of the liquid, add to kettle, and reheat to 190° F (88° C), and hold.

6. Add 30% H_2O at 212° F (100° C) to raise mash to 162° F (72° C), rest for 30 minutes.

7. Transfer most of the liquor in the mash tun - equal to roughly 38% of the total volume of mash liquor - to the primary kettle and begin to heat.

8. Add contents of kettle to mash to raise to 172° F (78° C), rest for 20 minutes.

8. Vorlauf to remove husks and chunks.

10. Sparge with 190° F (88° C) H_2O until gravity is less than 2 °P (1.008).

long term, a beer made with the turbid mash will be superior. According to Frank Boon, "the finest, most traditional lambics are produced from a turbid mash."

Brewers using a turbid mash to produce lambic wort traditionally sparge at temperatures too high for other beers— around 194° F (90° C). One of the common reasons to sparge is to wash any remaining sugars out of the mash. A turbid mash will have poor conversion of sugars, and a hotter than normal sparge will help to wash out remaining dextrins and unconverted starches. The higher temperature also will leach considerable tannins from the mash, something found undesirable in other beers. The tannins will precipitate out or break down over the long period of fermentation and do not contribute to a noticeable astringency in the resulting beer.

If the turbid mash just sounds too involved, and you still wish for some of the benefits of raw wheat, it will need to be

Wyeast Lambic Mash Schedule

Assume 2.35 quarts of H_2O/pound of grain (2.25 liters/450 grams). The folks at Wyeast Labs brew lambic on their pilot system. This simplified mash will extract the optimal amount of proteins and starches with a minimal number of rests and only one kettle.

1. Dough-in wheat with 10% of the barley malt and 75% of H_2O at 140° F (60° C).

2. Increase to 212° F (100° C), and hold for approximately 30 minutes.

3. Add the balance of the malt and H_2O. Adjust mash to 70° F (158° C), and hold for approximately 2 hours, stirring continuously. Rest 30 minutes.

4. Sparge with 203° F (95° C) H_2O.

gelatinized before it can be used in an infusion mash. The same holds true when using maize—common with Flanders beers. Both grains have a high gelatinization temperature, so they must be cooked in order to become soluble within the mash. Boiling allows the enzymes of the mash access to the starch and fermentable sugar of the grains. Cook a small portion of malted barley along with the unmalted grain to provide enzymes. First, mix the wheat or maize and small amount of malted barley (10%) with liquor, raise the temperature, and hold at a level conducive for saccharification—around 145° F (63° C). Then boil the mixture for 15 to 45 minutes, depending on the type of maize, or for 30 minutes when using wheat.

Brewers commonly use an infusion mash to produce most varieties of wild beer. The infusion mash provides a high fermentable sugar/high protein wort conducive to a quick

Flanders Mash Schedule

This mash schedule is very similar to the one used at Rodenbach. When using flaked maize you may omit steps 1 and 3.

Assume 1.33 quarts of H_2O/pound of grain (1.25 liters/450 grams).

1. Mash corn and 10% of malted barley at 145° F (63° C) for 15 minutes.
2. Dough-in grains and H_2O to hit 122° F (50° C), and hold for 20 minutes.
3. Add adjunct mash to main mash.
4. Raise to 145° F (63° C), and hold for 40 minutes.
5. Raise to 162° F (72° C), and hold for 30 minutes.
6. Raise to 169° F (76° C), and hold for 10 minutes (mash-out).
7. Sparge with 176° F (80° C) H_2O.

start to fermentation. This favors microorganisms dominant during the early phase of fermentation and reduces those most active during the later phases, mainly due to nutrient depletion but also to the presence of alcohol. This is one reason the by-products of *Brettanomyces* are so noticeable in traditional lambic but not in Flanders beers.

The lactic acid-producing bacteria require the starch, present in the adjunct grains, to produce their requisite by-products. When using adjuncts with an infusion mash, adding the boiling mixture of raw grain and malted barley helps raise the main mash from one temperature rest to the next during the saccharification phase. A variation that will provide additional starch to the wort involves adding only a portion of the adjunct mash at the first step to gain fermentable sugar, and the remainder once the enzymes have been denatured during the mash-out. Any beer that requires lactic acid development can benefit from some starch.

THE BOIL

Tired from all that mashing? When most brewers complete their brew day, many lambic brewers embark on a marathon boil. The Lindemans brewery once boiled wort for twelve hours, although six hours is now the maximum, and four hours is becoming increasingly more common. A long boil of five to six hours is traditional among most lambic producers; each may have their own beliefs as to why a long boil is desirable. The long, vigorous boil reduces the kettle volume, helps to precipitate excess proteins and tannins, and extracts compounds from the hops.

Considering the water-to-grist ratio during the mash and sparge, a long boil will reduce the volume of liquid in the kettle to arrive at the desired starting gravity of the wort. Boiling also helps to coagulate more of the excess proteins in the wort contributed by raw wheat. They will simply fall out of solution. Boiling aged hops for a long period of time will help to extract as much of the antibacterial humulones, hulupones, and preserving polyphenols as possible. The polyphenolic

The new brewhouse at the Lindemans brewery in Vlezenbeek.

tannins will confer some of the dry bitterness customary to the style. Many American brewers probably do not have a large enough kettle for a rolling five- to six-hour boil but should boil for at least two hours when producing a lambic.

Brewers in Flanders once boiled (simmered?) their worts for up to thirty hours. No producer of Flanders red or brown currently chooses to boil for longer than two hours. The popular myth that Flanders brewers achieve the color of their beer through a twelve-hour overnight simmer may have been unintentionally proliferated at the Liefmans brewery. Before production moved to Riva, boiling the wort did take as long as twelve hours. This wasn't simply to darken the color; the boiler was so inefficient, it took twelve hours to achieve what most kettles do in less than two. For patient brewers, a long, slow simmer will add a bit of reddish hue to the wort, but it is much easier and no less authentic to use malt to achieve the color.

The old wort cooler at Liefmans of Oudenaarde.

COOLING

The boil finally complete, the wort must be cooled. In many cases some form of heat exchanger, like in any modern brewery, cools the wort. Prior to refrigeration, a heat exchanger was a less mechanical device. The hot wort cascaded down over the surface of a series of copper pipes, connected the long way and turned on their sides like horizontal bars. Cold water ran through the pipes, resulting in a heat transfer between the hot wort and the cold water. The most classic cooling method, still in use today, is the coolship.

A huge, shallow, generally copper vessel, the coolship historically took up the entire top floor of the brewery. All breweries once had to use some form of a coolship. It is shallow to promote the greatest contact with the air to induce as rapid a cooling as possible. Windows or slats in the coolship room, open to the outdoors, allow the cool outside air to come into contact with the

The coolship—the highest point in the Cantillon brewery of Brussels.

beer. Except for lambic, fermentation begins so quickly that any organisms that infected the beer during the cooling process do not have the time to sour the wort before they are "out-competed" for food by *Saccharomyces*. "Thermo-bacteria" that produce unpleasant by-products do have an effect on lambic wort prior to the onset of fermentation (which is covered in depth in the next chapter). Ideally, the wort is cooled to about

Summary of Traditional Belgian Wild Beers

Lambic
70% Pilsener malt
30% unmalted white wheat
25 oz/bbl or 0.8 oz/gal (~6 g/l) of 3-year-old low alpha acid hops
Turbid mash
5- to 6-hour boil

Flanders Red
70-80% spring barley malt composed of Vienna, (Munich), cara-malts, and Special "B"
10-20% maize (or unmalted wheat)
10 IBUs (optionally of low alpha acid hops)
Infusion mash
2-hour boil

Flanders Brown
70% Pilsener malt
20% CaraVienna and CaraMunich
10% maize
25 IBUs (optionally of low alpha acid hops)
Infusion mash
2-hour boil

68° C (20° F), although on warmer days it might not drop that low. Trub will separate from the wort and fall to the bottom, left behind when the wort is transferred to a different vessel.

Today, many lambic breweries have fans in the coolship room to move the air. Mort Subite pumps air into cylindroconical fermenters to saturate the wort rather than using a coolship. That brewery also uses a wort cooler to chill the wort down to 95° F (35° C) before this takes place. "Quick cooling" eliminates the effect of "thermo-bacteria" on the fresh wort between 95 and 176° F (35 and 80° C). A bit less traditional, this cooling technique becomes desirable as some lambic brewers seek to avoid the unwanted by-products of "thermo-bacteria" in their beer (discussed in the next chapter).

The coolship gives wort intended for spontaneous fermentation the first taste of wild yeast and bacteria. This method of long, slow cooling also will lead to the formation of significant amounts of dimethyl sulfate, which will be scrubbed during the lengthy fermentation process. Contact with the greatest amount of surface area over a long-enough period of time, generally overnight, is important. The next day, the brewer racks the wort into a tank to separate it from the trub in the bottom of the coolship. The destination is sometimes referred to as the "horny tank," as whatever was inoculated overnight is now jumping and ready to go!

According to Frank Boon, much of the bacteria and some of the wild yeasts that ferment lambic come from the air, while *Brettanomyces* are generally found living in the wooden barrels used for fermentation. The concentration of microorganisms in the air alone, however, is not enough. What lives in the bare walls and wooden rafters of the brewery is of great importance.

The concentration of microorganisms found in the brewery air is far greater than that outside.

Says Karel Goddeau of the De Cam Geuzestekerij, "People always think it is the mystery of the air, but it is more in the building than in the air. The EU says we must clean up [paint] our walls, but the porous nature is very important. The bacteria live within the walls. This is what makes the brew of each brewery different, the location of the cooling vessel [and the barrels]." Many lambic brewers demonstrate near-superstitious behavior regarding the coolship. The brewers at Cantillon kept the old ceiling tiles in place when they replaced the roof over the coolship. The Lindemans brewers still used the old coolship, in the old building, after a new brewhouse was built. The importance of leaving the *terroir* of the brewery undisturbed will become even more evident in the next chapter.

six

Wild Fermentation

"The more man intervenes in the process, the less traditional and natural it becomes."

–John Matthys of Hanssens Artisanaal

I will discuss three types of wild fermentation: inoculated, spontaneous, and mixed. Inoculated fermentation involves introducing a concentration of one or more varieties of yeast and bacteria to wort to achieve fermentation. The introduction of various beer-souring microorganisms to mimic the fermentation of a lambic is, in fact, inoculation. Spontaneous fermentation assumes all of the microorganisms come from the air in the brewery and any porous materials (i.e. wood) around or in contact with the wort. Mixed fermentation involves the use of both a culture and microorganisms that grow in a wooden barrel for fermentation.

The by-products of yeast and bacteria the wild brewer consider friendly can be terribly distasteful in higher concentration. The producers of spontaneously fermented beer have no direct control over what actually inoculates the wort. Practitioners of mixed fermentation control the primary fermentation but lose that control during secondary fermentation to the microorganisms that reside inside their barrels. Brewers who inoculate their beer have the greatest—although never complete—control over fermentation. Pure cultures of wild yeast and bacteria can still exhibit unpredictable behavior. An understanding of the procedures surrounding fermentation with wild yeast and bacteria is essential to the production of a good wild beer. Let's consider the three types of fermentation in further detail. Understanding what occurs during a particular type of fermentation opens the potential to nudge it in a particular direction.

SPONTANEOUS FERMENTATION

Beer-fermenting and -souring microorganisms occur naturally, conditions favoring, everywhere in the world. Historically widespread, a number of indigenous fermented beverages still rely on spontaneous fermentation. Breweries in the United Kingdom and Netherlands produce spontaneously fermented, Belgian-influenced beer. Traditional lambic, however, remains the most widespread and consistent spontaneously fermented beer produced in the world.

Strictly speaking, spontaneous fermentation is easy: Simply allow unfermented wort to be exposed to wild yeast and bacteria, and then leave it to ferment for a period of time. Leaving exposed wort in the backyard overnight, however, will not produce a pleasant spontaneously fermented beer, at least not in most parts of the world. Don't be distraught—a batch of beer left open to ferment in Brussels' Grand Place probably wouldn't taste any better. The challenge of spontaneous fermentation lies

Fresh Fruit and Fermentation

The use of fresh fruit is a historical and comparatively easy way to introduce wild yeast to your beer naturally. If fruit is not boiled or frozen, there will almost certainly be some wild yeast on the skins that will induce some level of fermentation. Wine grapes and unpasteurized apple juice ferment without additional yeast.

The microorganisms residing on fruit may not be enough to completely ferment wort to a desired level. The best chance will occur when using extremely fresh fruit. For best results, crush or macerate the fruit prior to use to allow the sugars of the fruit to fully blend with the wort. Some tartness and acidity will definitely be conferred from both the fruit and resident microorganisms.

The addition of fresh, whole fruit to fermented wort will induce a "secondary spontaneous fermentation." Many brewers of fruit ales freeze or boil their fruit to avoid this occurrance, preferring only a pure culture of *Saccharomyces*

cerevisiae to perform the fermentation.

A type of secondary fermentation common in wine, malolactic fermentation, occurs due to the species of bacteria found in grapes. While winemakers generally control malolactic fermentation in order to avoid any "wild" results, resident bacteria, including *Pediococcus* and *Lactobacillus* sp. (though not *L. delbrueckii*), and those of *Leuconostoc* (especially *L. oenos*) will convert the "sharp" or "harsh" tasting malic acid present in many fruits into more pleasant lactic acid. The conversion lowers the total acidity and raises the pH, resulting in a more pleasant and palatable wine. Quite common in dry red wines and Chardonnay, winemakers avoid malolactic fermentation in sweeter wines where the acidity is needed for balance. Malolactic fermentation may occur during fermentation with grapes or in "uncleaned" wine barrels.

in achieving a product found pleasing. Many variables affect the results, and the brewer only has control over a few of them. Achieving the desired result occurs only over time. French enologist Emile Peynaud noted the presence of *Brettanomyces* on the walls and dirt floors of French wine cellars, and that "the winemaker should imagine the whole surface of the winery and equipment as being lined with yeasts." For hundreds of years, European winemakers have been returning the pressed-out skins of wine grapes to their vineyards as fertilizer. The naturally selected yeast strains that inhabit those skins have become so ingrained into the *terroir* that some winemakers can achieve consistent results with the spontaneous fermentation of newly pressed must. In the vineyards of the United States, however, such consistency, even in vineyards that have been around for more than a hundred years, may still be centuries away.

The favorable conditions for spontaneous fermentation along the Senne Valley were also no accident. The concentration of fruit trees and vines, combined with the abundance of traditional farmhouse breweries around Brussels, made an ideal environment for the necessary wild yeast and bacteria to become airborne and reside in the buildings. To add to matters, fruit flies and bees have been shown to spread *Brettanomyces* and other oxidative yeasts. Such insects were certainly an unavoidable part of farmhouse brewing. Lactic acid-producing bacteria live on raw grain and may be especially prevalent if grain is milled near the other brewing operations. One can only imagine what microorganisms were spread by the animals living in and around the farmhouse breweries at a time when sanitation was not considered a priority in brewing.

The brewery buildings in the Senne Valley have always been important to spontaneous fermentation within the region. The microorganisms necessary for spontaneous fermentation survive in the exposed wooden beams and floors and porous white-washed walls of the lambic brewery. Considering the loss of the Schaarbeek cherry orchards surrounding Brussels as a continuing source of fresh wild yeast, the buildings now play a greater role than ever before.

People sometimes ask why there have been no completely new spontaneous fermentation breweries opened in Brussels or the Payottenland, much less anywhere else? The problems surrounding a new brewery involve patience and money, and owners often have neither. The capital required to open a top- or bottom-fermentation brewery is generally raised with the expectation of a return on investment within a reasonable period of time. If everything goes right, a viable lambic product may be available within a few years and a blended product within five years. If everything goes according to plan . . . .

People serious about spontaneous fermentation should consider a number of factors. The first: a source of wild yeast. Consider locating your brewery (or home) downwind of a fruit orchard. A few fruit trees in the backyard may be enough for a homebrewer. A windy spot is a good idea. (The coolship room at the Melbourn Brothers brewery, high above the skyline of Stamford, is a bit like a wind tunnel.) If you are a fruit grower with a barn or extra wooden shed, you may have an entirely new opportunity.

Second, the wild yeast and bacteria necessary for fermentation require an environment conducive for their development. Porous items such as wooden beams, floors, ceilings, and unfinished walls do the trick in Belgium. The presence of beer in a room should eventually induce the "permanent" growth of various beer-fermenting and -souring microorganisms. To speed the process, splash some "live" beer, such as gueuze, around the space intended for fermentation. The more beer fermented in the space, the more the microorganisms will reproduce both in and around the beer.

While some brewers produce spontaneously fermented beers without the use of wooden barrels, they remain a part of the traditional fermentation process because they are porous and contain additional yeast and bacteria. All of the microorganisms do not come from the air. I discuss the variables involving the use of wooden barrels and potential substitutes in greater depth in the next chapter on maturation and wood.

Will following these suggestions result in a beer that tastes like a lambic produced in the Senne Valley? That question can only be answered on a case-by-case basis. Even in the Payottenland, a new brewery may not produce a quality lambic, at least not in a short period of time. The same microorganisms— *Pediococcus, Lactobacillus, Brettanomyces,* and even *Saccharomyces*—infect beer all over the world. With the proper facilities, it may be surprising how close a beer can come. The question remains, can a brewer produce a "local lambic" that tastes pleasant?

FERMENTATION CYCLE OF LAMBIC

Now let's consider the fermentation cycle of lambic. Among beers, it is the most unique in the world. There may be more than 200 different strains of microorganisms that take more than two years to complete their appointed tasks. That a similar

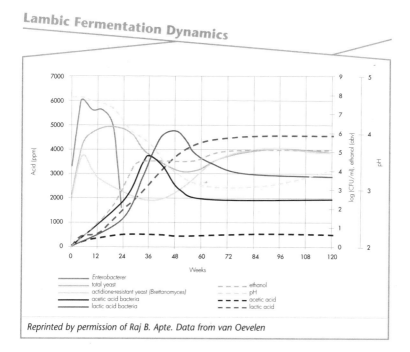

Lambic Fermentation Dynamics

Reprinted by permission of Raj B. Apte. Data from van Oevelen

product results time after time, albeit with a little help from the producers, virtually represents a "miracle" of brewing. Scientists and brewers alike have studied lambic fermentation, noted the by-products the dominant microorganisms produce, and have ascertained the stages through which a cask of lambic will pass. This teaches us both what to expect during spontaneous fermentation, and about the microorganisms necessary to effectively mimic the cycle of lambic fermentation.

The fermentation of lambic occurs in a specific sequence, each microbial species growing at different rates before reaching a high enough cell count to act, in turn, on the wort. The depletion of nutrients and oxygen, and the drop in pH caused by fermentation, results in each type of microorganism being dominant at a different time during the life cycle. The actual duration of each stage is not absolute but dependent upon the ambient temperature in the fermentation rooms and the particular concentration of microorganisms in each cask. These are two reasons why even the same batch of lambic will taste differently from cask to cask. Dr. Hubert Verachtert and his colleagues at the Catholic University of Leuven in Belgium conducted the research involved in determining the lambic fermentation cycle.

A seasonal beer, lambic is brewed and exposed to wild yeast and bacteria while in the coolship and allowed a "primary fermentation" during the cooler months. The onset of summer brings an increase in the population of lactic acid-producing bacteria. The fall brings with it a secondary alcoholic fermentation by highly attenuative yeasts. At Cantillon they say, "The beer must be inside the barrels for a summer and a winter." Once this time has passed, the young lambic may be served or blended. The onset of the second summer sees another increase in the population of lactic acid-producing bacteria. Lambic exhibits a viscosity during the summer that makes it unsuitable

Physical Movement of Lambic Wort During Production

Location	Time
Brew Kettle	2-6 Hours
Coolship	Overnight
"Horny" Tank	Until Full
Fermentation Vessel	Up to 3 Years

Lambic Fermentation Cycle

Dominant Microorganisms	Elapsed Time (Approximate)
Enterobacter and *Kloeckera apiculata*	3-7 Days
Saccharomyces	2 Weeks
Pediococcus	3-4 Months
Brettanomyces (and Other Oxidative Yeasts)	8 Months

for blending. After two years, the lambic is fairly mature, almost a finished product. A portion will mature an additional year to contribute the well-developed flavors of an old lambic when blended as gueuze.

Until this century, no producer incurred the expense for direct control over the temperature at which he fermented his lambic. Traditionally, the seasonal temperatures affect lambic fermentation. The location of the barrels of fermenting wort in the cellar, or in buildings with heavy stone walls and floors, resists any dramatic seasonal temperature changes. If the temperature stays at one extreme for too long, however, it can rise in the cellar and pose some problems.

A hot summer will adversely affect a cask of lambic, potentially turning it to vinegar. The lambic may become too acidic, as the lactic acid-producing bacteria can grow at alarming rates. According Jean Van Roy at Cantillon, anything above even 75° F (24° C) in the building is too high for more than one or two weeks. A complete summer where the temperature regularly reaches 86° F (30° C) may render lambic undrinkable and even unblendable. Lambic that was exposed to higher temperatures for an extended period of time may need to be dumped (or used to produce a bit of faro).

The temperatures in winter, too, can be a factor. Bacteria experience little growth and fermentation when the temperature drops below 50° F (10° C). Once the temperature reaches 40° F (4° C), the wild yeasts begin to go dormant. The longer the temperature rests below 40° F (4° C), the longer the current stage of fermentation will take to complete. The winter temperatures will not damage the lambic, only prolong the fermentation.

Lambic fermentation begins roughly three to seven days after cooling the wort. The first stage lasts for about one week. At this time, the dominant organisms are *Enterobacter* and strains of the yeast *Kloeckera apiculata*. Wort left without the suitable amount of *Saccharomyces* present during a "common" fermentation serves as an ideal breeding ground for aggressive microorganisms. *Kloeckera apiculata* produce a few volatile esters that likely dissipate during fermentation. Scientists believe the real contribution of this yeast to lambic fermentation involves breaking down proteins that did not precipitate out during the boil. *Kloeckera apiculata* are eventually overgrown by rising populations of *Saccharomyces* during the second stage of fermentation.

As you might expect from an organism commonly associated with food spoilage, *Enterobacter* can produce considerable off-flavors frequently characterized as vegetal or fecal, as well as copious amounts of acetic and even lactic acid. Some of the off-flavors and aromas contributed by the *Enterobacter* are "scrubbed" and dissipate during fermentation. The rapid growth of the *Enterobacter* during the early days of fermentation produces much of the acetic acid and ethyl acetate found in lambic. Additionally, according to Verachtert, the rapid consumption of amino acids by *Enterobacter* during this phase accounts for the slow start of alcoholic fermentation as compared to other types of beer.

All organisms require certain conditions where they can grow and survive. During fermentation both the composition and pH of the wort change dramatically. As a result, the viability of individual species of microorganisms varies as fermentation progresses. The fast growth of *Enterobacter* causes the production of acid, resulting in a significant decrease in the wort pH, from 5.1 to 4.6, according to Dr. Jean-Xavier Guinard. Generally absent after two months of fermentation, *Enterobacter* begins to die as the wort pH drops. While the contributions of *Enterobacter* are questionable, their presence in lambic wort is unavoidable without manual intervention.

Many, perhaps all producers seem to find the flavor, aroma, and sometimes-excessive amount of acid produced by *Enterobacter* to be undesirable. Additionally, the European Union has begun to question the (natural and centuries-old) presence of "potentially harmful" *Enterobacter* sp. during fermentation. Some lambic producers have chosen to take steps to inhibit the growth of these bacteria and fight their battles in other places.

Some lambic producers have begun to experiment with arresting the enteric stage of fermentation through the addition of lactic acid to the fresh wort. The addition of lactic acid will drop the pH of the wort and cause *Enterobacter* to die before growing to a significant cell count and producing any undesirable substances.

One method of introducing lactic acid involves inoculating wort with enough food-grade lactic acid to drop the pH to around 4. Other lambic producers add cultures of *Lactobacillus*—*L. delbrueckii* is generally blended with the wort as it is moved to the "horny tank." The lactic acid produced lowers the pH of the wort before too much proteolytic activity and resulting by-products from the *Enterobacter*. The introduction of lactic acid bacteria, as opposed to lactic acid, drops the pH naturally, and does not lend an acidic character without other balancing by-products. Inhibited by hulupones and by the falling pH, *Lactobacillus delbrueckii* also will die before producing any significant amount of lactic acid relative to the eventual flavor of the lambic.

Arresting the growth of *Enterobacter* will decrease the acidity of the final product, primarily acetic but also lactic. Also, if the *Enterobacter* do not consume their requisite nutrients (amino acids), it leaves more for consumption by yeasts such as *Saccharomyces* and *Brettanomyces*. This will presumably allow alcoholic fermentation to begin more quickly and serve to promote the growth of *Brettanomyces*. The lambic producer must decide whether to attempt to avert the eventual off-flavors and acidity the *Enterobacter* can cause while interfering with a natural part of fermentation.

Saccharomyces can begin alcoholic fermentation within three days to four weeks of being racked into the cask. The fermentation time is not absolute; temperature will influence the growth of *Saccharomyces*. The warmer the wort becomes, the quicker the alcoholic fermentation will begin and end. Some lambic breweries get as cold as 32° F (0° C) at night during the winter. Jean Van Roy told me of one extreme case where a cask did not

A barrel of lambic busily ferments at the Drie Fonteinen brewery in Beersel.

begin fermenting for six months, presumably due to cold temperatures. Generally, the alcoholic fermentation by various *Saccharomyces* sp. will take about three or four months. During this stage, roughly 60% of the total sugars will be fermented, and the density of the "average" wort will drop to around 1.022 (5.5 °P). *Saccharomyces* and *Kloeckera apiculata* also will begin to form capric acid, caprylic acid, ethyl caprate, and ethyl caprylate.

Since lambic is traditionally fermented in a single vessel, the trub and autolyzed yeast are not separated from lambic as is common in other brewing practices once alcoholic fermentation is complete. The nutrients contained within are used by the lactic acid-producing bacteria and *Brettanomyces* yeast to reproduce and become dominant during the next stages of fermentation.

The lactic acid fermentation occurs after the completion of the primary alcoholic fermentation: usually after three or four months, sometimes earlier, sometimes later. Bacteria of the genus *Pediococcus* perform this phase of fermentation; any growth of *Lactobacillus* is retarded by hop acids. The lambic tastes very sour during this phase, which lasts as little as three to four and usually no more than six or seven months. Seasonal temperatures play a determining factor in the speed of fermentation. During this stage, the gravity of the "average" wort further lowers to about 1.012 (3 °P) with roughly 80% of the total sugars being fermented. The substrates produced during the turbid mash are consumed over time by the lactic acid-producing bacteria and are essential to their proper growth.

As they say at Cantillon, "Before September, the beer will be sick." During the first warm day, certain strains of *Pediococcus cerevisiae*—sometimes known as *Bacillus viscosus bruxellensis*—give the beer viscosity. This condition is described in some texts as "ropiness" for the long strands of slime produced on the top

Nineteenth Century Lambic Fermentation

Dr. Jean-Xavier Guinard mentions that in the mid-nineteenth century, a ropy character was considered a defect in lambic and certainly was not as well understood as it is today as a natural part of fermentation. He cites the use of the vertical "heat exchanger" type of wort chiller, and says that only a portion of the wort was allowed to cool open to the surrounding air. Exposure to air was regarded as contributing to this "contamination." This being the case, a sizeable portion of the microorganisms would have come from the casks. George Maw Johnson wrote in 1917, "The original ferment was supposed to have been derived from wine lees, by the simple process of allowing wort to ferment in wine casks. No yeast was added." This underscores the importance of microorganisms from the wood.

Frank Boon on the changing character of lambic during fermentation

Lambic is indeed a funny beer. After three to four weeks, it is very full and very yeasty and has some bitterness. After four or five months, it can be very unpleasant. The bitterness disappears, the first trace of acidity appears, and it has less esters than the end. At certain moments it is very pleasant, and others it is not. Old lambic is similar to white wines, young lambic is similar to German *weizen* beers. In between there is a change where the beer is a bit strange. It is too bitter to be old and has too much acidity to be young. There is a lack of esters and a lack of fullness.

of the wort. All lambic must be "sick" at some point. "It's not bad—you can drink it—but it's a bit like oil," says Jean Van Roy. With the "sickness" comes the production of lactic acid, which gives the lambic its requisite tartness, and the characteristic ester ethyl lactate, which contributes fruitiness. The ropy character begins to disappear with the first cold night, after which the lambic will be ready to serve or blend.

After the summer comes and goes, a second alcoholic fermentation begins. The second alcoholic fermentation belongs to strains of the genus *Brettanomyces,* which will ferment nearly all of the remaining sugars. *Brettanomyces* do not wait for six to eight months to grow. They have been reproducing since their introduction to the wort and slowly fed on maltose and glucose before faster-growing populations of *Saccharomyces* consumed the bulk of those sugars. The *Brettanomyces* were not present in enough quantity to produce any notable by-products until this point in fermentation. Studies have shown *Brettanomyces* are difficult to detect during the early stages of fermentation, even in wines, when in the presence of other microorganisms. *Brettanomyces* contribute many acids and esters important to the final character of lambic. Levels of lactic acid and ethyl lactate increase, and the amount of acetic acid and ethyl acetate produced satisfies the palate of most lambic producers. Other acids (isovaleric, etc.) and esters (4-ethyl-guaiacol, etc.) are hopefully produced only in modest quantities. Compounds known as tetrahydropyridines, commonly attributed to *Brettanomyces* but also synthesized by certain strains of *Lactobacillus*, may contribute the objectionable "mousy" or "horsy" character. The concentration of these acids determines whether the character becomes complementary or offensive.

Brettanomyces will ferment for up to sixteen months, generally finishing after the second summer, at some point dropping the wort pH below 3.5. During this time they will form a characteristic pellicle on the top of the wort, which people believe prevents oxidation and also guards against *Acetobacter* while making use of atmospheric oxygen. *Brettanomyces* eventually begin to run out of sugars to ferment and will feed on nutrients present in autolyzed *Saccharomyces* at the bottom of the barrel. As time passes, the liquid in the barrels evaporates, and the wort will be exposed to oxygen and *Acetobacter* without the protective covering. This would not be necessary if the cask was filled every few months, as in winemaking, and some lambic producers may take this less-than-traditional step to further prevent acetification.

Brettanomyces do not share the dietary restrictions of *Saccharomyces* and have not found a sugar to be unfermentable, with the apparent exception of lactose in many strains. Over the course of this stage of lambic fermentation, virtually all of the

The Brouwerij Liefmans watches the river Schelde pass by from the eastern bank, as it has since 1930. Wort is now only fermented and aged at this classic brewery.

The entrance to the revered Brouwerij Rodenbach in Roeselare, West Flanders frames the historic malthouse, now part of a visitors center.

The thoroughly modern Brouwerij Bavik holds dear the Flemish traditions of wood-aged beer. The beer from many foudres will be blended to create Petrus Oud Bruin.

Armand DeBelder inspects a freshly cleaned barrel outside one of several barrel storehouses, all part of the Brouwerij Drie Fonteinen in Beersel, once home to many gueuze blenders.

Jean Van Roy, whose father set Brasserie Cantillon back down the path of traditional gueuze, prepares to take a sample of lambic from a classic pipe.

The foudres barely clear the ceiling of the cellar at the Brouwerij Verhaeghe in Vichte, West Flanders. The curved ceiling suggests the room once had a more formal use.

The coolship was an integral part of the traditional Flemish brewhouse, as is this one at De Dolle Brouwers in Esen, West Flanders.

The old mash tun and hop boiler are permanent fixtures in a living museum to lambic and gueuze at the Brasserie Cantillon in urban Brussels.

The neighbors have a front row seat for the copper at the now sizeable Mort Subite brewery in Kobbegem, the farthest north of the lambic producers.

The modern coolship begins to fill with near-boiling wort at Brouwerij Lindemans in Vlezenbeek. The "cage" beneath the fill pipe is intended to catch hops and other large residue.

The courtyard of the residence and geuzestekerij of Sidy Hanssens and John Mathys – Hanssens Artisanaal in Dworp.

The DeBelder family has been serving lambic, traditional Flemish cuisine and other fine dishes at their café in Beersel, south of Brussels, since 1961.

The café and former geuzestekerij of Herberg Moriau, in the historic town square of St. Pieters-Leeuw, where the language of gueuze is still spoken.

The Lindemans' farmhouse brewery as it has stood for more than 100 years. Behind the original building stand many newer structures encompassing a very modern brewery.

The gummy remnants of a turbid mash have almost been cleaned out of the tun at Brouwerij Boon in Lembeek.

Brettanomyces at work! A pellicle protects the spontaneously fermenting wort at the Gulpener Bierbrouwerij in the Netherlands, not very far from Brussels.

remaining carbohydrates in the wort will be fermented. Only the interruption of the process by pasteurization or the addition of artificial sweetener will result in a sweet lambic (or gueuze). Identified by Verachtert as "superattenuation," a lambic will reach a final apparent extract as low or lower than 0.1 Plato, nearly 1.000 SG. This condition is attributed to fermentation by the highly attenuative *Brettanomyces* yeasts in the presence of the other organisms found in lambic wort.

Floating to the top of the wort with *Brettanomyces*, other oxidative yeasts may contribute a modest winy/cidery character. The predominant species *Candida lambica* and *Pichia fermentans* have the ability to produce large quantities of acetic acid and ethyl acetate when aerated. Oxidative yeasts sometimes will become evident during the fermentation of wine, acting as a harbinger to the development of *Brettanomyces*. The vast majority of microbial activity now complete, lambic will mature and develop additional character for at least another year.

This "famous" graph (page 168) produced at the Catholic University of Leuven is still the best illustration of the compounds produced during traditional lambic fermentation.

MIXED FERMENTATION

Mixed fermentation first involves inoculating wort for primary fermentation, commonly in a stainless steel vessel. In some cases the inoculated culture will only involve *Saccharomyces cerevisiae*, while in other cases *Saccharomyces cerevisiae* will be in combination with beer-souring microorganisms, in what is known as a "mixed culture." The fermented beer ages for a period of time in wooden barrels containing beer-souring organisms to induce a secondary fermentation.

Lactic Fermentation Biochemistry

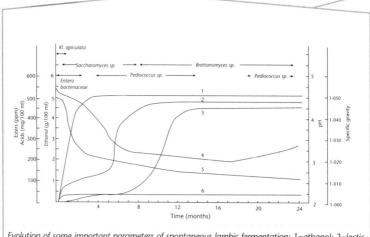

Evolution of some important parameters of spontaneous lambic fermentation: 1=ethanol; 2=lactic acid; 3=ethyl lactate; 4=pH; 5=real extract; 6=acetic acid, and sequence of microorganisms involved (Reprinted from Van Oevelen et al. 1977. J. Inst. Brew. 83:356-360).

Some producers prefer the use of a pure culture of *Saccharomyces cerevisiae* for primary fermentation. This promotes a cleaner alcoholic fermentation with no interference from lactic acid-producing bacteria. The souring of the beer occurs solely as the result of contact with microorganisms living in wood. Other producers prefer the use of a mixed culture. This allows souring in metal tanks immediately following primary fermentation, plus the ability to more closely maintain the balance of what organisms are in the beer and, therefore, what is introduced into the barrels.

Some brewers find the use of a mixed culture advantageous, owing to the possibility of "skimming" yeast from the top (or bottom) of wort during fermentation to "repitch" into successive batches. Commonly practiced in Flanders (and by less-than-traditional lambic producers), this centuries-old technique always assures a dose of the same microorganisms in succeeding batches of beer, even if not in the same proportions.

Mixed yeast cultures cannot be "repitched" forever. The bacteria eventually will grow at disproportionate levels to the yeast. Wyeast Laboratories found that with each repitching of its "Roeselare Blend," the lactic acid production became more pronounced, until the resulting beer was unpalatable. According to former Rodenbach brewer Peter Bouckaert, when lactic acid production from the primary Rodenbach culture became too harsh, it was washed at a pH of 2.1 for one hour to arrive at a lactic acid bacteria level below 5%. Acid washing of mixed cultures may not be practical to most small producers, and it may periodically be necessary to obtain a new culture from a different brewery or yeast company.

FERMENTATION OF FLANDERS RED BEERS

Flanders red beer experiences a mixed fermentation, often begun with a mixed culture. It undergoes a dual fermentation—a period of alcoholic fermentation followed by a lactic acid fermentation. Wort initially ferments for up to eight weeks. Once complete, the wort ages for eighteen months or longer, experiencing further acidification and fermentation by highly attenuative yeasts and lactic acid-producing bacteria. Sound simple? Read on.

The research into the fermentation of Flanders red ales is not as extensive as that into lambic fermentation. Dr. Hilde Martens, along with Verachtert, performed the bulk of the research at the Catholic University of Leuven. These studies

Flanders Red Fermentation Dynamics

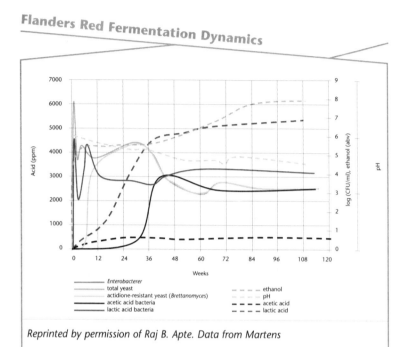

Reprinted by permission of Raj B. Apte. Data from Martens

looked specifically at beers known as "The Acid Ales of Roeselare," more commonly known as Rodenbach beers. Whereas lambic follows much the same path through fermentation, different Flanders red ales vary somewhat more in their fermentation and aging. I describe some of these different methods while referring specifically to fermentation as explained by Martens and Verachtert.

Very little mystery surrounds the use of a single, pure culture of yeast for fermentation, at least not when compared to the use of a mixed culture. These mixed cultures weren't arbitrarily developed from isolated strains of wild yeast and bacteria. Rodenbach, like other older breweries, once used a coolship (until 1992). I'm told at the brewery that Rodenbach spontaneously fermented

Flanders Red Fermentation Cycle

Dominant Microorganisms	Elapsed Time (Approximate)
Saccharomyces	1 Day
Lactobacillus	1 Week
Pediococcus	3 to 4 Weeks
Brettanomyces	8 Months

beer until around the mid-nineteenth century. (I'm also told Rodenbach attempted to make a "gueuze" as recently as 1970, and then stopped to focus on its primary red beer.) The mixed culture at Rodenbach was developed from microorganisms that naturally occurred in wort kept in that coolship.

According to Martens, the Rodenbach culture contains only *Saccharomyces cerevisiae* and lactic acid-producing bacteria—no *Brettanomyces* or other wild yeasts. Likely when developing that Rodenbach culture, the microbiologists isolated any naturally occurring wild yeasts, preferring those microorganisms to come from wooden barrels. The culture used today by several other Flanders breweries originated from the Rodenbach culture.

In spite of the mixed culture, the bulk of alcoholic fermentation still takes less than a week. Little acid is produced during this stage. In fact, the presence of acid-producing bacteria seems to have no effect as the wort reaches around 75% attenuation. The precise attenuation depends largely on the attenuative capabilities of the *Saccharomyces cerevisiae* strain(s) in the culture.

The time a wort spends in the primary fermenter depends upon the brewery. Rodenbach ferments the "heavy beer" (1.052, 13 °P) for four weeks—at 71 °F (22 °C) during primary alcoholic fermentation, and then at 59 °F (15 °C) during a secondary period of lactic acid formation. The "light beer" (1.044, 11 °Plato), on the other hand, ferments for up to eight weeks to promote greater lactic acid development (the heavy beer is aged, the light beer is blended directly from the stainless steel tanks). Once the primary alcoholic fermentation completes, *Saccharomyces cerevisiae* give way to growing populations of *Lactobacillus*, primarily strains of *Lactobacillus delbrueckii*. As lactic acid fermentation progresses, a noticeable increase in the amount of lactic acid occurs, and populations of *L. delbrueckii* give way to those of *Pediococcus parvulus*. *Lactobacillus delbrueckii* appears sensitive to the lactic acid produced, while *P. parvulus* has a lesser aversion. The attenuation of both worts may increase by around 5% while gaining an additional 0.5% abv during this period.

The next stage—tertiary fermentation in wooden vessels—is the most important stage for all beers experiencing mixed fermentation. During this period, many of the remaining sugars will be fermented by lactic acid-producing bacteria and highly attenuative yeasts producing alcohol and characteristic acids and esters. Tertiary fermentation may last from around eighteen months to as many as three years. The beer in a barrel may stop maturing after two years, and the difference between two and three, I'm told, is often negligible. The duration of tertiary fermentation depends on several factors, including the progress of the microorganisms in a specific barrel, the decision of the blender as to when the contents of a barrel is ready, and, economically speaking, how much product must be sold.

The amount of acetic and lactic acid will increase considerably during tertiary fermentation, as well as the esters ethyl lactate and ethyl acetate, produced by primarily *Brettanomyces* (most of the

Lactobacillus dies during the earlier stage). The balance between acetic acid, lactic acid, ethyl acetate, and ethyl lactate is very important. Brewers prefer a slower fermentation, as the microorganisms will more effectively produce acids and esters in balanced amounts over a longer period of time. Temperature contributes to the speed of wild fermentation. Simply put, warmer beer matures more quickly, because wild yeast and bacteria prefer warmer temperatures. Oxygen also influences fermentation. The greater the level of oxygen dissolved into the wort, the faster the fermentation. The porous nature of a barrel plays a key role in the amount of oxygen allowed into the wort, which will be covered in depth in the next chapter.

At some point during tertiary fermentation, the Rodenbach heavy beer may reach approximately 8% abv, while the pH may dip as low as 3.2. All Flanders beers experiencing mixed

fermentation will approach superattenuation, similar to lambic. The Flanders beers will come close to the terminal gravity of a lambic with a potential final apparent attenuation of 98%. (The sweetness attributed to some of the products on the market comes from blending with younger beer or sugar and pasteurization.)

Comparisons have been drawn between the fermentation cycles of lambic and Flanders red beers. The development of the major microorganisms during the tertiary fermentation is similar for both types of beer. Once the *Enterobacter* and *Saccharomyces* stages of lambic fermentation complete, similar fermentations occur involving *Brettanomyces* and *Pediococcus.* Virtually absent from the lambic fermentation is *Lactobacillus,* which lambic brewers scrupulously avoid, but plays a key role in the acid development of Flanders red ales.

Brettanomyces and *Pediococcus* appear to work best together at the fermentation of dextrins. Both experience optimal growth when present in the same wort. The relationship between *Brettanomyces* and lactic acid-producing bacteria during fermentation is still poorly understood.

A better explanation exists for the difference in the behavior of *Brettanomyces* between spontaneous and mixed fermentation. The Flanders worts contain a high concentration of fermentable sugars, most of which are consumed during the early stages of fermentation by "early adaptors," including *Saccharomyces cerevisiae* and lactic acid-producing bacteria. The supplies of glucose and maltose are quickly depleted, leaving a wort with fewer dextrins on which the *Brettanomyces* may feed than in a lambic wort. By the time *Brettanomyces* achieve optimal cell growth for fermentation, a lower amount of carbohydrates remain, thus a smaller amount of by-products. Also absent are the nutrients present in autolyzed *Saccharomyces*, since the Flanders acid ales are transferred from their primary fermenting vessel after the completion of primary and secondary fermentation.

The chart below compares a number of key characteristics between gueuze refermented in the bottle and unblended Flanders red ale (of Roeselare). Not a precise account of the composition of these two types of beer, the chart displays an approximate look at how they compare and differ. Most of the same dominant microorganisms are responsible for their fermentation and similar by-products for their flavor and aroma.

Comparison of Fermentation Products in Gueuze and Flanders Red Ale

	Gueuze (1)	Flanders Red (2)	Flavor Threshold
Highest Apparent Extract, °Plato	0.1 *	1.36	-
Ethanol, % abv	5.0-8.0 **	6.6-7.5	-
pH	3.25-3.45	3.19-3.26	-
Acetic Acid, ppm	656-1,238	1,511-2,489	300
Lactic Acid, ppm	1,890-5,277	4,248-6,272	400
Ethyl Acetate, ppm	61-167	92-127	30
Ethyl Lactate, ppm	361-483	215-289	50

Data taken from (1) Van Oevelen, et al., (1976) and (2) Martens, et al., (1996) except * from Kumara, et al., (1991) and ** compiled from commercial examples

INOCULATION

The most predictable way to make a "wild brew" involves the inoculation of wort with one or more microorganisms (not of *Saccharomyces* sp.) capable of fermentation and acidification. Different types of wort include one of a lambic profile, one that resembles a Flanders red or brown, or something completely different. Barrels intended for tertiary aging of wort must, in many cases, still be inoculated with beer containing fermenting and souring microorganisms that will become resident in the wood. Exceptions include obtaining a mature barrel from a traditional wild beer producer (dream on) or aging with the existing microorganisms in a used wine barrel (more on the second topic in the next chapter).

Unless you are able to practice complete spontaneous fermentation, at some point you will need to inoculate your wort with some type of culture or "cocktail"—a term some brewers use to refer to their mixed culture of yeast and bacteria. Many

An "open square" fermenter at De Dolle Brouwers in Esen.

possibilities exist, including a wort fermented with a strain of *Saccharomyces cerevisiae,* one fermented with a mixed culture of yeast and bacteria, aged with *Brettanomyces* or lactic acid-producing bacteria, or even fermented with only one or more *Brettanomyces* sp. (really!).

Pure cultures exist of the dominant yeast and bacteria necessary to reproduce a lambic (to some degree), a Flanders red-brown beer, or a new variation. Pre-mixed blends of yeast and bacteria also exist to replicate the balance of microorganisms needed to produce a lambic or Flanders red. The blends from the two major U.S. yeast companies—Wyeast Laboratories and White Labs—are detailed in the Appendix.

Yeast blends work under the concept that the cells of the individual microorganisms will grow proportionately to their original number in the blend, given the proper nutrients, temperature, and oxygen. The different concentrations of microorganisms in the blend reflect this balance. In simplest terms purchase one of the yeast blends, inoculate your wort, and wait. You may alternately choose to purchase the proper microorganisms separately to attempt to control the fermentation of a beer by inoculating (pitching) the microorganisms at different times throughout fermentation. Before discussing the specifics of inoculation, one of the classic styles uses this production method: Flanders brown/oud bruin.

FERMENTATION OF FLANDERS BROWN BEERS

Flanders browns remain the simpler of the two Flanders wild ales to ferment. The brewer inoculates all of the necessary fermenting and acid-producing microorganisms prior to primary fermentation. Flanders browns ferment for one week, generally in open

The open fermenter at Liefmans of Oudenaarde being filled with wort.

square vessels with a mixed culture. (The mixed culture at the classic East Flanders brewery Liefmans originated at Rodenbach.)

As wort ferments in an "open square," some wild microorganisms come into contact with the wort, most suppressed by healthily fermenting *Saccharomyces cerevisiae*. For this reason, breweries in the United Kingdom using "open squares" do not wind up with sour beer. (Those that do develop that taste due to poor sanitation.)

Similar to the Flanders red ales, alcoholic fermentation by strains of *Saccharomyces cerevisiae* lasts for about one week. The wort will be fermented to within roughly 75% of the starting gravity. Once primary fermentation completes, the brewer transfers the wort to temperature-controlled stainless steel tanks for a lengthy secondary fermentation.

The secondary fermentation consists of acidification performed by populations of lactic acid-producing bacteria. Populations of *Lactobacillus* and *Pediococcus* increase during a period of warm fermentation for up to two brewing seasons. Higher temperatures significantly favor lactic acid development. Stainless steel tanks eliminate the threat of exposure to oxygen or ambient temperature fluctuation. Heterofermentative *Lactobacillus* produces acetic as well as lactic acid, the latter being the more desirable. The longest aged worts in the tanks at Liefmans are significantly drier and more lactic than the eventual (blended) product available in bottles; however, they do not achieve superattenuation without the presence of *Brettanomyces*.

INOCULATED LAMBIC

A true lambic must be spontaneously fermented. A brewer pitches microorganisms dominant during lambic fermentation to effectively "mimic" the fermentation cycle to produce a beer often called a "pseudo-lambic." The first decision regards the choice between individual commercially available cultures of *Brettanomyces, Pediococcus cerevisiae, Saccharomyces cerevisiae,* etc., or the use of a blend. This choice depends largely upon your desire to "nudge" each different microorganism by adding them at a specific time or by allowing the microorganisms to follow the cycle on their own.

I feel if you are going to pitch all of the organisms at once, choose a blend for microbial balance, ease of use, and lower cost. I am a fan of the *laissez-faire* doctrine of pitching. The self-contained fermentative process of lambic cannot be precisely reproduced by inoculation. I do not, however, dispute the success of brewers using a "pitching schedule." Brewers and scientists differ on the best order to pitch each culture.

One schedule mirrors the microbial stages of lambic. Pitch the *Saccharomyces cerevisiae* immediately after cooling the wort to

68° F (20° C). After the completion of primary fermentation, add *Pediococcus cerevisiae*. Approximately six months later, when the pH is low, add *Brettanomyces*. This schedule attempts to introduce the microorganisms to the wort at a time when conditions favor their growth and production of their desired by-products.

A different schedule adds *Brettanomyces* immediately after the end of primary fermentation, prior to any lactic acid-producing bacteria. After six to eight months, add *Pediococcus cerevisiae* and wait. The theory behind this schedule is that you can always acidify the wort later. This may differ from the traditional cycle, but *Brettanomyces* grow slowly in lambic wort, and this schedule will give them a chance to reproduce without acid-producing bacteria competing for nutrients. If you are not using a turbid mash, which favors *Brettanomyces* growth, this schedule may be your best option.

A second decision regards *Enterobacter*. Commercially available lambic blends do not include species of this duly maligned genus of bacteria. (Nonpathogenic species are available by special order from Wyeast Laboratories, if you absolutely must have them.) Other homemade procedures such as the "kitchen inoculation"[1] were conceived to introduce what was once a largely unknown contributor to lambic fermentation. Considering the lambic producers' desire to avoid *Enterobacter*, in light of the undesirable effect they can have on lambic, I think it's best to leave them out of inoculated lambic. The other microorganisms responsible for fermentation should produce more than enough acid without objectionable side-effects.

[1]The "kitchen inoculation" involves exposing wort to *Enterobacter* commonly found where raw food is prepared. I do not recommend this procedure.

Traditional lambic fermentation involved dozens of different strains of microorganisms. Inoculated lambic does not have this array of microbial diversity. Homebrewers have found that periodically adding the dregs of a bottle of traditional lambic to the fermenter will add to the population of microorganisms and promote complexity.

The final point regarding inoculated lambic: Ferment the wort in a single vessel. Do not transfer/rack the wort until you are ready to age a portion on fruit or to blend/bottle. Use of a single vessel during all stages of fermentation allows the microorganisms to metabolize nutrients present in autolyzed yeasts. *Brettanomyces* will feed on these cells during the later phases of fermentation, when the supply of dextrins has been exhausted. *Brettanomyces* will grow and produce their by-products without autolyzed yeast, just not as effectively.

The fermentation of a lambic wort cannot be hurried. Lambic fermentation is the snail of the brewing world. Given the proper growth factors, the microorganisms will reproduce, ferment, and acidify the wort. If a batch doesn't have the desired characteristics, wait another six months and take another sample.

INOCULATED FLANDERS RED

The fermentation of a Flanders red does not occur as naturally as a lambic, making it easier to reproduce. Virtually identical microorganisms—*Brettanomyces, Pediococcus,* and *Saccharomyces cerevisiae*—with the addition of *Lactobacillus* and *Acetobacter* to the "cocktail," ferment and acidify the wort. A brewer does not inoculate *Acetobacter*, however; they "infect" wort via exposure to oxygen through wooden fermentation vessels or suitable alternative (covered in depth in the next chapter).

First, decide on pure cultures of each microorganism or a commercially available blend (see Appendix). If you chose a blend, simply cool the wort and pitch the mixed culture. If you choose not to use a blend, ferment your wort with a neutral *Saccharomyces cerevisiae* until it achieves the expected apparent attenuation, and pitch your homemade cocktail with the wort in a secondary fermentation vessel.

Unlike lambic fermentation, rack the wort into a different vessel for the next stage of fermentation. *Brettanomyces* only plays a supporting role in the acidification of a Flanders red, so the wort need not be fermented on top of autolyzed yeast. For the same reason, the involved pitching schedule of an inoculated lambic is unnecessary. An equivalent amount of patience, however, is required.

BRETTANOMYCES

The black sheep of the brewing yeast family for centuries, while strain after strain of *Saccharomyces* have been cultured for everyday commercial use, *Brettanomyces* are left to the fringe. Bring a beer you've made using *Brettanomyces* to a friend's brewery, and you may find yourself and your bottle being suddenly irradiated. Well, the *Wild Ones* finally get their day! *Brettanomyces* can ferment more than a few scraps of dextrins the *Saccharomyces* left at the table. *Brettanomyces* can ferment a wort without help from their more popular cousins or clean up the scraps once the meal is complete.

In other words, *Brettanomyces* can be used as the only microorganism to ferment a beer. *Brettanomyces* reproduce as readily—albeit more slowly—than *Saccharomyces cerevisiae*, conditions favoring. Variables include available oxygen, cell count, choice of species and strains, available carbohydrates, temperature, and alcohol.

During the traditional tertiary fermentation of Belgian wild beers, when *Brettanomyces* are most active, little oxygen is available. A study conducted at the Catholic University of Leuven found increasing the availability of oxygen increased the cell count but decreased "overall activity" of *Brettanomyces* during fermentation. *Brettanomyces* behave differently when fully aerated. They propagate faster and ferment very fast in a standard fermentation environment, sometimes faster than *Saccharomyces cerevisiae*. Too much oxygen can stress cell walls though, so don't go overboard with aeration.

One of the most important factors to a quick start to fermentation appears to be cell count. Most strains of *Brettanomyces* reproduce more slowly than *Saccharomyces cerevisiae*. Beginning fermentation with a higher cell count than normal appears to promote a quicker start to fermentation.

The other important factor regarding a successful *Brettanomyces* fermentation appears to be species/strain selection. Some strains may reproduce at a rate similar to *Saccharomyces cerevisiae*, some strains will grow more slowly, and others will show no signs of fermentation in a reasonable period after inoculation. Remember, also, *Dekkera* grows more slowly than *Brettanomyces*. Some brewers believe the production of compounds leading to a "mousy" character is strain dependent. The only way to know how a particular strain will behave comes from experience.

Brettanomyces must compete for nutrients during spontaneous and mixed fermentation. By the time *Brettanomyces* achieve a high enough cell count, a low amount of available carbohydrates—

mostly dextrins—remains. Introducing *Brettanomyces* to unfermented wort without other competing microorganisms provides a greater amount of carbohydrates to ferment.

Conditions favoring, *Brettanomyces* can ferment a wort of moderate starting gravity within a couple points of a "typical" finishing gravity within about one to two weeks. Temperature will influence the speed of fermentation. Fermentation temperatures as high as 78° F (26° C) promote a rapid fermentation. Temperatures over 80° F (27° C) may contribute to unpleasant characteristics. Temperatures under 70° F (21° C) promote a slower fermentation and give the *Brettanomyces* more time to form the requisite by-products.

Brettanomyces do not exhibit superattenuative properties as the only fermenting microorganisms in wort. They leave a higher amount of sugars unfermented, exhibiting a behavior similar to *Saccharomyces cerevisiae*. As a solo act, *Brettanomyces* appear to be satisfied with "fermentable" sugars, at least in the short term. While too new to understand long-term behavior following solo fermentation, a safe assumption is that *Brettanomyces* will continue to ferment dextrins at a slow rate.

Alcohol generally does not bother *Brettanomyces*. Gueuze and Flanders acid ale ferment to 7 to 8% abv; strong, aged English ales were commonly infected with *Brettanomyces;* and they can also live in wine to roughly 18% abv (although in laboratory tests they die at around 13% abv). The higher concentration of sugar prior to primary fermentation that is necessary to produce a stronger beer, however, may have a detrimental effect on the cell walls. *Brettanomyces* likely will get tired in higher alcohol beers—similar to *Saccharomyces*—and take a long time to complete fermentation or leave a higher finishing gravity.

Brettanomyces will readily form acids and esters during a long, slow fermentation, but not so easily during a conventional fermentation. Fermentation is a reductive process. *Brettanomyces* is an oxidative yeast; the production of acids is an oxidative process. The nature of each of the two processes is somewhat mutually exclusive. *Brettanomyces* will, therefore, produce alcohol more quickly than acid during a conventional fermentation.

Brewers often favor ethyl lactate, esterified from alcohol and lactic acid, for characteristically fruity aromas. There may be little or no lactic acid produced during primary fermentation by *Brettanomyces*. Simply adding lactic acid to the fermenter can con-

tribute a harsh sourness. As a more desirable solution, add some acidulated malt to the grist. Another more natural method—suggested by Peter Bouckaert—involves taking a portion of the first runnings of the mash and acidifying with *Lactobacillus*, then adding the solution to the kettle at the end of the boil. Not much lactic acid is required; don't bother with a sour mash.

Brettanomyces can still fill their role as complementary yeast to *Saccharomyces cerevisiae*. One or more strains can be added to a beer at bottling. Wild character will develop and become stronger over time and can be accelerated a bit by higher temperatures. *Brettanomyces* will slowly ferment dextrins, but the beer will not reach superattenuation.

No studies have been conducted on *Brettanomyces* for use as the sole source of fermentation. More traditional characteristics occur during slower fermentation. Rushing the fermentation with aeration, higher cell counts, and temperatures may reduce the traditional "wild" character.

Studies on yeast strains suitable for the fermentation of beer concentrate on *Saccharomyces cerevisiae*, because funding comes from large brewing companies. The bulk of what we know about *Brettanomyces* comes from studies on lambic and from the wine industry. Generally seen as an overall contributor to fermentation, *Brettanomyces* generally appear during the later stages of fermentation. Only very recently a select few American breweries have begun breaking their own ground and trying entirely new things with *Brettanomyces*.

LACTIC ACID-PRODUCING BACTERIA

Lactic acid can be pleasant as the only sour character in a beer, though not in more than a relatively modest quantity. Beers from the Fantôme brewery in Belgium often develop a "house" lactic character, particular to the *terroir,* that ranges from pleasingly complementary to terribly oppressive. Lactic acid-producing bacteria can grow out of control without warning.

Lactobacillus and *Pediococcus* will produce copious amounts of acid when pitched with high enough cell counts and at the optimal temperature. If pitched along with *Saccharomyces cerevisiae*, the yeast generally dominate the bacteria. In most cases *Lactobacillus* and *Pediococcus* do not come into play until most of the simple sugars have been fermented, and the bacteria must feed on the remaining complex sugars at a much slower rate.

Lactic acid will develop over time, and production may be accelerated by warmer temperatures and retarded by alcohol. *Lactobacillus* and *Pediococcus* both produce lactic acid. Some species of *Lactobacillus* (i.e., *L. delbrueckii*) produce only lactic acid but react negatively to hop acids. Other species (i.e., *L. brevis*) have no aversion to hop acids but produce a number of other acids and diacetyl. *Pediococcus damnosus* is rather hop-tolerant and produces not only lactic acid but also high levels of diacetyl.

One interesting way of acidifying a beer was proposed by Martens, who suggested a split fermentation involving the same or similar worts in two fermenting vessels. Inoculate one fermentation vessel with a *Saccharomyces cerevisiae*, the other with *Lactobacillus* and/or *Pediococcus*. Blend the eventual beers (to taste) to make the final product. To increase the amount of lactic acid produced, ferment the batch containing lactic acid-producing bacteria at a warmer temperature, as high as 98° F (37° C). This technique is sometimes used in the production of Berliner weisse. A split fermentation, however, concentrates on lactic acid production without other flavor and aroma components, including acetic acid, ethyl acetate, and ethyl lactate.

Don't feel that the addition of lactic acid to a beer will lend a character comparable to that contributed by lactic acid-producing bacteria. The flavors resulting from the addition of lactic acid, on its own, have been described as harsh and medicinal without other balancing by-products produced by bacteria. This book is about wild brews, not sour beers.

seven

Fermentation and Maturation Vessels

"They [the barrels] keep secrets even I do not know."
–Rudi Ghequire of Brouwerij Rodenbach

Most brewers find the choice of a fermentation vessel a simple one. Commercial brewers generally choose stainless steel cylindroconical tanks. The homebrewer commonly chooses glass—a 5-gallon glass carboy. Wood is extremely important to wild brewers. Most traditional producers of wild beers age at least a portion of the final product in wooden barrels for several years.

While the wild brewer may desire the flavors and aromas that may be imparted from the wood, more importantly, the wooden barrel provides beer-souring microorganisms with a place to live and breed. Many of these microorganisms require at least small amounts of oxygen to live and propagate. *Brettanomyces*, in particular, ferments better in the presence of oxygen. Wood's porousness, both for the potential for "infection" by microorganisms and for permeability to small amounts of oxygen, accounts for its value in transforming the flavor and aroma of wort.

Anatomy of a Barrel

Stave	A narrow strip of wood forming part of the sides.
Stave Joint	The point where two staves meet. Sometimes sealed with reeds or attached with dowels (wooden pegs), particularly in larger barrels.
Hoop	Metal ring(s) that hold the barrel together.
Head	The round(ed) sections, one on either end.
Croze	Groove in the staves that receives the head.
Bung Hole	Small round opening on a side and/or in the head of a barrel through which liquid is poured or drained.
Bung	Wooden stopper used to seal the bung hole.
Entryway	Opening at the base of larger barrels through which can pass liquid or people (not at the same time).
Spigot	A small "faucet" placed in the bunghole of a cask for the removal of liquid.
Spile	Wooden peg used to repair "end grain" leaks, usually near the croze, or to plug up a bung that has been breached.
Wedge	Angled piece of wood used to repair a leak in a head or stave.

The lambic brewers consider the microorganisms living in the barrels as important as those that inoculate wort overnight in the coolship. For Flanders beers, many, if not all, species of microorganisms—save perhaps *Saccharomyces cerevisiae*—live in the wood. According to Frank Boon, "The finest *Brettanomyces* survive in the wood."

Wooden barrels hold a special relationship to the fermentation and maturation of traditional and not-so-traditional wild beers. Key points to learn about barrels include the different types, the wood used in construction, level of toast or char, flavor, and aroma contributed to a beer, and how a barrel has been used. Once familiar with those points, it's time to learn about selection, cleaning, usage, and ongoing care of a barrel. But don't be discouraged if you feel the use of wooden barrels is beyond your current desire or capabilities. I also discuss alternatives such as oak chips and glass, plastic, and stainless steel fermenters that will achieve credible if not precisely comparable results. First, onto wood!

CHARACTERISTICS OF WOOD AND BARRELS

Factors including the type of wood, method of production, size, and prior use will affect the amount of character imparted from a barrel to the liquid stored within. A brewer must first understand these factors in order to properly select a barrel for the fermentation and/or maturation of a wild brew.

Traditional brewers favor oak as the primary wood used to produce their barrels for its strength, resistance to decay, and general ease of use. Oak will always impart some of its own character to a beer. The wild brewer desires barrels already used to age an alcoholic beverage, as the character contributed by a new barrel will be oppressive.

The designation "oaky" refers to the aroma or flavor of a liquid that has interacted with the oak while in a barrel. More than 200 components of wood may directly contribute to an alcoholic beverage, although only about a dozen are detectable by the human palate, and three deserve closer attention. One of the primary compounds contributed is vanillin. This compound will lend a vanillalike aroma and corresponding sweetness, even in barely detectable amounts. Oak also contributes tannins. This compound adds a drying, astringent, acidic character often present in red wines. A third—the unique spicy character contributed by methyloctalactones—differs according to the origin (country, region, and even forest) of the wood.

The classic wood for the production of wine barrels comes from French oak—either the fragile European oak (*Quercus sessiliflora*) or the English oak (*Quercus robur*), also known as "common oak" to arborists. Ideal for its high level of tannin, French oak exhibits a highly porous nature. Additionally, the forests (some of which date back to the time of Napoleon) are close to the great wine-producing regions. The oak from different French forests each lend slightly different "spice" characteristics. The high production costs associated with French oak mean the barrels will generally be expensive.

Finally gaining acceptance around the world for wine barrel production, the strong North American oak (*Quercus alba)* or white oak is commonly used to make barrels destined for Kentucky or Tennessee to age bourbon or whiskey. Barrels made from American oak will contribute a high degree of vanilla and toastiness. "Spice" flavors contributed by American oak vary more widely from different states and different forests than do those contributed by French oak. Barrels made from American oak typically cost less than half the price of French oak barrels.

The perception of American oak as inferior to French oak was once accredited to a problem with the wood. Experts now attribute the cause to the preparation of the wood and method of barrel construction. The traditional French method of producing barrels involves air-drying the wood for at least twenty-four months to attain the necessary seasoning. The newer American method, which uses a kiln to dry the wood, is more suited to whiskey and bourbon than wine. Additionally, the staves for whiskey and bourbon barrels are sawn, while French barrelmakers split the wood along the grain. These two differences in the French method produce barrels with a more subtle effect on wine.

The way the wood is treated exhibits a great deal of influence on the amount of character the barrel will impart. During construction, a cooper places a partially assembled barrel over a wood fire. During this step, the inside of the barrel will be "charred" in a kiln to produce whiskey and bourbon barrels or "toasted" over a fire for use with wine. Essentially produced with light, medium, or heavy toast/char, the amount or depth has an effect on the eventual contents of the barrel. The heavier the toast/char, the greater the character imparted. The decision on the level of toast for wine barrels depends on the grape variety and style of wine to be produced. American whiskey or bourbon producers often prefer a heavy char to impart greater oak and often a "burnt" character to their liquor.

By the middle of the twentieth century, most barrels used to hold beer were "pitched"—lined with an organic resin or wax to isolate the beer from the actual wood. This served to effectively eliminate any sour character imparted from microorganisms living in the barrel. It also eliminated any character the wood imparted to the beer. Producers of other alcoholic beverages generally did not follow this practice, as they desired the contributions from the wood.

The contributions of oak aging are considered essential to many fine wines. Producers of specialty wines, including cognac, port, and sherry, consider oak barrels an irreplaceable part of their production. Distillers commonly age Scotch, other whiskeys, and bourbon for more than a decade in oak. Even beer was once commonly fermented and aged in barrels, but that is now reserved for only a select number of products. Aging one of these alcoholic beverages in an oak barrel will extract some of the compounds, rendering the effects of the oak less pronounced on succeeding batches;[1] eventually, this process leaves a barrel well suited for use by the wild brewer.

Each batch of alcoholic liquid matured in a barrel extracts tannins and other compounds, leaving less and less in the wood, until the barrel has little to contribute. A barrel used to mature six batches of wine, for instance, will have less character to contribute than one used only three times. The age of the barrel is also important. One cooperage in Bordeaux states a barrel will contribute aromatic compounds to a wine for two years and allow fermentation for another three, before sediment and oxidation will end its useful life for the winemaker.

Used barrels have little use to winemakers. To remedy this, barrels may be subjected to a reconditioning or "retoasting" process, which cleans the barrel and replaces the toast lost during the previous fermentations. This process involves disassembling, stripping off a portion of the wood, toasting, and reassembling the barrel. One Bordeaux cooperage warns of using "retoasted" barrels, saying they can contribute a "burnt character." This

[1]Some distilled beverages (bourbon, for instance) are required by law to use only new barrels for aging.

appears largely dependent on the actual process; some are less abusive to the barrel than others. The reconditioning processes "revive" the oak character subdued by years of aging wine by stripping the inner surface of the barrel to reveal fresher oak underneath. The oak character will be more aggressive, and the barrel staves thinner, as a result, neither of which is desirable to the wild brewer.

Common Barrels Used in Belgium

Barrel	Volume (liters)	Volume (gallons)
Bordeaux	225	59.4
Burgundy	228	60.2
Tonne	267	70.4
Pipe	650	171.7
Foudre	10,000-30,000	~2,500-8,000

SIZES OF BARRELS

Barrels come in many different styles. Most of the famous wine-making regions (e.g., Bordeaux, Burgundy) have traditional shapes to their barrels (and bottles). Barrels come in different sizes and have variations in the thickness of the staves. You may find a barrel as small as 5 or 10 gallons (~20-40 liters), although the beginning (standard) size for a commercial wine or whiskey barrel in the United States is 53 gallons (200 liters). Many larger variations exist up to the type known as *foudres*, ceiling-high barrels of varying capacity, as large as nearly 8,000 gallons (300 hectoliters).

Traditional brewers consider size an important factor in the fermentation and maturation of beer. Simply put, larger barrels produce more complex wild beer. The surface-to-volume ratio—the contact between the inner surface of the barrel and the volume of the wort—contributes to the speed of fermentation.

A foudre *in the Mort Subite brewery in Kobbegem. Note the bottle at the center of the barrel, for scale.*

The surface-to-volume ratio gets smaller, as the size of the barrel increases. In a small barrel, you have a low volume of wort, but it is proportionally in contact with a greater amount of wood. As the size of the barrel increases, less liquid actually comes in contact with wood. Wood is porous—permeable to oxygen. The lower the surface-to-volume ratio, the less oxygen diffused into the beer.

The thickness of the barrel staves also influences the amount of oxygen diffused into the beer. The thickness of the staves increases with the size of the barrel. Thicker staves allow less oxygen to pass into the beer. The larger the barrel, the less proportional oxygen diffused into the beer.

Oxygen speeds fermentation by *Brettanomyces,* which ferment better in the presence of oxygen. Acid and ester production, however, do not proportionally increase with the speed of fermentation. Oxygen also promotes the growth of *Acetobacter* and retards the growth of *Pediococcus* and *Lactobacillus.* Higher

Oxygen Diffusion Into Selected Wooden Casks

Type	Volume [liters/gallons]	O$_2$ cc/L/year
Rodenbach Wooden Tun (Large)	20,000/5,280	0.53
Rodenbach Wooden Tun (Small)	12,000/3,168	0.86
Wine Barrel	300/79.2	8.5
Small "Homebrewer's" Barrel	40/10.6	23

Reprinted by permission of Raj B. Apte

levels of oxygen will cause acetic acid and ethyl acetate to be produced more quickly than balancing lactic acid and ethyl lactate. Too much acetic acid, and you have vinegar, not a quality product.

Oxygen also speeds the fermentation of a wild beer and promotes growth of only certain microorganisms. Slower fermentation produces a more complex beer of potentially higher quality. The microorganisms in a barrel take time to produce their respective by-products, which must be in balance and contribute to the complexity of the beer. Additionally, exposure of the wort to more oxygen increases the risk of oxidation, a flaw in any beer.

The size of the barrel also helps to determine how much the changes in ambient temperature will affect the beer. A liquid can only absorb and lose so much heat at a time. The amount of time required for wort to gain or lose heat increases with the volume of the wort. A larger volume of liquid will maintain a consistent temperature longer than a smaller volume. Temperature extremes throughout the year do not concern brewers with larger barrels as much as those with smaller barrels.

SELECTING BARRELS

Many choices confront the wild brewer when selecting one or more barrels. They include the type of wood, toast or char level, size, prior use, and condition. The brewer also must decide what he/she expects from a barrel. Do you desire only the microbial contents, a pleasant oaky character, or one of heavy char and whiskey flavor? Don't be limited to only one broad characteristic. The importance of a number of barrels with different characteristics will become evident during the chapter on blending. While reading this section, consider all of the potential options and characteristics available when selecting one or more barrels.

Traditional wild beers generally receive minimal contributions from the actual oak. Still, as one Flanders brewer mentioned, "Oak stays oak; you will never entirely lose that character." Depending on the character you find pleasant in a lambic, Flanders acid ale, or unique interpretation, a complementary oaky character may be desirable. Producers of wild beers consider the character imparted by a new barrel, however, to be quite oppressive. You will want to choose a used barrel from a number of possible sources.

Preferred for lambic and Flanders acid ales, wine barrels present both a mellow character and microorganisms already resident in the wood. Specialty wine barrels, such as those used

Pilsner Urquell barrels have found a new home at the De Cam Geuzestekerij in Gooik.

to ferment cognac or port, maintain a unique character contributed to the wood by the specific wine. Whiskey and bourbon barrels will contribute a powerful character, although it is generally considered too dominant for traditional wild beers. Other less aggressive distilled spirits leave barrels acceptable for many styles of wild beer. Two traditional gueuze blenders prefer used beer barrels, although few breweries use barrels any longer to age beer.

How extensively a barrel was used also determines residual character. The potential character imparted from the wood to a beer decreases with each "filling." Conversely, the character imparted from the previous contents of a barrel increases with time and use. Cleaning the barrel directly influences residual character, which is discussed in the next section.

The level of toast also has a direct effect on how much the barrel will influence its contents. Lambic and Flanders red brewers generally prefer medium toast; for other types of beer, it depends on how much wood character the brewer desires in a beer. A higher toast will lend a more aggressive, oaky character. I mentioned brewers consider the heavy char of bourbon and whiskey barrels too assertive for the traditional wild beers. If one of these barrels is your best option, don't fret; some potential solutions are described in the next section on cleaning the barrel.

The type of oak is an important factor in selection. While the debate over the character contributed by French and American oak rages on, the wild brewer considers French oak ideal for a different reason. French oak is generally thought to be more porous than American oak, which aids in oxygen diffusion. Many of the resident microbes require small amounts of oxygen to feed and propagate. American oak, meanwhile, has more "water channels" that can block the air. The small producer, however, must often face a compromise based on availability and cost.

Five- or 10-gallon (~20-40 liter) barrels appear very compatible with the batch size of a homebrewer, but wineries and distilleries consider them impractical. Small barrels can be found at shops that cater to home winemakers, but they'll generally be new and quite expensive. The price of a barrel does not drop in proportion to the size. The most common size in the United States will be the 60-gallon (227-liter) wine barrel or 53-gallon (200-liter) bourbon barrel. A winery or distillery may be looking to unload a used barrel at a fraction of the original cost. While larger barrels produce more complex results, the small producer and homebrewer also must consider availability and the ability to fill and cellar a particular size of barrel.

Smaller casks do present a few advantages to the smaller producer. First, they are more manageable. Smaller barrels are easier to move and to cellar; require less beer to fill and less effort to empty. Second, if time is a factor, beer in smaller barrels will mature more quickly. In the long run, the beer might not have the same complexity, but you will have a finished product sooner using smaller barrels. Third, you potentially have a greater variety of flavors and aromas when it comes time to blend. Since each barrel is unique, using the same volume of beer in a number of smaller casks offers greater possibilities than using fewer larger casks.

Reconditioned barrels do not present an ideal option. I have never heard any of the producers I speak with mention the use of reconditioned barrels (and they often feign ignorance of the process). Traditional producers have their own cleaning process, which is more applicable to fermenting and aging wild beer. Also, do not select a pitched barrel, which is effectively sealed from any microbial growth, or you will have to remove the pitch before using the barrel.

Whether you purchase a used car or a used barrel, the condition is of utmost importance. How was it treated, and how will it perform once you are the owner? There are, of course, a number of factors to consider. Avoid barrels with any off-aromas, as they may be evidence of harmful bacteria and/or mold that you may not be able to remove. An obvious ring or clumps of sediment around the inside of the barrel also may be evidence of unwanted growth and be difficult to clean effectively. Ask when the barrel was last emptied—that affects the condition of the wood. A freshly emptied barrel will be more likely to be "watertight" and less likely to have mold growth.

Any growth inside the barrel may also signal the presence of oxygen due to a leak or because the barrel has dried out. Check the condition of the wood and joints. The barrel should be free of any small holes or bores (from insects), spiles or wedges, or other obvious repairs. These may jeopardize the barrel's ability to hold liquid without leaking over a long period of time. Check the heads. They should fit cleanly into the croze without any obvious gaps. Don't be afraid to kick the tires. If the barrel is big enough, climb in and poke around a bit. If not, give the barrel a good inspection with a flashlight. Don't wind up with a lemon!

BARRELS AND MICROORGANISMS
Wooden barrels present an ideal breeding ground for wild yeast and bacteria. But how do they get in there, and how do we know they will produce a tasteful product? The answer to the first question is rather concise: You put them there. The second answer is also short but a bit harder to accept: You don't know until your wort has completed fermentation and maturation. The long answer to both questions can swing a few variables in the brewer's favor.

OK, I simplified a bit; microorganisms likely already live in used barrels. Wine (and beer) barrels certainly have a plethora of microbes more than happy to at least partially ferment and acidify wort. *Brettanomyces* find their way into even fresh barrels containing unfermented wine. Distillers' barrels will not contain any microorganisms due to the presence of greater amounts of alcohol in the aging spirits. Empty that or any barrel, let the alcohol evaporate, and allow it to dry, and colonies of lactic acid-producing bacteria will feel quite at home. Microbes that grow after a barrel has been emptied are usually not terribly friendly toward beer. A process of preparation and inoculation will help stabilize the unknown ecosystem of a used barrel.

When I say "you put them there," I mean remove the residue and microorganisms that live on the inner surface of the barrel and replace them with the microorganisms that were inoculated into a beer. By filling a barrel with inoculated, unfermented wort, the brewer exposes the barrel to the microorganisms in the wort, which will make a (hopefully) happy home of the "new" barrel. But before filling a "new" barrel, it should be cleaned.

Outsiders frequently mistake the conditions surrounding the barrels in many "wild breweries" as a disregard for hygiene

Kris Herteleer's barrels at De Dolle Brouwers in Esen.

and sanitation. This is not true. I believe the wild brewer has more to consider about hygiene than any other type of brewer in the world. Most brewers use a combination of chemicals to hopefully rid the brewery of all microorganisms. The chemicals designed to clean the modern brewery are unacceptable for cleaning barrels, as they will have a negative effect on and will leach into the wood and, eventually, your beer.

The wild brewer fights to keep wild yeast and bacteria at bay, while never completely destroying them. Wood is porous and virtually impossible to totally disinfect. Besides, the wild brewer doesn't want to disinfect a barrel completely. The wild brewer wishes to eliminate the "weaker," more plentiful microorganisms while allowing the "stronger" ones to survive. Generally, good, strong microorganisms that produce a "pleasant" character live deeper in the wood. The cleaning regimen of the traditional producer rids the barrels of residue and promotes "the survival of the fittest."

I don't wish to discount the brewers who use unrinsed wine barrels. The lees present in a freshly emptied wine barrel can help to age a very pleasant beer. I emphasize the word "fresh." Wait very long, and the barrel will be ripe with unwanted growth of bacteria and mold. Ridding the barrel of unknown yeast and bacteria before replacing them with microorganisms present in your own beer simply represents a more predictable solution.

PREPARING A BARREL FOR FIRST USE
A fresh barrel arrives at your doorstep. Time to roll up your sleeves. The steps necessary to prepare a barrel for use include rinsing, scraping, and "disinfecting" the barrel.

Some producers start with a cold-water rinse of the barrel, while others prefer warm water of not more than 140° F (60° C). Some wineries recommend water as hot as 170° F (77° C), although many traditional producers feel the use of very hot water may cause the wood to warp and promote leaks. Wineries and breweries use both low-pressure and high-pressure rinses, although some producers believe a high-pressure rinse may damage the wood. Some form of rinsing is necessary to remove most of the residue from the previous contents of the barrel.

The pores of the wood have been closed by the years of fermentation and aging of alcoholic liquid in the barrel. They must be reopened to promote oxygen diffusion and the growth of yeast and bacteria. You also need to remove winestone and beerstone[2] from the inner surface. Some lambic brewers have a machine that rotates sharp chains through the barrels to perform this task. Others brewers use stiff, sharp brushes to scrape the insides of their barrels. If your barrel is large enough, you can just hop in and scrape away. It is usually only necessary to remove a millimeter or less of inner surface wood, so a paint scraper or similar tool is adequate. The most difficult, traditional method is to partially or completely disassemble a barrel[3] and shave the inner surface, often with some type of wood planer. If you have acquired a barrel with a heavy char layer and wish to reproduce the classic styles, you may need to disassemble it to effectively remove that layer. (One U.S. brewer tells me a

---

[2]Beerstone is an inorganic, insoluble, scalelike deposit composed primarily of calcium oxalate (C_2CaO4) that accumulates in beer-storage vessels. Winestone is a similar insoluble deposit composed of tartar and potassium tartrate.

[3]This book cannot do justice to the specific details of disassembling and reassembling a barrel. If you choose to undertake this task, I recommend you consult resources on coopering—the art of building and maintaining barrels.

strong, hot water spray will remove a portion of the layer of heavy char.)

After rinsing and scraping, sulfur dioxide will eliminate mold, yeast, and bacteria remaining on the inner surface but not the ones deeper in the wood. Yeast and bacteria can penetrate 6 to 7 millimeters (approximately one-quarter inch) into the inner surface of the barrel. Burning a sulfur stick suspended on a wire through the bunghole into the barrel releases sulfur dioxide. Careful, it's very hot and harmful to inhale! Another option—use a solution of cold water and potassium metabisulfite or sodium bisulfite, which release sulfur dioxide when dissolved in liquid. These compounds are commonly used in the wine industry and are available from winemaking resources. If the barrel has dried or it will dry before you are ready to use it, store the barrel with a sulfite solution, which will retard the formation of mold and other contaminants.

Some brewers and winemakers choose steam as an alternative cleaning and sanitizing method. Steam will expand to touch the entire inner surface of the barrel. Steam contains energy, known as the heat of vaporization that was necessary to change water from a liquid to a gas. As the steam comes in contact with the inner surface, it condenses to liquid and transfers that energy, effectively removing the residue and heating the inner surface. Steam burns skin nearly on contact, as it will almost instantly transfer heat of vaporization to the skin.

Steam generally does not present a cost-effective option to merit its use for occasional cleaning. The size of a barrel should also be considered. The larger the barrel, the more time and energy required to raise the temperature of the wood to an adequate level. For a *foudre*, the wood is too thick to raise the temperature to an acceptable level over a reasonable period of time.

After cleaning, there should be no residue on the inner surface of the barrel. The only remaining microorganisms survive within the wood. The aroma of what was previously in the barrel may still be evident. The characteristics of the previous contents are commonly noticeable in the first batch or two of beer aged in the barrel. This character will diminish with use, and blending with beers from older barrels will minimize the effect in the final product (covered in the next chapter).

INOCULATING BARRELS

Time to put those microorganisms into the barrel. The microbes still residing in the wood after cleaning will not sufficienly ferment the first batch. Most wild brews enter the barrel with some portion of the microorganisms necessary to ferment and acidify. The new wild brewer must choose whether to follow the example of the lambic or of the Flanders acid ale producers.

Lambic wort becomes inoculated (overnight, in the coolship) with many of the species of microorganisms necessary to ferment and acidify. Whether wort has been spontaneously inoculated or done so with one or more cultures of yeast and bacteria, it has a population of microorganisms ready for fermentation. Add your wort to the barrel, and be (very) patient.

After a barrel in a Flanders brewery has been cleaned, it is customary to add a portion of "older" wort—around 10%—from an "established" barrel. This means using wort nearing the end of its maturation cycle from a barrel that has been producing consistent results. This wort will pass along the microorganisms responsible for a "quality" batch of beer to the new wort and barrel. "Old" beer should be used, as younger beer likely will not contain large enough populations of microorganisms to effectively reproduce in the fresh wort and inoculate the barrel.

Traditional producers of lambic and Flanders acid ales alike desire a barrel that will have a consistent effect on the beer, time after time. Brewers desire the correct combination of microorganisms in a barrel that will produce a consistent, pleasant beer. A *foudre*, given the slow diffusion of oxygen and slower resulting speed of fermentation, will achieve greater consistency than smaller barrels.

Beer from a large established barrel represents an excellent source of healthy microorganisms for fresh wort and new barrels. This technique has been practiced for centuries by the brewers of Flanders, but historically is considered taboo in the world of

Just climb right in this used wine barrel at New Belgium Brewing in Fort Collins, Colorado, and scrub away!

spontaneously fermented traditional lambic. No longer unheard of in lambic production, the use of old beer to promote consistent fermentation presents one solution to the reported problems with the microflora surrounding Brussels. A small U.S. producer may never achieve the consistency of the traditional Belgian producers, at least not without devoting many years, many dollars, and many barrels to the cause. Even in Belgium, one barrel seldom produces a product ideal for consumption without blending. Still, the perfectionists in Flanders, the Payottenland, and Fort Collins did not develop overnight. Beginning wild brewers first must simply strive to produce an enjoyable product without comparing the result to the beers of a hundred-year-old Belgian brewery.

MAINTAINING BARRELS

Similar to wine or spirits, each batch of beer aged in a barrel has a cumulative effect on the wood. Succeeding batches of beer, aged in a barrel, will have a detrimental effect. Wild yeast and bacteria multiply as beer ages in the wood. Acid-producing bacteria tend to grow at a faster rate than other microorganisms, which naturally results in higher and higher levels of acid production. Over time, the beer aged in a barrel can become too acidic for consumption. Also, beerstone will form on the inner surface of the barrel, as it will on any surface left in contact with beer. Beerstone eventually can lead to a partial or total blockage of the pores of the wood, thereby cutting off the microorganisms from oxygen, reducing the effectiveness of the barrel.

The continuing growth of microorganisms within a barrel prohibits indefinite use without proper care. The traditional producers religiously clean their barrels. Lambic producers may put a barrel through the regimen of rinsing, scraping, and disinfecting prior to every new filling. Flanders brewers go through this process as often as every two fillings. The coopers at Rodenbach will completely disassemble and clean a *foudre* at least once every twenty years. The size of the barrel influences the cleaning schedule. A *foudre* producing consistent beer likely will do so for a longer period of time than will a smaller barrel, largely due to the diffusion of less oxygen and slower resulting growth of *Acetobacter* and production of acetic acid.

The small producer's cleaning schedule should be based primarily on the quality of beer coming from a barrel and, realistically, how much effort he/she wishes to expend at any given time. I've met brewers in the United States who initially prepare their barrels and then accept whatever effect the wood and resident microorganisms have on the beer. Over time, the resulting product can become highly acidic (even for my palate). Too much acid and you have vinegar, not a quality wild beer.

Try not to let a barrel run dry between fillings. This leads to the growth of mold and unwanted bacteria that will unpleasantly acidify beer. (I speak from experience!) If a barrel runs dry, give it a thorough cleaning, particularly a filling with a potassium metabisulfite or sodium bisulfite solution.

With proper care, a barrel might outlast its owner. Does a barrel ever need to be retired? Only the owner can make that decision. High levels of acidic liquid stored for long periods of time can permanently damage wood. The brewer ultimately must be happy with the character a barrel gives to beer. If not, and the problem cannot be corrected with a thorough cleaning, then it may be time to feed the campfire or add a new planter to the patio.

Solera for Brewers

The traditional method of aging sherry, known as the sherry solera, can give the brewer some new ideas about aging wild beer. The solera—a series of casks—can vary in number. The sherry producer blends the final product from multiple casks, similar to lambic and Flanders red-brown beers. Blended sherry contains no more than one-third of the oldest product. When the sherry blender removes a portion of the oldest cask, he or she replaces it with sherry from the next oldest cask, and so on until the youngest cask receives only new wine. The presence of old sherry significantly affects the newer sherry while in the barrel. Applied to wild beer, a solera will not maintain the consistent taste desired by traditional blenders. Peter Bouckaert states that with each filling, even with as little as 10% old beer, the taste of a cask can be quite different. To the new wild brewer, however, a solera represents yet another option to produce interesting beer.

OXYGEN IN THE BARREL

Beer-souring microorganisms require small amounts of oxygen, diffused into the wort through the barrel staves. Any additional oxygen can be detrimental to the beer. More oxygen diffuses through thinner, smaller barrels than thicker, larger ones. Head space—the layer of air between the top of the wort and the top of the inner layer of the barrel—also will expose the wort to oxygen.

Head space inevitably increases as wort evaporates. This happens over time to any liquid exposed to air. Head space also increases when the brewer removes beer from the barrel for tasting or serving. Tasting maturing beer is a mixed bag. Beer must be tasted in order to determine its "readiness," but the process creates more head space and introduces more oxygen into the barrel. This leaves the beer open to oxidization and the influence of acetic acid. Too much acetic acid combined with ethanol, oxidized into acetaldehyde, and you have only vinegar.

Brettanomyces (and other oxidative yeasts) will essentially protect a lambic from air in the cask by forming the characteristic pellicle on the top of the wort. (While *Brettanomyces* also play a role in the fermentation of Flanders acid ales, no mention is ever made of the pellicle.) This white layer of yeasts will use available oxygen during the fermentative process and not allow it to diffuse into the wort. Due to the pellicle, lambic brewers do not traditionally "top-off" a cask with additional wort—common with must during the aging of wine. The pellicle plays an important role during the long fermentation of a cask of lambic.

Removing beer through the bunghole using a "wine thief" will disturb the protective layer of oxidative yeasts and introduce oxygen directly into the wort. The pellicle can "reseal" to some extent, so be careful to produce as small a hole as possible. Without the pellicle, traditional producers will blend or bottle the beer.

The traditional brewer prefers to remove beer through a spigot, which leaves the pellicle completely intact. A spigot can be added to a barrel that doesn't already have one. Drill the proper-sized hole into the head but be careful; not to large or it will leak. Some producers keep a cork in the hole during fermentation, preferring to drive the cork into the liquid when time to bottle, like a keystone on a cask of real ale.

Flanders brewers cover the top of the wort in the barrel with a quantity of aged hops—a sort of manmade pellicle—to reduce

Notes on the Manufacture of Vinegar—1917

There was another process in Belgium by which they sometimes made vinegar unintentionally. In Flanders they had a curious beer called "Lambic," which was a hopped malt-and-wheat wort allowed to ferment "spontaneously" in casks. The original ferment was supposed to have been derived from wine lees, by the simple process of allowing wort to ferment in wine casks. No yeast was added. The casks, of course, were not sterilized, and so the "wine ferment" started the fermentation. Lambic took from two to three years to ferment, and one of the great enemies was mother vinegar. Occasionally, they got a cask apparently half filled with that tenacious growth, and when a cask started making vinegar, it did not make beer. The strange thing was that the vinegar and the alcoholic fermentation appeared to go on simultaneously, or in any case alternately, acetifying following fermentation.

C. Ainsworth Mitchell, B.A., F.I.C.
From a discussion by George Maw Johnson

acetic acid and oxidization from head space. This layer of hops will not only protect the wort from oxidation but will also block any fungus that might grow in the head space from making contact with the wort. Examination of this layer on a beer after an extended period of aging reveals a white substance, likely mold, growing on the top.

Topping-off a barrel with fresh or even partially fermented wort presents a tradeoff. Topping-off will reduce the effects of oxygen and *Acetobacter* but can change the character of fermenting wort. Common among wine producers, Flanders brewers (and even the occasional lambic producer, if no one is looking) sometimes employ this technique. Adding a layer of CO_2 on top of the beer represents a short-term solution to head space. The

CO_2 will eventually diffuse, but is heavier than O_2 and should hang out on top of the beer for a while.

THE LAMBIC CELLAR

The lambic cellar is a place most revered—and rightly so—in the world of fermentation. Dozens of different strains of microorganisms busily go about their work inside each oak cask, from the smallest barrel to the largest *foudre*. A term for the room(s) filled with barrels, the cellar can be any room in the brewery (or blendery).

Condition often comes to mind when people think of the lambic cellar. Images of dirty places where undisturbed cobwebs and spider webs and insects and spiders are necessary for fermentation spring to mind. More of a practical issue than a necessity, the dark, damp environment of most any cellar promotes the growth of cobwebs. Says Frank Boon, "If you clean off the cobwebs they come back in two or three weeks. It is best to put efforts in other areas." Brewers do respect the spider, since they eat unwanted insects that often gather wherever fermentation occurs. No lambic brewer would step on a spider!

Fermentation runs rampant throughout the lambic cellar during the brewing season. The kraeusen of fermentation bubbles freely up and out of the bungholes of recently filled casks. No blowoff tube here; fermentation is *au naturel*. The yeast foam rising from the cask plays an important role, as it will solidify around the bunghole, effectively sealing the cask. Some producers have become dissatisfied with this closure, preferring to bung the cask when obvious signs of fermentation begin to slow.

Barrels of all sizes may adorn the cellar. *Foudres* require large rooms with tall ceilings. These "airplane hangars" of the lambic world may contain more than two dozen of the monstrous casks. That's a lot of lambic! Smaller casks are staggered, stacked two (sometimes three) high by two across in long rows. The brewer or blender (and lucky guests) may periodically taste these casks during the course of fermentation to check their progress.

Lambic blenders have wort from several different breweries in their cellars. It's not unheard of to find the stray barrel of a different lambic even in a brewery, just for variety during blending. Symbols on the casks denote the brewery of origin. A single letter often denotes the brewing season when the wort was produced.

Casks represent a great moving puzzle to the producer. What casks are ready, how much do I need to blend, and where is there space for fresh wort? The brewer/blender prefers to empty and fill a cask all at once to avoid introduction of oxygen, but this may not be practical. A *foudre* generally takes more than one batch of wort to fill. Imagine blending with that much lambic! Even one smaller barrel might be filled with just one batch or two or more, depending on how much room remains.

A barrel must not be left partially empty for long. Oxygen is the bane of every brewer once fermentation has begun. Beyond the small amount diffused through the wood, additional oxygen during the aging or transfer of wort will have a detrimental effect. It can oxidize the lambic and help turn it to vinegar. Frank Boon has gone to the length of equipping his *foudres* with stainless steel pipes to allow the transfer of wort without any oxygen coming into contact with his beer.

A brewery will commonly add new barrels both for additional capacity and to account for normal wear and tear on older casks. When a lambic brewery adds new casks, they actually mean used casks from a winery, distillery, or top/bottom-fermentation brewery. New barrels are well cleaned but will still add flavor to the resulting beer for at least one filling before the original character ages out in favor of the lambic. Reportedly, some lambic connoisseurs can identify the character of a new distinctive barrel, such as a port or cognac barrel, in a blend. Jean Van Roy of Cantillon tells me a "real lambic" is produced in a cask used many times. It often takes two to four fillings before a cask produces a beer with the particular "house character" of the brewery. Perhaps it's a Brussels thing: Cantillon and Belle-Vue have barrels constructed of chestnut in addition to those of oak. The cellar is truly the heart of the lambic brewery.

ALTERNATIVE MATERIALS

Most traditional producers of wild brews believe you cannot produce their product without wooden casks. The most successful U.S. producers also use oak barrels to ferment and age their beer. I do believe a long aging in wood imparts a complexity— which may or may not include an oaky character—largely absent with other methods. Wooden barrels, however, may be impractical for some brewers. Alternatives to the use of wooden casks by both commercial and homebrewers include fermenting and aging in stainless steel, plastic, glass, and the use of pieces of oak.

Some Belgian brewers produce Flanders red and lambic in stainless steel tanks. Dirk Lindemans of the Lindemans brewery lists less risk of oxidation, a consistent temperature, and ease of cleaning as advantages over oak barrels. Beers produced in stainless steel never appear to quite reach the same level of complexity or attenuation as those aged in wood. Very credible examples of lambic and Flanders red may be fermented and aged in stainless steel, but they will not have characteristics identical to those aged in wood.

One problem with stainless steel tanks is that they have a smooth, solid inner surface with no place for microorganisms to live and breed. By design, stainless steel tanks effectively keep air away from the fermenting beer. Brewers who use stainless steel fermenters largely ignore the topic of oxygen. The oxygen-poor environment of a cylindroconical tank favors bacterial growth at the expense of wild yeast.

The commercial brewer must consider how long he or she must tie up valuable tank space. Traditional Belgian lambics

Plastic barrels with aging kriek at Cnudde in Eine.

and Flanders acid ales age for several years, a long time to take a tank out of commission. This may be one reason why lambic and Flanders red ales aged in stainless steel are aged for less time than those aged in wood. The quicker fermentation time needed for a beer fermented entirely with *Brettanomyces,* however, makes that type of beer an ideal candidate for a stainless steel fermenter.

The glass carboy is to the homebrewer what the cylindroconical tank is to the commercial brewer. Glass, too, does not allow oxygen to diffuse into the contents nor microorganisms to breed within the walls. A glass carboy does, however, have an opening on the top through which oxygen will diffuse at different rates depending on the type of stopper (see chart on page 220). Glass represents an excellent alternative to the wild homebrewer lacking any inclination towards using barrels. Glass also allows the brewer to view the pellicle formed by *Brettanomyces* (providing hours of entertainment on cold winter nights).

Plastic fermentation vessels, designed for the wine industry, start at five gallons and rise in size to many hundreds of gallons. Commonly made from standard food-grade high-density polyethylene (HDPE), plastic fermenters exhibit a high permeability to oxygen—actually too permeable for wild fermentation. While plastic has the reputation of allowing bacteria to live in surface scratches, that potential characteristic does not effectively mimic the staves of a barrel.

The chart below illustrates the amount of oxygen diffused through a number of popular fermentation/maturation vessels. The data represents vessels used by both commercial and home brewers. While a 10-gallon oak barrel allows roughly three

Oxygen Diffusion Through Selected Fermentation Vessels

Type	Volume [liters/gallons]	O₂ cc/L/year
Rodenbach Wooden Tun (Large)	20,000/5,280	0.53
Rodenbach Wooden Tun (Small)	12,000/3,168	0.86
Wine Barrel	300/79.2	8.5
Flextank HDPE Fermenter	200/53	20
Homebrew Barrel	40/10.6	23
Homebrew HDPE Bucket	20/5.3	220
Glass Carboy w/Silicone Stopper	20/5.3	17
Glass Carboy w/Wooden Stopper	20	0.10
Glass Carboy w/30 cm Vinyl Immersion Tube	20	0.31

Table by Raj Apte, reproduced by permission

times the oxygen that a "standard" wine barrel does, this pales in comparison to the average plastic homebrew fermenter. Also note that a small (10-gallon) oak barrel compares favorably to a significantly larger HDPE vessel. Based primarily on oxygen diffusion, a glass carboy (or small oak barrel) presents better options for fermentation than a plastic fermenter.

Several commercial brewers and plenty of homebrewers add oak chips, oak cubes, or chunks of (French) oak barrel staves to their fermenters to account for the absence of wood. But why are pieces of wood in the fermenter desirable or even necessary? Traditional producers use oak barrels for their porous surface and permeability to oxygen rather than flavor and aroma contributions of the oak. How will a small amount of oak chips immersed in liquid fulfill that role? The answer is, it won't, but oak in wort will give a few other contributions.

Pieces of oak will, of course, actually contribute some oak character to wort, if you desire those traits in your beer. Some of the same considerations apply here as when using oak barrels. Chips, cubes, and segments generally come in medium or heavy toast, with medium preferred. New oak will contribute a far too aggressive character to your beer. Some brewers recommend boiling the oak chips in a few changes of water to remove the tannins. Alcohol, however, can leach out tannins that boiling water or even chemicals will not. From personal experience, I know that you cannot age a beer for years on boiled new oak chips without the oak character becoming too dominant. The best results come from first aging them in beer, any kind of beer, to minimize that character.

Pieces of oak can also be used to give a "spontaneous" boost to sluggish fermentation. Soak some oak in beer, and leave it exposed, overnight, near your coolship (or equivalent) to become inoculated with the resident microorganisms. The next day, add them to your fermenter. The oak will provide additional microorganisms for fermentation where the current populations in the wort are not sufficient.

Oak still provides a contribution to *Brettanomyces*, even without oxygen. *Brettanomyces* will metabolize cellubiose from toasted wood. Even though oak chips at the bottom of a

Solera for Homebrewers

Homebrewer Jeff Renner conceived a method of souring beer in a single vessel he called solera. Begin with a vessel of beer, and let it age. After a period of time, remove a portion (to consume), and replace it with new beer of a different style. At some point very early in the solera, add a reasonably dark beer. The reduction capacity of dark malts may help the beer to age more gracefully. Over time, the beer will develop "aged" flavors from the introduction of new beer. Unless completely sterile, bacteria will be introduced and grow in the beer. Autolyzed yeasts will provide nutrients, so filtered beer should be avoided. Jeff uses a stainless steel keg, and the resulting fermentations do produce CO_2, so the keg must periodically be vented to purge the gas.

fermenter will not provide oxygen, they will provide a valuable carbohydrate for *Brettanomyces*.

The appropriate quantity of oak to add to wort varies by form. A value of 0.5 ounces per gallon (3.75 grams/liter) or roughly one pound per U.S. barrel (385 g/hl) of oak cubes or chips is often considered "new barrel' extraction rates for wine. The extraction goes a bit slower on the staves, which contain less "end-grain" wood, so generally about 1.5 ounces per gallon or three pounds per U.S. barrel (1.2 kg/hl) Many red wines contain more oak character than commonly desirable in a wild beer, so err on the side of caution, particularly when using fresh or boiled wood. Most brewers find "new barrel" character undesirable in many wild beers.

eight

Finishing the Beer

"You must know by heart what all the barrels are doing, like a painter knows all of his colors."

–Frank Boon of Brouwerij Boon

The traditional producers of wild beers in Belgium don't have much direct control over fermentation. Even the newer producers in Belgium and the United States, who have adapted some modern brewing practices, often find unexpected results when working with *Brettanomyces* and lactic acid-producing bacteria. Identically produced worts may have different characteristics following fermentation and maturation.

A single batch of wild beer can be very different in the bottle as compared to immediately following maturation. The decision to serve one batch as a finished product, blend and further age all or a part of that batch with fruit, or blend with a number of other different batches gives the wild brewer some control over the product offered to the consumer. Refermentation in the bottle, too, will change the character of the beer. These decisions all come into play once the wild brewer decides when a beer is ready to serve or blend.

WHEN IS THE BEER "READY"?

Producers of lambic age beers for roughly one to three years, while Flanders acid ale producers age their beers for eighteen to twenty-four months. These "standard" periods regarding lambic and Flanders acid ales are approximations based on traditional processes and materials over centuries of experience. Taken away from the natural setting, the processes may be incomplete, the yeasts and bacteria may behave differently. A predefined time required for complete fermentation and flavor and aroma production does not exist. The brewer must rely on tasting to best determine the readiness of a beer both in North America and in Belgium. Does the batch of beer exhibit the desired characteristics?

A beer is ready when it tastes ready. The meat of that statement lies in the use of the word "ready." To determine when a batch of beer is ready is to know what you will do next with the beer. For example, a lambic that is only one year old may be ready to serve on draft in a café. That same lambic may also be ready to blend as a portion of a gueuze but requires older beer as a part of the blend. Our young lambic will not be ready to blend with fruit, nor is it ready for bottling. The wild brewer must understand how different characteristics and finishing steps go hand-in-hand to produce a finished product.

BLENDING 101

The art of lambic and Flanders acid ales, blending was popular throughout England in the 1800s, a signature of the classic Ballantine Ale in the United States during World War II, and an essential production step in larger breweries. Blending is the brother of assemblage: "The blending together of component wine lots to form a final composite intended for bottling, for aging, for sparkling wine production or some other use by the winemaker." A brewer blends beer for two basic reasons: to change the character of the beer and/or to produce a consistent result not possible from a single batch. Sometimes the traditional producer finds the occasional exemplary batch of beer. He will bottle the standout as a "special *cuvée*." Most often, however, only the result of a blend or several batches produces a truly sublime result. A single batch of beer will taste different from the batch in the next barrel or in the one down the row and to the right. Differing characteristics make blending possible.

Here the artisanal brewer and the mass-producer do something for one of the same reasons: consistency. Whether brewed in Brussels or St. Louis, every single batch of beer will not taste exactly the same each and every time. Only by blending several batches can a consistent result be achieved. With so many variables involving beer-souring organisms, this hold exponentially true with wild brews.

Anheuser-Busch carefully controls every step of the brewing process and still blends to achieve an extremely high level of consistency. Traditional Belgian producers don't try to achieve that same level of control but still blend to reach a level of consistency that is sufficient for "brand identity."

The traditional producer blends a beer with his "signature" that the consumer will recognize and enjoy, time after time. Smaller producers and homebrewers, however, do not have to be so bound to consistency. Many craft beer drinkers consider the differences of a seasonal beer offering a part of the fun of visiting a brewpub in the United States. While many beer consumers in the United States turn up their noses at inconsistency, aficionados of wild beers usually revel in differences from vintage to vintage.

Beyond consistency, the wild brewer blends to achieve a complexity not possible from a single fermentation of beer. Blending does not simply disguise inferior batches, a misconception sometimes held in the United States; blending achieves the creation of new, unique products. Consider four basics when determining the components of a blend: different casks produce different results, "young" beer and "old" beer each contribute something different to a blend, fruit will completely change the character of a beer, and not all characteristics of beer and/or fruit blend well together.

BLENDING WITH FRUIT

Fruit and beer have gone together almost since beer was invented. Fruit contributes wild yeast, fermentable sugar, and new flavors and aromas when blended to create a completely different beer.

Belgian producers traditionally brewed only one type of beer. This limited the selection of beers available at the local café. The café owner blended fruit with beer to create a new beer. Belgian breweries and brewery groups that produce an entire range of different beers only surfaced in the twentieth century. Despite the vast selection of different beers available at many specialty beer bars and cafes, people still enjoy the taste of fruit in beer.

One common misconception regarding traditional wild ales is that fruit is added to sweeten beer. This does hold true regarding modern examples of kriek, framboise, and other fruit beers. Large breweries add fruit, or more commonly, fruit syrup, and pasteurize the resulting blend. Without yeast to start a refermentation, the sugars from the fruit remain in the very sweet end product often more reminiscent of fruit juice than actual beer. Live yeast present in traditional wild beer will completely ferment the sugars in the fruit.

The resulting fermentation occurs in every traditional wild beer. Sugar plays a key role in the characteristics of fruit. The blender considers balance between sweetness and acidity essential to a pleasant fruit. That same sweetness can overpower the character of the resulting beer. The refermentation changes the sugars into alcohol and carbon dioxide. The carbon dioxide escapes from the fermenting beer. The alcohol, along with the remaining flavor and aroma components of the fruit, produce new characteristics in the beer. The marriage of flavors, fruit, and beer, as a result of the refermentation, contributes a complexity not achieved by the addition of fruit syrup.

Consider the characteristics of the available beers and the fruit when deciding on the components of a blend. The blender searches for a "soft beer"; the beer chosen to blend with fruit should not have too much bitterness, which does not complement fruit flavor. The traditional producer will not put too much "character beer" with the fruit. "Character beer" refers to the more aggressive, acidic batches, which may overpower the fruit character, and is traditionally reserved for blending without fruit. Consideration also must be given to acidity when blending. Both the beer and fruit contain acid; neither should be overtly acidic. Acidity increases as the blend matures. Too much acid produced will result in vinegar come bottling time. A cool temperature during refermentation will help control acid production. For a truly excellent blend, the character of the beer, the fruit, and the acidity must be in balance. The judgment of what constitutes "in balance," however, is very subjective, and a part of the art of blending.

The blender must also consider the age of a beer. Another common misconception exists among U.S. brewers regarding when to add fruit to beer. Fruit should not be added to very young beer. Consider the lessons regarding the bitterness, acidity, and character of beer ideal for blending with fruit. The brewer cannot predict the eventual character of young beer. Enough time must pass for the wild yeasts and bacteria to produce acids and esters before adding fruit. The acidity contributed by the fruit may harm the microorganisms before they can produce their requisite by-products.

Lambic producers wait at least one year, and often two, before blending fruit with their beer. Flanders acid ale producers will wait at least six months, and even eighteen to twenty-four months, when the fermentation cycle is complete, before blending fruit. A portion of young beer may be used to encourage fermentation of the sugars in the fruit. One producer uses as much as 35 to 40% of young (one-year-old) lambic—which contains a higher concentration of wild yeasts than older lambic—as a component of a blend.

The thought of adding fruit to wooden barrels is quite romantic though not terribly practical. Working with hundreds of pounds of cherries in a space as small as a standard wine barrel presents an arduous task. Think of it as stuffing a bowl of popcorn into a gallon milk jug. Many homebrewers can empathize by considering the task of getting 10 to 20 pounds of cherries through the opening of a standard 5-gallon carboy. Additionally, fruit will contribute flavor to wood that is not easily removed.

Even traditional Belgian brewers generally referment beer with fruit in stainless steel tanks. Tanks are easier to access and clean than barrels and leave little worry of oxidation. Small producers in the United States may choose to directly add fruit to the barrel and undertake some extra cleaning after the completion of fermentation or devote that barrel to the specific production of fruit beer. Plastic fermenters of various sizes may be used, although their permeability to oxygen should be taken into consideration. Homebrewers will find carboys with larger openings the ideal choice.

The lessons on head space and exposure to air from the previous chapter remain applicable. Excessive air space can promote the growth of *Acetobacteria* and cause beer to turn to vinegar. The volume of liquid should be as close to the capacity of the secondary fermenter as possible. Refermentation will not be as vigorous as primary fermentation so does not require any notable head space.

The traditional brewer generally allows the beer and fruit to ferment from six to nine months. By the end of the refermentation, the fruit may be virtually unidentifiable. Generally, no more than 5%—often less—of the sugar from the fruit left remains in solution. Six to nine months should be ample time for the wild yeast and bacteria to sufficiently reduce the amount of sugar. Without the equipment for a precise reading, a simple gravity reading and taste test should be sufficient as to the readiness of a beer. The beer should have virtually no noticeable sweetness and be extremely dry on the palate. The gravity must be very low, an important factor when considering the total amount of sugar available for refermentation in the bottle.

Eric Rose, Tomme Arthur and Vinnie Cilurzo add cherries to a barrel at Russian River Brewing.

The fruit may be lightly pressed to extract any remaining character, but carefully, so as not to extract any bitterness. The residue of the fruit contains juice as well as polyphenolic matter, which contributes to the taste and color of the lambic. Without these compounds, some homebrewed examples do not always exhibit the expected character of the fruit. The beer may be lightly filtered to remove pulp and skins but not any microorganisms. The fruit lambic may be served "as-is" or blended with young lambic for carbonation once the microorganisms have finished fermenting the sugar contributed by the fruit.

BLENDING LAMBIC

"We are beermakers in the brewhouse, but here we are more winemakers," says Bruno Reinders, plant manager at Mort Subite, regarding the blending of lambic. Similar to the blending of Champagne from different batches of wine, the blender combines different batches of lambic to produce gueuze. Simply put, a gueuze contains a blend of one-, two-, and three-year-old lambic. Old lambic contains a well-developed profile of acids and esters, while young lambic provides fermentable sugars and active yeasts to ferment sugar and produce carbonation in the bottle. Young lambic also may be blended with fruit lambic to provide that same carbonation.

Gueuze blending is an art. The traditional gueuze blender expresses himself using a liquid media the same way a painter uses paint and a canvas. The goal of the gueuze blender is to either accentuate or soften characteristics of the available batches of lambic to suit the blender's palate. Less romantically, the blender also provides sugar as a source of refermentation. To accomplish these goals, the gueuze blender makes use of the different characteristics of one- , two- , and three-year-old batches of lambic. The "young" one-year-old lambic has not completed fermentation. The young lambic still contains sugars that will be fermented in the bottle, producing carbon dioxide (and alcohol). The use of young lambic in the blend gives gueuze the characteristic high level of carbonation. The amount of young lambic blended for refermentation differs from brewery to brewery. One producer may use as little as 10%, while others use a more even proportion to "old" lambic. The amount of sugar remaining in the lambic determines the eventual level of carbonation in the gueuze.

"Old" lambic, of two to three years, has completed fermentation. The old lambic contains the acids and esters that give gueuze the myriad of different flavors and aromas. While fermentation finishes after two years, a third year of aging allows the acids and esters to develop fully. The three-year-old lambic is the most complex but also the most acidic. The two-year-old lambic is more mellow and will balance the acidity of the three-year-old lambic. Many brewers state the use of even proportions of one- , two- , and three-year-old lambic, although they do not base the actual decision solely on this generalization.

The combination of the lambics of different ages from different barrels produces a complex, effervescent product. The flavors and aromas present in a gueuze seldom exist in a single barrel of lambic. Each cask contains a potential ingredient for the blend. The gueuze blender considers all of the characteristics of the available lambics, including bitterness, sweetness, body, acidity, fruitiness, spiciness, oakiness, and what was previously aged in the barrel, plus more intangible characteristics, including softness and the "lasting properties" of the lambic. The gueuze blender tastes everything, and then begins to "piece the puzzle." The blender knows what he wants to achieve in the end product and considers what proportion of each available cask of lambic is necessary to reach that goal.

The blender who uses lambic from different brewers has additional variables to consider. If a house lambic has many tastes, the beers from other brewers present many more. The blender understands very well what to expect from the lambic of each different brewery. The thought process of the blender takes into consideration what each lambic will contribute to a blend based on their knowledge and experience with each different lambic.

The age of a barrel also contributes to the character of a lambic. "Younger" barrels, particularly ones containing an inaugural batch of lambic, may impart a noticeable character of what was previously aged in that barrel. Lambic from younger barrels makes up only a small portion of a blend.

The size of a barrel also must be considered when blending gueuze. Smaller barrels allow greater amounts of oxygen to come into contact with the beer. Lambic from smaller barrels will be more oxidized and, therefore, drier. To dry the blend, the blender may use beer from a smaller barrel. Mature lambic often comes from larger barrels, where less oxygen comes in contact with the beer.

The tradeoff between practical considerations and the complexity of the beer often determines the size of the blender's barrels. Frank Boon uses many different sizes of barrels, but his "favorites" are the large *foudres*, preferred for the "quality" of lambic they produce. Given the high volume of gueuze blended by Boon, smaller casks are impractical to age the necessary volume of lambic. Tasting the different lambics is also an easier task with fewer, larger barrels.

Blending is simpler with fewer casks, but fewer possibilities exist. Each barrel of beer will have a unique flavor. This fact drives both the complexity of the blend and the consistency of the final product. Twenty smaller casks allow for potentially more variety than one or two *foudres*. One *foudre* may be only one taste; twenty barrels may be twenty different tastes. (According to Boon, however, beer matured in large casks may taste more like a "finished product" prior to blending than does lambic from smaller casks.) The variety of flavors and aromas presented to the gueuze blender by many smaller barrels carries with them a greater challenge of arriving at a reasonably consistent end product.

Even the most experienced gueuze blender can't make exactly the same gueuze time after time. If the art of the blender lies in creating complexity and balance, the science lies in producing a reasonably consistent product. The individual house character present in every bottle is unique to the brewery and identified by the consumer as the unique product of that producer. Only through experience does the blender learn how to take each factor into consideration and arrive at a signature gueuze.

The gueuze blender cannot adequately control the effect of the different seasons on the fermenting lambic. During the summer, a lambic will be "sick" and ropy due to the predominance of lactic acid-producing bacteria in the fermentation during the hot weather. Gueuze is, therefore, never blended during the summer. The viscous, ropy character of lambic during hot weather will become a part of the blended beer, and that character will not quickly fade. Additionally, gueuze normally takes roughly one year for adequate refermentation in the bottle. If you blend with a "sick beer," it may take two to three years or even longer to referment. A fully developed gueuze takes roughly four years, from the production of the oldest portion of the blend to the end of refermentation in the bottle. The lambic producers, like every other brewery, need product to sell and don't want to add to the already long life cycle of the gueuze.

BLENDING FLANDERS BEERS

Flanders brewers blend their acid beers year-round. Blends generally consist of two components—young beer and aged beer, although some blends consist solely of aged beer.

The aged beer has matured in oak casks for eighteen months to three years. The precise time depends on the specific brewery, and when the blender decides the beer in a particular barrel has

developed the correct attenuation and acid and ester profile. The aged beer is very dry—though not to the degree of a lambic—with the bulk of the sugars consumed by wild yeast and bacteria. A well-aged Flanders acid ale often will be even more acidic than a comparably aged lambic. The acidic character differs between the beers of West and East Flanders. The acidic character of the West Flanders red will be sharper, as acetic acid plays a larger role in the flavor and aroma due to the exposure to oxygen in oak casks. Lactic acid dominates the profile of the East Flanders browns due to the aging in stainless steel tanks impermeable to oxygen. Strains of *Pediococcus* produce any acetic acid present in the brown beer.

Two varieties of young beer (aged up to eight weeks) exist: acid beer and ordinary top-fermented beer. The top-fermented variety is a lightly bittered, sweet, malty brown ale. The acid beer has not aged long enough to achieve a very high attenuation. The young acid beer displays some sweetness, although this is balanced by the presence of lactic acid due to the use of a mixed culture during fermentation. The comparatively brief period of fermentation will not allow time for the production of much if any acetic acid.

Aged beer provides the complex acid and ester profile characteristic of Flanders acid ales. Young beer may or may not provide acidity but will contribute sweetness to the blend. Historically, Flanders beers were very volatile, as the wild yeast and bacteria present in the aged beer would consume the sugars of the young beer, leaving no sweetness. The acceptance of pasteurization throughout Flanders solved this "problem," and maintained the sweet character. Sugar or artificial sweetener added to the blend will contribute additional sweetness, producing the "sweet and sour" profile commonly found in many modern Flanders acid ales. Homebrewers often ponder how to achieve the malty sweetness present in some of the blended commercial products. Those products are pasteurized; the wild yeast and bacteria aren't given a chance to achieve a high level of attenuation within the blend.

Taste largely determines the proportions of aged and young beer in the blend. The blender considers both the acidity of the aged beer and "which acid" contributes the dominant character. Too much acetic acid means the blend should contain more young beer with balancing sweetness and/or lactic acid. The blend commonly contains from 10 to 30% of aged beer.

The blender generally considers a blend of young and aged beer for a relatively wide audience but intends a blend consisting

of different vintages of aged beer for the aficionado. The balance of lactic and acetic acid still drives the blend, although the acidic character will be more assertive without the sweetness contributed by the young beer. The blend may be sweetened with sugar, and pasteurized to blunt the acidic character, or released "straight-up," perhaps as a bottle-conditioned product.

BLENDING WITH OTHER BEER STYLES

What if you asked a lager-brewing compatriot to give you some of his fine Pilsener beer? What if you told him you wanted to blend it with your lambic? He may just walk away mumbling something about *Reinheitsgebot.* Blending aged, wild beer with another completely different beer is both traditional and can produce some very tasty results.

Commercial examples exist as introductions to the realm of possibilities. They include the blend of lambic and *Bink Blond* (*Reuss*), Boon kriek lambic and New Belgium blond ale (*Transatlantique Kriek*), and *Lindemans Kriek* with Brewery Ommegang's Belgian-style dark strong ale (*Three Philosophers*). Canada's Unibroue uses "spiced cherry juice" from Liefmans— likely *Gluhkriek*—to create *Quelque Chose.*

Blending will introduce a tart character to the profile of an otherwise non-sour beer or, alternately, soften the tart character of a wild beer. The character of two beers may be complementary or be very different and strike a curious balance. Consider the esters and the tartness of a lambic combined with the esters and bitterness of a Belgian golden ale, or the fruitiness of a kriek complementing the rich maltiness of a Belgian dark ale.

Flavor and aroma primarily drive the blender, but sugar remains an important consideration. The wild yeast and bacteria have the ability to ferment a great deal of the commonly "unfermentable" sugar in the non-sour beer. This creates some very explosive possibilities! The amount of sugar remaining in the average beer is more than sufficient to produce an extreme level of carbonation. A blend of wild and "ordinary" beer should be consumed relatively quickly, even from a keg, or pasteurized for stability.

BLENDING YOUR OWN

So you want to be a blender? The art of blending is traditionally passed down in Belgium from father to son or, perhaps, master to apprentice. Armand DeBelder of Drie Fonteinen describes blending as something unspoken, a look or a feeling when reaching the perfect combination, as Armand and his father had done so successfully together for decades. In more concrete terms, a person can be taught to blend by someone with a more experienced palate or attempt to dive in headfirst. If your apprenticeship at a lambic brewery hasn't yet been approved, here are some points for the aspiring blender in you to consider.

A successful blend results from knowing the character of the available beers, the eventual goal, and how to achieve that result. For starters, understand the base beers well. The character of the available beers determines what can be accomplished with a blend. Each batch of beer will contribute its own character to the blend, so understand the qualities of each batch. One cask might be fruity, another oaky, and another acidic. The characteristics of each cask are often not so simply described but may have a single, dominant quality. The many complex flavors and aromas present in multiple casks of wild beer may cause the blender a moment of indecision.

The second trait of a successful blender, therefore, is the ability to envision the desired end result. Do not blend haphazardly; have an end product in mind based on the characteristics of the available beers. Should the beer have oak, a notable acidity, quite a bit of fruitiness, or a balance of all three? The successful blender understands the flavors and aromas of all of the components and determines what proportions of each different beer is necessary to achieve the end result. Experienced blenders have their "signature" in mind, and influence the beers throughout the entire life cycle to have the necessary characteristics when the time to blend arrives.

Exacting this degree of control is admittedly easier said than done for the beginner. The novice often learns best through trial and error. Start out by blending different beers in different quantities to decide what will work together, what best reflects individual tastes, and what will arrive at the desired result. Develop an understanding of the component batches and the end results possible from different combinations.

Start small. Begin by taking small samples of each batch. Mix the samples together and note precisely the proportions used. Do not arrive at that perfect destination only to forget the route. With an understanding of the possibilities, invite a few friends over to assist. One or two other people have different palates and will likely try something different. Besides, tasting beer with friends is more fun than tasting alone.

Don't decide the time to blend; let the beers make that decision. A wild beer cannot be rushed. If a batch isn't quite ready, leave it to age a bit longer. If the character in the beers to arrive at an ideal blend does not exist, envision a different outcome or blend at a later date. Don't blend hoping a character will develop or fade. Only a highly experienced blender understands how the beers will taste in the future.

In reality, blending involves not so much understanding what the beer will taste like, but what must be sold (or drunk) in the future. How much beer must be brewed this year and the next and the next? The lead times range from eighteen months to three years before a single blend of lambic or Flanders acid ale can be produced. Many beers must be produced during that period to eventually have enough different beers to blend. Blending involves a bit of predicting the future; understanding how much beer is needed as much as four years down the road.

CONDITIONING

Before the advent of stainless steel and compressed carbon dioxide, beer was naturally carbonated and served from the wood. Around the turn of the nineteenth century, 90 to 95% of all lambic was served on draft from the cask; gueuze represented only a very small volume. One hundred years later, most people drink gueuze.

Europe abolished heavy taxes on glass in 1865. No longer a luxury item, less-expensive glass made the disposal of used Champagne bottles very common. An inexpensive source of nonreturnable glass bottles helped make highly conditioned gueuze readily accessible to the public. Traditional gueuze is a naturally carbonated product, refermented in the bottle.

The dark, sourish beers of Flanders also conditioned in the cask, similar to their blended counterparts across the channel in England. The Flemish found a gentle, low, natural carbonation popular during the days of Alexander Rodenbach in the late 1800s. The use of bottles grew in popularity during the twentieth

A "classic" bottle filler still used by John and Sidy at Hanssens Artisanaal in Dworp.

century, but unlike traditional gueuze, bottle-conditioned Flanders acid ales are seldom (ever?) produced in Belgium.

Producers of Flanders acid ales state the advantage of fil-tration, pasteurization, and force-carbonation as an aid to the stability of the beer in the bottle. The modern approach also facilitates the production of sweeter beers. Without pasteurization, the microorganisms in the bottle would consume virtually all of the sugars. The sweet/sour character in Flanders acid ales that became popular during the second half of the twentieth century would be nearly impossible to achieve if wild yeast and bacteria were left to ferment in the bottle. The reliance of Flanders brewers on modern methods of conditioning beer draws our attention to gueuze during the final stage of wild beer production.

TRADITIONAL REFERMENTATION OF GUEUZE

Many people compare gueuze to Champagne both in character and production methods. A sparkling wine produced by *Méthode Champenoise* is a blend of dry white wines to which sugar (*tirage*) and yeast are added at bottling. A secondary fermentation in the bottle produces carbonation and alcohol. Vintners slowly tilt and periodically turn Champagne bottles (*remuage*), then remove the sediment (*lees*) resulting from the refermentation once it gathers in the neck (*disgorge*). By contrast, the lees remain in a bottle of gueuze. The viable microorganisms will help the beer to mature for a considerable period of time.

Blending young lambic with old gives the wild yeasts in a bottle of gueuze a source of sugar to referment, producing a high level of carbonation. Both gueuze and Champagne are highly carbonated products. To arrive at appropriate carbonation, Frank Boon recommends 14 to 16 grams of sugar per liter (about 2 ounces per gallon) of lambic. Boon says half of the sugar produces alcohol during fermentation, the other half CO_2. Refermentation of this amount of sugar at a cellar temperature of around 55 to 60° F (13 to 16° C) will produce roughly 4.8 to 5.3 volumes of CO_2 and about 0.33 to 0.38% additional alcohol by volume. A bottle of Coors, in contrast, contains about 2.8 volumes of CO_2.

Most gueuzes don't contain a high volume of alcohol, as beers go. Commonly between 5% and 6.5% abv, a few gueuzes reach as high as 7 to 8% abv. Alcohol helps beer to age gracefully. A blender produces a gueuze of higher alcohol with the intention of being conserved (cellared) for a longer period of time before being consumed.

Traditional lambic producers agree that some period of conservation in the cellar during refermentation helps to ensure a quality gueuze. The necessary carbonation, flavors, and aromas must have time to develop. A rule of thumb states a bottle should sit in the cellar for roughly one year to pass through the cycle of refermentation. Unfortunately, modern economics may cause the cellaring time to vary. One traditional gueuze is cellared for only one week, while the stronger gueuzes may be conserved for several years. Ideally, the blender releases a gueuze only when the beer has reached maturity.

Professor Hubert Verachtert monitored the growth and activity of the different microorganisms found in a bottle of gueuze. Verachtert categorized the refermentation into three phases. During the first phase, aerobic yeasts such as *Candida*, *Torulopsis*, and *Pichia* reproduce respective to how much the beer is inadvertently aerated during transfer and bottling. Aerobic yeasts live in the pellicle on the surface of fermenting lambic.

The second phase begins about three weeks after bottling. *Brettanomyces* and *Pediococcus* reproduce and ferment virtually all of the sugar in the beer and produce additional acids and esters. Studies suggest *Brettanomyces* require the presence of *Pediococcus* to achieve a complete fermentation. This slow process of fermentation produces a character not available from artificial carbonation. The third phase sees the death and autolysis of most of the cells of *Brettanomyces* and *Pediococcus*.

Brewers store the bottles of gueuze in *caveaus*, literally small cellars. Visually, picture a collection of bottles (sometimes hundreds) from the same blending, turned on their sides and stacked in many horizontal rows somewhere against a wall. A *caveau* may be a massive wall-to-wall, floor-to-ceiling collection of bottles.

The temperature in the cellar will have an effect on the *caveaus* of gueuze. The changing seasons produce ambient temperatures in lambic cellars that may vary from roughly 36 to 75° F (2 to 24° C), hopefully never reaching 80° F (27° C). Bottles of gueuze first conserved prior to the winter months will start refermentation more slowly than those in the summer.

A caveau of gueuze refermenting at Hanssens Artisanaal in Dworp.

A slower refermentation is advantageous, just as a slower fermentation was desirable to the different batches of lambic used to blend the gueuze. The different microorganisms responsible for the refermentation of gueuze have different optimal temperatures desirable for their growth. Warmer temperatures will promote a quicker start, as well as the production of acids, while cooler temperatures will prolong the refermentation and limit acid production.

The cement floors of the lambic cellars are often colder than the ambient temperature of the room, so bottles at the bottom will ferment more slowly at lower temperatures than those at the top at higher temperatures. The bottles may differ in taste and in quality. While a slower fermentation is better, if a bottle is too cold there will be no refermentation at all. To help alleviate this problem, some blenders had pipes flowing with warm water beneath the *caveaus* to keep the bottles warm in the winter. A consistent temperature during the winter months promotes a consistent refermentation.

A lambic blender needs only to look at a bottle of gueuze to measure the degree of refermentation. A growing amount of sediment, and how well it adheres to the bottom of the bottle, denotes a healthy refermentation. The yeast should resemble a fishbone and cling to the side of the bottle. Some producers have a clear bottle on the top of every *caveau* to better observe the progress of refermentation. Growing occurrences of stagnant refermentation in the bottle contributed to the popularity of bulk refermentation and forced carbonation of gueuze beginning around the 1950s. The refermentation of traditional gueuze remains a natural process; modern methods of conditioning beer simply don't produce as refined a product.

PACKAGING AND CONSERVING LAMBIC AND GUEUZE

The brewer or blender generally bottles traditional gueuze and old lambic. Lambic and gueuze may be consumed shortly after leaving the brewery or conserved for years. The proper way to serve a traditional gueuze is another piece of the art that is lambic.

The refermentation of gueuze can generate five to six atmospheres of pressure. Similar to a bottle of champagne, the pressure in a bottle of gueuze may be between 70 and 90 pounds per square inch. That's two to three times the pressure of the average car tire and, as Mom cautioned, can put your eye out. Traditional blenders use heavy Champagne bottles and corks to withstand the tremendous pressure.

A cork seals a bottle of gueuze, like a bottle of wine, secured in place with a wire basket to stop the pressure from launching the cork into the nearest wall or ceiling. The look of a cork-finished bottle is both traditional and appealing. Ah, nothing like the pop of a cork in a lambic café to signal that someone has ordered a bottle of traditional gueuze!

Corks have the potential to dry out, allow carbonation to escape, grow mold, and/or contribute a "corked" flavor and aroma to the gueuze. Like a bottle of wine, a gueuze should be stored on the side if conserved for an extended period of time in order to keep the cork moist. A high-quality cork will experience fewer problems than a cheaper alternative. After producing a premium product, don't skimp on one of the final details. Most lambic producers use Champagne corks to seal their gueuze. Champagne corks will withstand a greater amount of pressure and will not dry out as easily as other types of corks.

Corks

Cork comes from the bark of the cork tree (*Quercus Suber*), a species of oak that grows best for commercial use in Western Europe and Northern Africa along the Mediterranean coast. The bark consists of a honeycomb of small cells of suberin, a waxy, complex fatty acid, filled with an airlike gas. The bark can be compressed to half its size without losing any flexibility and will instantly attempt to return to the original size. The resulting cork maintains a very constant pressure against the surface of the bottleneck, producing a tight seal, and has a high level of tolerance against changes in temperature and pressure.

Natural (straight) cork is a cylindrical stopper that has been punched directly from cork tree bark and reduced to the correct length. It is said that natural cork is the only sealing material that allows wine to "live" and "mature" in the bottle.

Champagne corks are straight-sided and only develops the mushroom shape after being jammed into a bottle. They are not solid cork but disks of cork separated by a cork mash. They are designed to maintain very high pressure in the bottle and to stop gas from escaping.

Colmated or pore-filled cork goes through an extra operation of filling the pores inherent to all corks, although this is usually performed only on lower grades, since the top grades are of a quality high enough not to require pore filling.

Agglomerate cork is produced from cork granules that are combined with cork oak resins using heat treatment while under pressure. These corks are generally used on wines that will be consumed within two or three years.

1 + 1 cork is composed of a cylindrical body of agglomerate cork and a disc of natural cork at each end and is commonly used for wines that are not designed for long aging.

Corks, cont.

Corks commonly come in four different sizes:

#9 x 1-1/2" (24mm x 38mm)

#9 x 1-3/4" (24mm x 45mm)

#8 x 1-1/2" (22mm x 38mm)

#8 x 1-3/4" (22mm x 45mm)

A bottle of gueuze traditionally had no label. Simple markings such as a white slash of chalk served to denote the contents, as well as which side to keep up during refermentation so as not to disturb the busy yeast. Often a white mark signified a gueuze, while a red mark denoted a kriek. This method of identification was as much practical as entailing less effort. Lambic cellars can be damp and moldy. Labels would peel or simply disintegrate. The sale of gueuze far beyond the blender's own walls, as well as laws created by the European Union, prompted the use of proper labels.

While American brewers argue over "born-on dates," all bottles of beer in Belgium must contain a "best before date." For example, strong beers such as the Trappist *Rochefort 10* have a "best before date" of three years beyond the bottling date, even though connoisseurs realize bottles will conserve for a longer period of time. A gueuze will keep for years—some perhaps decades—similar to a fine wine. Jean Van Roy of Cantillon wonders why, if there is no date on a bottle of wine, must there be one on a bottle of gueuze? Some traditional lambic producers have made their point by setting the best before date at twenty years after bottling.

Traditional gueuze is alive, like any bottle of "real ale." The flavors and aromas will evolve for many years. Many connoisseurs conserve a bottle of gueuze for roughly one to two years after it leaves the brewery. How the character of the gueuze develops may be different with every single bottle,

Bottles of various lambics for sale at the Cantillon brewery in Brussels.

although the blender strives to achieve a reasonably consistent product every time. Aging any alcoholic beverage carries no guarantees. It is just as possible to age a gueuze for too long a time as it is to age it for too little a time. With a good cellar (generally dark, free of vibration, at a reasonable humidity, and a stable, moderate temperature) and without any problems with the cork, a bottle of gueuze may pleasantly mature for decades. The oldest bottle in the Cantillon brewery dates back to around 1970!

Pouring gueuze is an art form among Belgian publicans, and an improperly poured gueuze will detract from the quality. Serve the gueuze no colder than 54° F (12° C)—cellar temperature. If the gueuze was stored horizontally, serve the bottle using a (wine) basket. Pop the cork with a flourish, as with a bottle of fine Champagne. The high level of carbonation, warm serving temperature, or oxidation may cause the liquid to gush out of the bottle.

Twirl the glass as you pour the first part of gueuze. The foam will stick to the sides and allow you to fill the glass with beer. Pour quickly but gently, leaving the sediment in the bottle. The sediment will detract from the flavor of the gueuze. A glass of gueuze will have a thick, moussey, everlasting layer of foam on top of the beer. (High carbonation promotes foam on beer, while a low pH promotes stability.)

Traditionally, if a person found the gueuze too sour, he or she dissolved a lump or two of sugar in the beer. The *stoemper*—a flat disk attached to a handle, functioning as a sort of mortar—crushed the sugar in the glass. This tradition seems preferable to the production of filtered, sweetened, pasteurized gueuze!

Casks present another traditional manner for serving lambic or gueuze in cafés. Casks, however, have the same problem in any country: freshness. The beer must be consumed quickly, or oxidation will occur. Both lambic and gueuze may be served directly from the cask or via a traditional handpump. The British do not have the sole claim on handpulled ales.

I REFERMENT, THEREFORE I AM

American brewers favor refermentation in the bottle to finish their wild beer. A cork-finished bottle helps a beer to stand out as "something special." Many considerations exist for successful refermentation, including available sugar, viable yeast, acidity, alcohol, time, temperature, and oxygen.

Blending young beer to provide sugar for refermentation can be a difficult process to master. The science of blending involves knowing how much sugar remains in the young beer (and lambic producers are not against taking a precise reading of the sugar content). Trusty old priming sugar represents a viable option. Even lambic breweries don't always use young lambic as a component of a blend. Jean Van Roy of Cantillon feels young lambic may dilute the character of the old lambic. He produces special releases, blended from his favorite batches of old lambic, conditioned to the effervescent level of a gueuze with a solution of priming sugar.

The exact level of carbonation for many wild beers focuses largely on a matter of personal taste. A gueuze by definition, however, is highly conditioned. Roughly 2 ounces (57 grams) of sugar per gallon of lambic at a comfy cellar temperature around 55 to 60 °F (13 to 16 °C) will provide the level of carbonation appropriate for a gueuze—a tremendous five volumes of CO$_2$! Common longneck bottles may not be sturdy enough to contain that level of pressure. Heavy Champagne bottles not only look attractive, they will withstand tremendous pressure. Flanders acid ales generally contain a more ordinary 2.0 to 2.5 volumes of CO$_2$. About 0.5 to 0.75 ounce (14 to 21 grams) per gallon of sugar will provide a pleasant carbonation.

Highly acidic and/or highly alcoholic wild beers, or those that have undergone a lengthy fermentation, may be devoid of enough viable yeast for a successful refermentation. A high level of acidity and a low pH can often harm *Saccharomyces cerevisiae*. Pitching a new *Saccharomyces* culture may be necessary. A strain of *Saccharomyces* must be fairly tolerant of acidity and neutral in flavor. Wyeast Laboratories recommends its *German Ale Yeast (1007)*, while White Labs recommends its *California Ale Yeast (WLP001)*. Both strains perform well under harsh conditions and settle nicely in the bottle. Dried yeast also may be acceptable, although you will need to determine if a particular strain can withstand high levels of acidity. Some brewers chose to "repitch" all of the microorganisms used in fermentation to help assure viability.

Oxygen remains a source of concern for the wild brewer throughout the entire life of a beer, right up until a bottle is opened and consumed. Care must be taken during transfers, bottling, and aging to avoid exposing the beer to oxygen. The presence of oxygen promotes the growth of *Acetobacter*, which will produce acetic acid and turn the beer to vinegar. Oxygen will also promote the growth of aerobic yeasts such as *Candida*, *Torulopsis*, and *Pichia*, which cause beer to gush from the bottle.

Colder temperatures will slow refermentation. Warmer temperatures promote the growth of lactic acid-producing bacteria. Refermenting beer should not be exposed to either extremely hot or extremely cold temperatures. Be careful when transferring the beer not to disturb the sediment at the bottom of the fermentation vessel to avoid carrying over a high density of *Pediococcus* and autolyzed yeast. A high density of *Pediococcus* will promote acid production and potentially an oily ropiness.

The successful refermentation of a wild beer takes time. Even a fresh, healthy culture of *Saccharomyces cerevisiae* will ferment more slowly, if at all, when faced with the level of acidity commonly found in a wild beer. *Brettanomyces*, too, react poorly to high levels of acidity, although the beer may continue to ferment for years in a bottle. A wild beer has followed a long path from "bacteria to bottle." Don't be reluctant to allow a wild beer to age for months or even years. The good news: They usually keep getting better with age!

nine

Do It Yourself

"If you want to be good, you're going to have to dump some beer."
—Peter Bouckaert of New Belgium Brewing

Don't let Bouckaert's "near famous" quote discourage you; dumping beer just appears to be a part of the traditional wild brewer's way of thinking. Not an easy choice, traditional producers only consider dumping a final solution for an unblendable batch of beer. You will hopefully never have to dump a batch, but you should never be afraid to take a chance and try something new because you face an uncertain result. To assist you, I have provided some hopefully interesting recipes. A few represent "classic styles," others, some newer ideas.

The following recipes are intended as samples. The options for each recipe provide some potential variations that I feel go well with the base beer. While each recipe will produce a very nice wild beer, do not let them constrain you. Once you reach a comfort level using microorganisms beyond *Saccharomyces cerevisiae*, develop your own unique recipes. Fortunately, the unpredictability of *Brettanomyces* sp. and lactic acid-producing bacteria means two brewers using the exact same recipe may achieve different results. Allow the "house character" of your beers to develop and define a signature of your own. Don't let narrow style guidelines restrain your creativity. There is life beyond competitions! Payottenland brewers never set out to copy a style; the brewers created indigenous beers, and someone eventually decided to define the beer as lambic. Here's to our own house beers!

Lambic

Malt Type	Color (ASBC)	Grist % by Weight
Pilsener	1.6	60.0%
Wheat (unmalted)	3.5	40.0%

Mash Schedule: Turbid mash (See Page 141)

Boiling Time: 4 hours

Bittering Hop Addition: 0.8 oz/gal (6 g/l) or 1.5 lb/bbl (580g/hl). Suggested variety: Any low alpha acid variety aged roughly 3 years (pellets 5-7 years).

Finishing Hop Addition: None

Original Gravity: 12-14 °P (1.048-1.057 SG)

Fermentation: Wyeast #3278 or Whitelabs WLP655. Cellar temperature for 1-3 years.

Secondary Storage: N/A

Options:
1. Serve the lambic after one year
2. Age 2-3 years, and prime with sugar or blend with other batches of lambic to produce gueuze
3. Add fruit after 1-2 years

Comments: A lambic may be brewed to various starting gravities depending on the intended use. A lower gravity is applicable for producing fruit lambics, while higher gravities are helpful for long aging.

Flanders Red Ale

Malt Type	Color (ASBC)	Grist % by Weight
Vienna	7	50.0%
Carahell	10	9.0%
CaraVienna	20	9.0%
Aromatic	20	9.0%
Special "B"	115	3.0%
Maize	n/a	20.0%

Mash Schedule: See Page 143

Boiling Time: 2 hours

Bittering Hop Addition: 10-12 IBUs. Suggested varieties: Hallertaur, Styrian Goldings, East Kent Goldings.

Finishing Hop Addition: None

Original Gravity: 12-14 °P (1.048-1.057 SG)

Fermentation: Wyeast #3763 at 68° F (20° C) for 1 week.

Secondary Storage: 80° F (27° C) for 8 weeks, or cellar temperature for up to 3 years.

Options:
1. Substitute maize with unmalted wheat
2. Blend with cherries after 12-18 months
3. Blend with other batches
4. Blend with a malty brown ale
5. Serve unblended, primed with sugar

Comments: A base wort intended for brief or lengthy fermentation. A short fermentation at higher temperatures produces more lactic acid, while a longer fermentation will produce an attenuated beer with a complex acid profile.

Flanders Pale Ale

Malt Type	Color (ASBC)	Grist % by Weight
Pilsener	1.6	90.0%
Carahell	10	10.0%

Mash Schedule: See Page 143

Boiling Time: 1.5 hours

Bittering Hop Addition: 25 IBUs. Suggested varieties: Hallertaur, Styrian Goldings, East Kent Goldings.

Finishing Hop Addition: None.

Original Gravity: 14 °P (1.057 SG)

Fermentation: Wyeast #3763 at 68° F (20° C) for 1 week.

Secondary Storage: Cellar temperature for up to 3 years.

Options:
1. Blend with a batch or two of Flanders red
2. Blend with a malty brown ale
3. Serve unblended, primed with sugar

Comments: The hop character in this pale beer will be more prominent than in darker, maltier worts.

Flemish Provision Brown Ale

Malt Type	Color (ASBC)	Grist % by Weight
Pilsener	1.6	70.0%
CaraVienna	20	10.0%
CaraMunich	60	10.0%
Maize	n/a	10.0%

Mash Schedule: See Page 143

Boiling Time: 2 hours

Bittering Hop Addition: 25 IBUs. Suggested variety: Hallertaur.

Finishing Hop Addition: None.

Original Gravity: 18 °P (1.074 SG)

Fermentation: Wyeast #1007 or Whitelabs WLP001at 68° F for 1 week.

Secondary Storage: Wyeast #4335 and #4733 or Whitelabs WLP672 and WLP661 at cellar temperature for up to 2 years.

Options:
1. Blend with cherries or raspberries after 1 year
2. Blend with one or more batches of different ages
3. Serve unblended, primed with sugar

Comments: The modern interpretation of a Flemish oud bruin. A higher gravity makes this beer ideal for "laying down." The addition of fruit will produce a beer of considerable alcohol.

Flemish Session Brown Ale

Malt Type	Color (ASBC)	Grist % by Weight
Pilsener	1.6	75.0%
CaraVienna	20	5.0%
CaraMunich	60	15.0%
Maize	n/a	5.0%

Mash Schedule: See Page 143

Boiling Time: 2 hours

Bittering Hop Addition: 20 IBUs. Suggested variety: Hallertaur.

Finishing Hop Addition: None.

Original Gravity: 12 °P (1.048 SG)

Fermentation: Wyeast #1007 or Whitelabs WLP001 at 68° F (20° C) for 1 week.

Secondary Storage: Wyeast #4335 and #4733 or Whitelabs WLP672 and WLP661 at cellar temperature for up to 2 years.

Options:
1. Blend with cherries or raspberries after 1 year
2. Blend with one or more batches of different ages
3. Serve unblended, primed with sugar

Comments: The more traditional interpretation of a Flemish oud bruin. The lower gravity makes this beer suitable for everyday drinking. The addition of fruit will produce a classic Flemish kriek or framboise.

Singularité

Malt Type	Color (ASBC)	Grist % by Weight
Pilsener	1.6	88.0%
Wheat	2.5	8.0%
Acidulated	2.5	4.0%

Mash Schedule: 90 minutes at 148° F (64° C)

Boiling Time: 1.5 hours

Bittering Hop Addition: 25 IBUs. Suggested variety: Crystal

Finishing Hop Addition: 0.5 oz/5 gal (4 g/liter) or 3 oz/bbl (72 g/hl) during the final 2 minutes of the boil. Suggested variety: Crystal.

Original Gravity: 15.3 °P (1.062 SG)

Fermentation: Wyeast #3110 or Whitelabs WLP645 at 65° F (18° C) for 2 weeks or 78° F (26° C) for less than 1 week.

Secondary Storage: 2-4 weeks at 55° F (13° C) or less.

Comments: A pale beer fermented with a "single" strain of *Brettanomyces*. Primary fermentation with *Brettanomyces anomalus* produces the bulk of the flavor and aroma. Bitterness is moderate and malt character low to accentuate the yeast character. No *Saccharomyces* will be harmed during the fermentation of this beer!

Sans Le Chat

Malt Type	Color (ASBC)	Grist % by Weight
Pilsener	1.6	90.0%
Wheat	2.5	5.0%
Acidulated	2.5	5.0%

Mash Schedule: 90 minutes at 148° F (64° C)

Boiling Time: 1.5 hours

Bittering Hop Addition: 20 IBUs. Suggested variety: Willamette.

Finishing Hop Addition: 0.25 oz/5 gal (7 g/ 19 l) or 1.5 oz/bbl (36 g/hl) during the final 2 minutes of the boil. Suggested variety: Willamette.

Original Gravity: 15.3 °P (1.062 SG)

Fermentation: Wyeast #3112 and/or #3536 or Whitelabs WLP650 and/or WLP653 at 65° F (18° C) for 2 weeks.

Secondary Storage: 2-4 weeks at 55° F (13° C) or less.

Comments: A pale beer fermented with two (or more) strains of *Brettanomyces*. Primary fermentation with *Brettanomyces lambicus* and/or *Brettanomyces bruxellensis* produces the characteristic wild, fruity aromas and flavors. The malt and hop character is kept very low. A slower, cooler fermentation increases the development of "traditional" flavors and aromas.

Flemish Nouveau

Malt Type	Color (ASBC)	Grist % by Weight
Pilsener	1.6	85.0%
Wheat	2.5	7.5%
Vienna	14	7.5%

Mash Schedule: 90 minutes at 150° F (66° C)

Boiling Time: 1.5 hours

Bittering Hop Addition: 25 IBUs. Suggested variety: Sterling.

Finishing Hop Addition: 0.75 oz/5 gals (21 g/19 l) or 4.5 oz/bbl (110 g/hl) during the final 2 minutes of the boil. Suggested variety: Crystal.

Original Gravity: 18 °P (1.074 SG)

Options: Steep fresh heather flowers in wort for 1 hour after cooling.

Fermentation: Wyeast #3942 or Whitelabs WLP410 at 70° F (21° C) for 1 week.

Secondary Storage: Wyeast #3112 and/or #3536 or Whitelabs WLP650 and/or WLP653 for 3 months at cellar temperature.

Comments: My "new Flemish ale" was inspired by the beers produced with *Brettanomyces* at De Proef with some help from those ancient brewers, the Picts. *Brettanomyces* provide flavor and aroma development in the "classic" method—after the completion of primary fermentation. Fresh heather flowers, a historic brewing ingredient, may introduce *Brettanomyces* without using any actual additional cultures. You may wish to decrease the amount of finishing hops if you choose to use heather.

Lacto In De Heuvels

Malt Type	Color (ASBC)	Grist % by Weight
Pilsener	1.6	85.0%
Wheat	2.5	5.0%
Vienna	7	5.0%
Munich	14	5.0%

Mash Schedule: 90 minutes at 150° F (66° C)

Boiling Time: 1.5 hours

Bittering Hop Addition: 20 IBUs. Suggested variety: Sterling.

Finishing Hop Addition: 0.5 oz/5 gals (14 g/19 l) or 3 oz/bbl (73 g/hl) during the final 2 minutes of the boil. Suggested variety: Crystal.

Original Gravity: 18 °P (1.074 SG)

Fermentation: Wyeast #3942 or Whitelabs WLP410 at 70° F (21° C) for 1 week.

Secondary Storage: Wyeast #3112 and/or #3536 or Whitelabs WLP650 and/or WLP653 for 3 months at cellar temperature.

Options:

1. Age with a variety of wine grapes for an additional 3-6 months

Comments: Inspired by some of the classic wild beers brewed near the Ardennes, which isn't terribly far from the growing region of Champagne grapes. *Lactobacillus* and/or *Pediococcus* will feed on the "scraps" of sugar left unfermented by *Saccharomyces*. Grapes not only provide flavor and aroma but also may encourage acid development (malolactic fermentation). The use of both lactic acid-producing bacteria and wine grapes may produce quite a tart beer, so some experimentation is required.

Donkere Geneeskunde

Malt Type	Color (ASBC)	Grist % by Weight
Pilsener	1.6	66.0%
Wheat	2.5	6.0%
Munich	14	6.0%
Aromatic	20	6.0%
CaraMunich	60	6.0%
Special "B"	115	2.0%
Chocolate	300	2.0%
Sugar	n/a	6.0%

Mash Schedule: 90 minutes at 152° F (67° C)

Boiling Time: 2 hours

Bittering Hop Addition: 25 IBUs. Suggested variety: Challenger.

Finishing Hop Addition: 0.5 oz/5 gals (14 g/ 19 l) or 3 oz/bbl (73 g/hl) during the final 2 minutes of the boil. Suggested variety: Styrian Goldings.

Original Gravity: 21 °P (1.087 SG)

Fermentation: Wyeast #1214 or #3763 or Whitelabs WLP530 at 68° F (20° C) for 1 week.

Secondary Storage: Wyeast #3278 or Whitelabs WLP655 for 6+ months at cellar temperature.

Options:
1. Age with fresh dark cherries
2. Age in a used bourbon or wine barrel

Comments: Literally "dark medicine," this recipe may (or may not) have been inspired by Tomme Arthur's *Cuvée de Tomme*. Dark malt plays a large role in the flavor and aroma profile. Wild character gradually increases with age, as microorganisms commonly found in lambic produce their respective by-products. Use of fruit or a barrel with residual character further increases complexity.

Appendix

"And if any man think that he knoweth any thing, he knoweth nothing yet as he ought to know."

–1 Corinthians 8:2

Before putting all of this information about producing wild beers to the test, a few questions remain. Namely, where to find the bugs, some stinky old hops, and an unwanted barrel (or three)? I have compiled a few sources to help you on your quest.

BEER-SOURING MICROORGANISMS
In spite of what you may have heard, culturing your own microorganisms is not a simple task. It requires knowledge, equipment, and patience. Even after following prescribed methods, there is no guarantee as to what you have actually grown. If you have interest in this sort of thing, other publications can provide the appropriate information. I choose to fight my battles at the macroscopic level and leave the bug ranching to the professionals.

The Big Two yeast suppliers—Wyeast Laboratories and Whitelabs—both carry unique blends and other seemingly identical strains of yeast and bacteria. While they are of the same species, don't be fooled; each company sells different strains that have different characteristics. The American Type Culture Collection is an option for brewers who like to "grow their own."

Wyeast Laboratories

P.O. Box 146

Odell, OR 97044

(541) 354-1335

www.wyeastlab.com

The folks at Wyeast Laboratories carry two blends of yeast and bacteria as well as three strains of *Brettanomyces* and two strains of lactic acid producers. The blends—Belgian Lambic Blend and Roeselare Blend—offer a single-package source of the most popular microorganisms necessary for fermenting a lambic and Flanders red respectively; no additional yeast is required. Other strains and species of yeast may be available by special order. Products are available by direct sales to commercial breweries and through retailers to homebrewers.

Cultures are available in 125ml XL packages, 0.25- , 0.5-, 1-liter, and multiple liters for direct inoculation. Wyeast suggests purchasing pitchable quantities due to the differential rates of growth with multiple organisms.

The commonly available products are:

3278 Belgian Lambic Blend

A blend designed for the fermentation of classic lambic-style beers. Contains a selection of *Saccharomyces* and non-

Saccharomyces, which include Belgian-style wheat beer yeast, sherry yeast, two *Brettanomyces* strains, and lactic acid-producing bacteria. No additional yeast is necessary for primary fermentation. While this mixture does not include all of the possible cultures found in Belgian lambics, it is representative of the organisms that are considered most important to produce the typical flavor characteristics.

Flocculation—low to medium; Apparent Attenuation—Variable; (60-80° F, 15-27° C)

3763 Roeselare Blend
A blend designed for the fermentation of classic Flanders red and brown beers. This blend is a mix of yeast and bacteria, including *Saccharomyces, Brettanomyces,* and lactic acid-producing bacteria. No additional yeast is necessary for primary fermentation. This culture is carefully maintained to keep the balance of these organisms intact. As the culture is repitched into successive beers, the lactic acid bacteria continue to increase, until the resulting beer is too sour to drink.

Flocculation—Medium; Apparent Attenuation—Variable; (60-80° F, 15-27° C)

3110 Brettanomyces anomalus
Wild yeast of unknown Belgian origin. May produce a distinct fruity character. This strain is a vigorous fermenter that will produce a thick layer of foam on the top of the fermenting wort. Reacts well to elevated temperatures.

Flocculation—Low; Apparent Attenuation—Medium to High; (60-80° F, 15-29° C)

3112 Brettanomyces bruxellensis
Wild yeast isolated from brewery cultures in the Brussels region of Belgium. Produce a classic horsy character. Ferment best in worts with lower pH after primary fermentation has begun. This strain is generally used in conjunction with *Saccharomyces cerevisiae* and other wild yeast and lactic bacteria. Produces some acidity and should form a pellicle in casks and sometimes in bottles.

Flocculation—Medium; Apparent Attenuation—High; (60-85° F, 15-29° C)

3526 Brettanomyces lambicus
Wild yeast isolated from brewery cultures in the Payottenland region of Belgium. Produce a pie–cherrylike flavor and sourness. Ferment best in worts with lower pH after primary fermentation has begun. This strain is generally used in conjunction with *Saccharomyces cerevisiae* as well as other wild yeast and lactic bacteria. Produces some acidity and should form a pellicle in casks and sometimes in bottles.

Flocculation—Medium; Apparent Attenuation—High; (60-85° F, 15-29° C)

4335 Lactobacillus delbruckii
Lactic acid bacterium isolated from a Belgian brewery. This culture produces moderate levels of acidity and is commonly found in many types of beers, including Flanders red and brown ales. Always used in conjunction with *Saccharomyces cerevisiae* and often with various wild yeast. *(60-100° F, 15-38° C)*

4733 Pediococcus cerevisiae
Lactic acid bacterium used in the production of Belgian-style beers where additional acidity is desirable. Commonly found in gueuze and Flanders red beers. A high acid producer, which usually increases overall acid levels in beer as storage time increases. Always used in conjunction with *Saccharomyces cerevisiae* and often with various wild yeast.

(60-100° F, 15-38° C)

WHITE LABS
7564 Trade Street
San Diego, CA 92121
(858) 693-3441
www.whitelabs.com

White Labs carries one blend of yeast and bacteria, as well as three strains of *Brettanomyces* and two strains of lactic acid producers. The blend—Belgian Sour Mix I—offers a single-package source of the most popular microorganisms necessary for fermenting a lambic; no additional yeast is required. Other strains and species of yeast and blends may be available by special order. Products are available by direct sales to commercial breweries and through retailers to homebrewers.

Cultures are available in standard tubes, designed for direct inoculation into 5-gallon batches or in larger sizes for commercial breweries.

The commonly available products are:

WLP645 Brettanomyces claussenii
Low intensity, mutant strain found in lambic and currently finding favor with brewers in California and Colorado. More

aroma than flavor contribution, with a fruity, sometimes pineapplelike aroma.

Flocculation—Low; Apparent Attenuation—High; (60-85° F, 15-29° C)

WLP650 Brettanomyces bruxellensis
Classic, medium-intensity strain responsible for much of the wild character in Brussels lambics.

Flocculation—Low; Apparent Attenuation—High; (60-85° F, 15-29° C)

WLP653 Brettanomyces lambicus
High-intensity strain characterized by horsy, smoky, and spicy flavors.

Flocculation—Low; Apparent Attenuation—High; (60-85° F, 15-29° C)

WLP655 Belgian Sour Mix I
A blend of all the organisms necessary to ferment a beer in the lambic style.

Flocculation—low to medium; Apparent Attenuation—Variable; (60-80° F, 15-27° C)

WLP661 Pediococcus damnosus
Aggressive lactic acid bacterium commonly found in lambic and Flanders beers. Produces copious amounts of diacetyl but often favored for its high acid production.
(60-100° F, 15-38° C)

WLP672 Lactobacillus brevis
Moderate lactic acid producer for Flanders beers and other styles. Ideal for wort souring, this strain is hop resistant, which allows it to grow well in many beer styles.
(60-100° F; 15-38° C)

AMERICAN TYPE CULTURE COLLECTION (ATCC)
P.O. Box 1549
Manassas, VA 20108
(703) 365-2700
www.atcc.org/
Founded in 1925, ATCC is "the world's leading biological resource center." Its mission is to "acquire, authenticate, preserve, produce, develop, and share biological materials for the advancement of scientific knowledge." ATCC is a good source for people versed in working with yeast and bacteria cultures to acquire a particular critter that neither of the W-labs stock. For the rest of us, the website is useful as a handy reference to the microscopic world. It's quite amazing how many organisms exist that will ferment and/or acidify beer (and other sugary liquids).

AGED HOPS
Some hop merchants may sell old hops at a discount but usually on a reasonably large scale and not to individuals. The following hop grower will sell used hops in smaller quantities:

Puterbaugh Farms
686 Green Valley Road
Mabton, WA 98935
(888) 972-3616
www.hopsdirect.com/

Puterbaugh Farms is a family-run hop, apple, and cherry grower. It advertises 4- to 5-year-old whole leaf "debittered" Tettnang at 0% alpha acid, or Choice "Debittered" Type 90 Hop Pellets, also at 0% alpha acid. It also sells some dandy Bing cherries.

USED BARRELS

If you live in wine, whiskey, or bourbon country, you may be able to procure a barrel for a reasonable price from a winery or distillery once one has outlived any usefulness to their product. The following posting service for buying and selling used wine barrels may be helpful:

Wine Business Exchange (Wine Business Online)
110 W. Napa Street
Sonoma, CA 95476
(707) 939-0822
www.winebusiness.com/usedbarrels

To aid you in selecting a quality barrel, an excellent article on inspecting barrels can be found at:
www.practicalwinery.com/mayjun02p68.htm

Glossary

acetic acid (CH_3COOH). A pungent, colorless liquid commonly known as vinegar, the product of the oxidation of alcohol by a variety of bacteria and certain types of yeast. Naturally occurring in a variety of fruits and other foods.

Acetobacter. A genus of aerobic, rod-shaped bacteria that grows in the presence of alcohol and secures energy by oxidizing organic compounds to organic acids, e.g., alcohol to acetic acid.

acidic. Having a sour taste/aftertaste.

adjunct. Any unmalted grain or other fermentable ingredient added to the mash.

aeration. The action of introducing air to the wort at various stages of the brewing process. Proper aeration before primary fermentation is vital to a vigorous ferment.

aerobic. Requiring the presence of oxygen to survive and reproduce (aerobic bacteria).

airlock. *See* fermentation lock.

air space. *See* ullage.

alcohol by volume (v/v). The volume percentage of alcohol in beer. To calculate the approximate volumetric alcohol content, subtract the final gravity from the original gravity and divide the result by 0.0075. For example: 1.050 – 1.012 = 0.038 ÷ 0.0075 = 5% v/v.

alcohol by weight (w/v). The percentage of alcohol in beer based on the weight of the alcohol. To calculate the approximate alcohol content by weight, subtract the final gravity from the original gravity and multiply by 105. For example: 1.050 – 1.0212 = 0.038 x 105 = 4% w/v.

ale. Historically, an unhopped malt beverage. Now, a generic term for hopped beers produced by top fermentation, as opposed to lagers, which are produced by bottom fermentation.

all-extract beer. A beer made with only malt extract, as opposed to one made from barley or a combination of malt extract and barley.

all-grain beer. A beer made with only malted barley, as opposed to one made from malt extract or from malt extract and malted barley.

all-malt beer. A beer made with only barley malt with no adjuncts or refined sugars.

alpha acid. A soft resin in hop cones. When boiled, alpha acids are converted to iso-alpha-acids, which account for 60 percent of a beer's bitterness.

alpha-acid unit. A measurement of the potential bitterness of hops, expressed by their percentage of alpha acid. Low is 2 to 4 percent; medium is 5 to 7 percent; high is 8 to 12 percent. Abbreviation is AAU.

anerobic. The inability to survive and reproduce in the presence of oxygen (anaerobic bacteria).

antioxidant. A reducing agent that delays oxidation and prolongs useful life of an organic product.

attenuation. The reduction in the wort's specific gravity caused by the transformation of sugars into alcohol and carbon dioxide.

astringent. A drying, tannic aftertaste.

autolysis. A process in which yeast feed on each other, producing a rubbery odor. To avoid this, rack beer to remove excess yeast as soon after fermentation as possible.

bacteria. Unicellular microorganisms that may typically infect wort and beer.

beer engine. Device used to draw beer from a cask by the use of suction created by pulling a handle. Also called a handpump.

beta acid. Hop resin essentially insoluble in liquid, unless oxidized, and cannot be isomerized by boiling. Exhibits a powerful antibacterial effect against the growth of thermophilic, gram-positive, lactic acid-producing bacteria.

bitter. A sharp taste and aftertaste associated with hops, malt, and yeast.

Bittering Units (BU). A measurement of the American Society for Brewing Chemists for bittering substances in beer, primarily iso-alpha-acids, but also including oxidized beta acids. *See also* International Bittering Units.

blending. The mixing together of different batches of beer to form a final composite intended for bottling.

blow-by (blow-off). A single-stage homebrewing fermentation method in which a plastic tube is fitted into the mouth of a carboy, and the other end is submerged in a pail of sterile water. Unwanted residues and carbon dioxide are expelled through the tube, while air is prevented from coming into contact with the fermenting beer, thus avoiding contamination.

bottle-conditioned. A beer in which carbonation is the result of the fermentation of sugar by yeast in the bottle.

Brettanomyces. A yeast common in the fermentation of wild beers and often resident in the equipment and vessels of breweries that make such beers. Produces very distinctive acid and ester profiles.

calcium carbonate ($CaCO_3$). Also known as chalk. Added during brewing to increase calcium and carbonate content.

calcium sulfate ($CaSO_4 \cdot 2H_2O$). Also known as gypsum. Added during brewing to increase calcium and sulfate content.

carbohydrates. A group of organic compounds including sugars and starches, many suitable as food for yeast and bacteria.

carbonation. The process of introducing carbon dioxide into a liquid by: (1) injecting the finished beer with carbon dioxide; (2) adding young fermenting beer to finished beer for a renewed fermentation (kraeusening); (3) priming (adding sugar to) fermented wort prior to bottling, creating a secondary fermentation in the bottle.

carboy. A large glass, plastic, or earthenware bottle.

catalyst. A substance, such as an enzyme, that promotes a chemical reaction.

chill haze. Haziness caused by protein and tannin during the secondary fermentation.

cold break. The flocculation of proteins and tannins during wort cooling.

coolship. A large, shallow tank historically used to cool and settle freshly boiled wort. Also used to expose wort to yeast and bacteria for spontaneous fermentation.

cuvée. A special product produced by a brewery.

decoction. A method of mashing that raises the temperature of the wash by removing a portion, boiling it, and returning it to the mash tun.

diacetyl. A compound contributing an objectionable butterscotch character.

dimethyl sulfide. A naturally occurring beer constituent that originates in malt. While it contributes to favorable beer flavors at low levels, in increased concentrations DMS contributes an objectionable cornlike or cooked vegetable character.

dry-hopping. The addition of hops to the primary fermenter, the secondary fermenter, or to casked beer to add aroma and hop character to the finished beer without adding significant bitterness.

dry malt. Malt extract in powdered form.

European Brewery Convention (EBC). The scientific body that establishes measurement standards and test methods for use in brewing in Europe. *See also* Standard Reference Method.

Enterobacter. Any of various gram-negative, rod-shaped bacteria of the family *Enterobacteriaceae,* which includes some pathogens, including salmonella.

esters. A group of compounds in beer that impart fruity flavors and aromas.

ethanol. Ethyl alcohol; the colorless, odorless, alcohol of beer, wine, and spirits.

extract. The amount of dissolved materials in the wort after mashing and lautering malted barley and/or malt adjuncts such as corn and rice.

fermentation lock. A one-way valve that allows carbon dioxide to escape from the fermenter while excluding contaminants.

filter. To extract solids, generally yeast and protein, from beer.

final gravity. The specific gravity of a beer when fermentation is complete.

fining. The process of adding clarifying agents to beer during secondary fermentation to precipitate suspended matter.

flocculant yeast. Yeast cells that form large colonies and tend to come out of suspension before the end of fermentation.

flocculation. The behavior of yeast cells joining into masses and settling out toward the end of fermentation.

framboise. French. A beer fermented with raspberries.

fusel alcohol. High molecular-weight alcohol, which results from excessively high fermentation temperatures. Fusel alcohol can impart harsh bitter flavors to beer as well as contribute to hangovers.

gelatin. A fining agent added during secondary fermentation, clarifying the beer.

genus. A taxonomic category ranking below a family and above a species, generally consisting of a group of species exhibiting similar characteristics.

glucose ($C_6H_{12}O_6$). An easily fermentable sugar used in brewing, sometimes contributing a cidery character in higher quantities.

grist. The milled malt and adjuncts prior to mashing.

gueuze. A blend of different batches and ages of lambic beer, which undergoes an additional fermentation in the bottle due to the presence of yeast and fermentable sugar.

hedgehog. Small, prickly mammal found primarily in European countries.

Homebrew Bittering Units. A formula invented by the American Homebrewers Association to measure bitterness of beer. Calculate bittering units by multiplying the percent of alpha acid in the hops by the number of ounces. Example: if 1.5 ounces of 10 percent alpha acid hops were used in a 5-gallon batch, the total homebrew bittering units would be 15: 1.5 x 10 = 15 HBU per 5 gallons.

hop pellets. Finely powdered hop cones compressed into tablets. Hop pellets are 20 to 30 percent more bitter by weight than the same variety in loose form.

horny tank. Tank employed after the coolship and before a fermenter at a time when the yeast and bacteria are jumping and ready to go.

humulone. Synonym for alpha acid.

hydrometer. A glass instrument used to measure the specific gravity of liquids as compared to water, consisting of a graduated stem resting on a weighed float.

infusion mash. *See* step infusion.

inoculation. Introduction of microorganisms to wort for the purpose of fermentation or acidification.

IBU (International Bittering Units). The measurement of the European Brewing Convention for the concentration of iso-alpha-acids in 34 milligrams per liter (parts per million) in wort and beer. *See also* Bittering Units.

infection. Growth of microorganisms in wort or beer detrimental to flavor or aroma.

Irish moss. Copper or lead "finings" that help precipitate proteins in the kettle. *See also* cold break.

isinglass. A gelatinous substance made from the swim bladder of certain fish and added to beer as a fining agent.

isomerization. The extraction (inversion) of hop alpha acids by boiling in wort.

kilning. The final stage in the malting process, when malt is exposed to high temperatures to halt modification and increase color and character.

kraeusen. *n.* The rocky head of foam that appears on the surface of the wort during fermentation. *v.* To add fermenting wort to fermented beer to induce carbonation through a secondary fermentation.

kriek. *Flemish.* A beer fermented with cherries.

lactic acid ($C_3H_6O_3$). A clear, odorless acid found in beer, sour milk, and fruit.

Lactobacillus. Any of various rod-shaped, aerobic bacteria of the genus *Lactobacillus* that ferment lactic acid (and often others) from sugars.

lager. *n.* A generic term for any bottom-fermented beer. Lager brewing is now the predominant brewing method worldwide, except in Britain, where top-fermented ales dominate. *v.* To store beer at near-zero temperatures in order to precipitate yeast cells and proteins and improve taste.

lambic. A spontaneously fermented beer produced with a portion of unmalted wheat, generally containing specific characteristics due to various acids and esters. Also used to describe the unblended form of the beer—as opposed to gueuze—commonly served young on draft or old in bottles.

lauter tun. A vessel in which the mash settles and the grains are removed from the sweet wort through a straining process. It has a false slotted bottom and spigot.

liquefaction. The process by which alpha-amylase enzymes degrade soluble starch into dextrin.

liquor. Water intended for brewing.

Lovibond (°L). The scale used to measure beer color. *See also* Standard Reference Method.

lupulone. Synonym for beta acid.

malt. Barley that has been steeped in water, germinated, then dried in kilns. This process converts insoluble starches to soluble substances and sugars.

malt extract. A thick syrup or dry powder prepared from malt.

mashing. Mixing crushed malt with water to extract the fermentables, degrade haze-forming proteins, and convert grain starches to fermentable sugars and nonfermentable carbohydrates.

Méthode Champenoise. A blend of wine or beer, refermented in the bottle to produce a sparkling, effervescent product.

microorganism. An organism of microscopic or submicroscopic size, such as a bacterium.

mixed fermentation. Use of both a culture and microorganisms that grow in a wooden barrel for fermentation.

modification. 1. The physical and chemical changes in barley as a result of malting. 2. The degree to which these changes have occurred, as determined by the growth of the acrospire.

moldy. An objectionable earthly aftertaste often caused by damp, unsanitary conditions during the fermentation or aging of beer.

nitrogen content. The amount of nitrogen in malt as a percentage of weight.

oaky. Exhibiting the characteristics commonly associated with oak, e.g., vanilla, tannic.

old beer. Beer that has undergone sufficient fermentation and aging as to be considered of a mature flavor and aroma profile.

original gravity. The specific gravity of wort before fermentation. A measure of the total amount of dissolved solids in wort.

oxidation. A chemical reaction involving oxygen, detrimental to beer.

pasteurization. Exposure to heat to destroy microorganisms present in beer (or other food products susceptible to infection).

Pediococcus. A genus of gram-positive, facultative, anaerobic bacteria whose growth is dependent on the presence of a fermentable carbohydrate.

pH. A measure of acidity or alkalinity of a solution, usually on a scale of 1 to 14, where 7 is neutral.

phenols. Volatile compounds in beer contributing a pleasant spicy character or objectionable plastic or medicinal character.

pitching. The process of adding yeast to the cooled wort.

Plato. A saccharometer that expresses specific gravity as extract weight in a 100-gram solution at 68° F (20° C). A revised, more accurate version of Balling, developed by Dr. Plato.

polyphenols. An antioxidant phytochemical that tends to prevent or neutralize the damaging effects of oxygen and free radicals.

primary fermentation. The first stage of fermentation, during which most fermentable sugars are converted to ethyl alcohol and carbon dioxide.

priming sugar. A small amount of corn, malt, or cane sugar added to bulk beer prior to racking or at bottling to induce a new fermentation and create carbonation.

racking. The process of transferring beer from one container to another, especially into the final package (bottle, keg).

recirculation. Clarifying the wort before it moves from the lauter tun into the kettle by recirculating it through the wash bed.

reduction. A reaction by which oxygen is removed from a compound.

refermentation. An additional fermentation, generally in the bottle, with the intention of producing carbonation as well as additional alcohol.

saccharification. The naturally occurring process in which malt starch is converted into fermentable sugars, primarily maltose.

saccharometer. An instrument that determines the sugar concentration of a solution by measuring the specific gravity.

Saccharomyces. Any of several single-celled yeasts belonging to the genus *Saccharomyces,* many of which ferment sugar. Yeasts of the genus *Saccharomyces cerevisiae* are the most common in brewing.

secondary fermentation. 1. The second, slower stage of fermentation, lasting from a few weeks to many months depending on the type of beer. 2. A fermentation occurring in bottles or casks and initiated by priming or by adding yeast.

solventy. An objectionable aroma and flavor of higher (fusel) alcohols, reminiscent of acetone.

sour. A sharp, acidic taste and aftertaste.

sparging. Spraying the spent grains in the mash with hot water to retrieve the remaining malt sugar.

species. A fundamental category of taxonomic classification, ranking below a genus, consisting of related organisms capable of interbreeding.

specific gravity. A measure of a substance's density as compared to that of water, which is given the value of 1.000 at 39.2° F (4° C). Specific gravity has no accompanying units, because it is expressed as a ratio.

spontaneous fermentation. A method of fermentation by which all microorganisms necessary for fermentation are naturally occurring in the brewery; the brewer adds no cultures of microorganisms.

Standard Reference Method (SRM) and **European Brewery Convention (EBC).** Notations used to indicated two different analytical methods for color. Degrees SRM, approximately equivalent to degrees Lovibond, are used by the American Society of Brewing Chemists (ASBC), while degrees EBC are European units. Both methods are based on spectrophotometer readings at the same wavelength, and conversion between the two is calculated by this equation: ($^\circ$EBC) = 1.97 x $^\circ$Lovibond.

starter. A batch of fermenting yeast, added to the wort to initiate fermentation.

step infusion. A method of mashing whereby the temperature of the mash is raised by adding very hot water, then stirring and stabilizing the mash at the target step temperature.

strain. A group of microorganisms of the same species, having distinctive characteristics but not usually considered a separate species.

strike temperature. The initial temperature of the water when the malted barley is added to it to create the mash.

style. Characteristics, generally flavor and aroma, by which beers are categorized.

superattenuation. Achieving a final apparent extract as low or lower than 0.1 Plato, nearly 1.000 SG, attributed to fermentation by the highly attenuative *Brettanomyces* yeasts in the presence of the other organisms.

sweet. Having the taste of sugar or resembling sugar.

tannin. Various soluble, astringent, phenolic substances, often present in yeast, malt, and wood.

terroir. A unique combination of environmental conditions, present in every place where alcoholic beverages are produced, largely contributing to the character of wild beer and wine.

tertiary fermentation. An additional period of aging when beer is left to fully mature due to the presence of various microorganisms.

torrefied wheat. Wheat that has been heated quickly at high temperature, causing it to puff up, which renders it easily mashed.

trub. Suspended particles resulting from the precipitation of proteins, hop oils, and tannins during boiling and cooling stages of brewing.

tun. Any open tank or vessel.

turbid mash. A method of mashing involving the boiling of liquid from a mash consisting of a portion of unmalted grain, resulting in a highly dextrinous wort.

ullage. 1. The empty space between a liquid and the top of its container. Also called air space or head space. 2. Waste beer, often left over from handpumps or the bottom of casks.

viscous. Having a glutinous consistency and the quality of sticking or adhering.

v/v. *See* alcohol by volume.

vorlauf. To recirculate the wort from one mash tun through the grain bed to clarify.

w/v. *See* alcohol by weight.

water hardness. The degree of dissolved minerals in water.

whirlpool. A method of bringing cold break material to the center of the kettle by stirring the wort until a vortex is formed.

wild beer. Any beer fermented or matured with yeast and/or bacteria other than those belonging to the genus *Saccharomyces.*

wort. The mixture that results from mashing the malt and boiling the hops, before it is fermented into beer.

yeast. Generally, any of various unicellular fungi used in fermentation, most commonly members of the genus *Saccharomyces,* especially *S. cerevisiae.* In wild brews, yeasts from other genera also play a role. See *Brettanomyces.*

young beer. Beer that has not undergone sufficient fermentation and aging as to be considered of a mature flavor and aroma profile. Usually contains significant concentrations of viable microorganisms and sugars.

Bibliography

Apte, Raj. "How to Make Sour Ale: An Inquiry," 2004. Available at: www2.parc.com/eml/members/apte/flemishredale.shtml.

Arnold, J. P. *Origin and History of Brewing From Prehistoric Times to the Beginning of Brewing and Science Technology.* Chicago: Alumni Association of the Wahl-Henius Institute of Fermentology, 1911.

Battcock, Mike, and Sue Azam-Ali. *Fermented Fruits and Vegetables. A Global Perspective.* FAO Agricultural Services Bulletin 134. Rome: Food and Agriculture Organization of the United Nations, 1998.

Benoit, Yves, personal communication, 6 April 2004.

Boakes, John. *Making a Barrel.* West Yorkshire, England: Smith Settle Ltd., 2001.

Boon, Frank, personal communication. 14 April 2004.

Bouckaert, Peter. "Brewery Rodenbach: Brewing Sour Ales." Online posting to *Lambic Digest* No. 846, 9 May 1996. Available at http://brewery.org/brewery/library/Rodnbch.html.

Bouckaert, Peter, personal communication, April, September, October 2004.

Brande, W. *Town and Country Brewery Book*. London: Dean and Munday, 1830. Reprint. Newbury, Ohio: Raudins Publishing, 2003.

Brown, Tony, personal communication, 26 November 2004.

Cornell, Martyn. *Beer: The Story of the Pint*. London: Headline Book Publishing, 2003.

DeBelder, Armand, personal communication, 19 April 2004.

De Boeck, Guido. *Un 'BEER'ably Delicious: Recipes for Cooking With Artisan and Craft Beers*. Arlington, Va.: Dookus Publishing, 2002.

De Keersmaecker, Jacques. "The Mystery of Lambic Beer." *Scientific American* 275, no. 2 (August 1996): 74-80.

De Keukeleire, Denis. "The Hop in the Brewing Process and As a Medicinal Plant." www.bierengezondheid.be/.

Devolder, Filip, personal communication, 5 April 2004.

Dunson-Todd, Jason. "Beer From the Wood—From Ancient Times Past to Present, Oak Remains a Perennial Source of Special Character." *Brewing Techniques* 5, no. 4 (September 1997): 60-71.

Egli, Christoph, and Thomas Henick-Kling. "Identification of *Brettanomyces/Dekkera* Species Based on Polymorphism in the rRNA Internal Transcribed Spacer Region." *American Journal of Enology and Viticulture* 52, no. 3 (2001): 241-247.

Fix, George and Laurie. *An Analysis of Brewing Techniques.* Boulder, Colo.: Brewers Publications, 1997.

Fix, George. *Principles of Brewing Science.* Boulder, Colo.: Brewers Publications, 1989.

Forster, A., B. Beck, and R. Schmidt. *Hop Polyphenols: A Substance Group of Importance for Brewing Technology.* Wolnzach, Germany: Hopfen-Extraktion HGV Barth, Raiser, & Co., 1995. Available at: www.johbarth.com/scientific/55.html

Forster, A., B. Beck, and R. Schmidt. *Investigations on Hop Polyphenols.* Text for the poster made for the 25th EBC Congress, Brussels, 1995. Wolnzach, Germany: Hopfen-Extraktion HGV Barth, Raiser, & Co. Available at: www.johbarth.com/scientific/51.html

Franson, Paul. "The Threat of *Brett.*" *Vineyards and Winery Management* 27, no. 5, (September-October 2001). Available at: www.vwm-online.com/Magazine/Archive/2001/Vol27_No5/Brett.htm

Ghequire, Rudi, personal communication, 6 April 2004.

Gilliland, R. "*Brettanomyces*. I. Occurrence and Characteristics." *Journal of the Institute of Brewing* 67 (1961): 257-261.

Goddeau, Karel, personal communication, 15 April 2004.

Guinard, Jean-Xavier. *Lambic*. Boulder, Colo.: Brewers Publications, 1990.

Herteleer, Kris, personal communication, 3 April 2004.

Hitchcock, Ed. "Kitchen Anthropology: Home Brewing an Ancient Beer." *Brewing Techniques* 2, no. 5 (September-October 1994): 38.

Hornsey, Ian. *Brewing*. Cambridge, England: The Royal Society of Chemistry, 1999.

Inglis, Tom. "Hops and Beer Flavours," IOB Technical Symposium, HoChiMinh City, Vietnam, April 2001. Available at: www.nzhops.co.nz/articles/flavours.htm.

Jackson, Michael. *The Great Beers of Belgium*. 1st ed. Antwerp: CODA, 1991.

Jackson, Michael. *The Great Beers of Belgium*. 4th ed. London: Prion Books, 2001.

Jackson, Michael. *Michael Jackson's Beer Companion.* Philadelphia: Running Press, 1993.

Jackson, Michael. *The New World Guide to Beer.* Philadelphia: Running Press, 1988.

Johnson, G. M. "A Belgian Mashing System Suitable for Light Beers." *Journal of the Institute of Brewing* 15, no. 6 (1916): 237-251.

Johnson, G. M. "Brewing in Belgium and Belgian Beers." *Journal of the Federated Institutes of Brewing* 1 (1895): 450-470.

Kumara, S., and H. Verachtert, "Identification of Lambic Superattenuating Micro-Organisms by the Use of Selective Antibiotics." *Journal of the Institute of Brewing* 97, no. 2 (1991): 181-185.

Kumara, S., S. De Cort, and H. Verachtert. "Localization and Characterization of Beta-Glucosidase Activity in *Brettanomyces Lambicus.*" *Applied and Environmental Microbiology* (August 1993): 2352-2358.

Liddil, Jim. "Brewing in Styles: Practical Strategies for Brewing Lambic at Home, Part I—Wort Preparation." Edited by Martin Lodahl. *Brewing Techniques* 5, no. 3 (May-August 1997): 27-35.

Liddil, Jim. "Brewing in Styles: Practical Strategies for Brewing Lambic at Home, Part II—Fermentation and Culturing." Edited by Martin Lodahl. *Brewing Techniques* 5, no. 4 (September 1997): 38-49.

Liddil, Jim. "Brewing in Styles: Practical Strategies for Brewing Lambic at Home, Part III—The Finishing Touches." Edited by Martin Lodahl. *Brewing Techniques* 5, no. 5 (October-November 1997): 26-37.

Liker, J., T. Acree, and T. Henick-Kling. "What is '*Brett*' (*Brettanomyces*) Flavor? A Preliminary Investigation." *Chemistry of Wine Flavor.* A. L. Waterhouse and S. E. Ebeler, eds. American Chemical Society Symposium Series 714 (1999): 96-115.

Lindemans, Dirk, personal communication, 16 April 2004.

Lodahl, Martin. "Lambic: Belgium's Unique Treasure." *Brewing Techniques* 3, no. 4 (July-August 1995): 43-46.

Martens, H. "Microbiology and Biochemistry of the Acid Ales of Roeselare." University of Leuven. (1996).

Martens, H., D. Iserentant, and H. Verachtert, "Microbiological Effects of a Mixed Yeast-Bacterial Fermentation in the Production of a Special Belgian Acid Ale." *Journal of the Institute of Brewing* 103, no. 2, (1997): 85-91.

Martens, H., E. Dawoud, and H. Verachtert, "Synthesis of Aroma Compounds by Wort *Enterobacteria* During the First Stage of Lambic Fermentation." *Journal of the Institute of Brewing* 98, no. 6 (1992): 421-425.

Matthys, John, personal communication, 18 April 2004.

Mosher, Randy. "Notes From a Fruit Beer Fancier: Aesthetics, Practicalities, and Utter Trickery." *Zymurgy* 25, no. 4, (July-August 2002): 22-25.

Mosher, Randy. *Radical Brewing.* Boulder, Colo.: Brewers Publications, 2004.

NaturalCork Quality Council, www.corkqc.com.

Noonan, Greg. *New Brewing Lager Beer.* Boulder, Colo.: Brewers Publications, 1996.

Nummer, Brian. "Brewing With Lactic Acid Bacteria." *Brewing Techniques* 4, no. 3 (May-June 1996): 56-63.

Overbeck, O. "Low Alcohol Beers." *Journal of the Institute of Brewing* 15, no. 1 (1916): 3-12.

Perrier-Robert, Annie, and Charles Fontaine. *Belgium by Beer, Beer by Belgium.* Luxembourg: Schortgen, Esch/Alzette, 1996.

Piatz, Steve. "Lambic Brewing." *Brew Your Own* 10, no. 6 (October 2004): 44-48.

Rajotte, Pierre. *Belgian Ale.* Boulder, Colo.: Brewers Publications, 1992.

Reinders, Bruno, personal communication, 15 April 2004.

Renner, Jeff. "Solera Ale: Beer That Gets Older As You Drink It." *Zymurgy* 25, no. 1 (January-February 2002): 26-29.

Rotter, Ben. "Improved Winemaking." members.tripod.com/ ~Brotter.

Rutten, Paul, personal communication, 9 April 2004.

Sakamoto, Kanta. "Beer Spoilage Bacteria and Hop Resistance in *Lactobacillus brevis*." Groningen, Netherlands: University of Groningen (2002). Available at: www.ub.rug.nl/eldoc/dis/ science/k.sakamoto.

Schramm, Ken. *The Compleat Meadmaker*. Boulder, Colo.: Brewers Publications, 2003.

Siebel, J. E., ed. *One Hundred Years of Brewing: A Complete History of the Progress Made in the Art, Science, and Industry of Brewing During the Nineteenth Century*. Chicago: H.S. Rich & Co., 1903.

Spaepen, M. and H. Verachtert, "Esterase Activity in the Genus *Brettanomyces*." Journal of the Institute of Brewing 88 (1), pp. 11-17, (1982).

Spaepen, M., D. Van Oevelen, and H. Verachtert, "Fatty Acids and Esters Produced During the Sponteneous Fermentation of Lambic and Gueuze." *Journal of the Institute of Brewing* 84, no. 5 (1978): 278-282.

Unger, Richard. *Beer in the Middle Ages and Renaissance.* Philadelphia: University of Pennsylvania Press, 2004.

Van Oevelen, D., and H. Verachtert. "Slime Production by Brewery Strains of *Pediococcus Cerevisiae.*" *Journal of the American Society of Brewing Chemists* 37, no. 1 (1979): 34-37.

Van Oevelen, D., De L'Escalle, F., and H. Verachtert. "Synthesis of Aroma Compounds During the Spontaneous Fermentation of Lambic and Gueuze." *Journal of the Institute of Brewing* 82, no. 6, (1976): 322-326.

Van Oevelen, D., M. Spaepen, P. Timmermans, and H. Verachtert. "Microbiological Aspects of Spontaneous Wort Fermentation in the Production of Lambic and Gueuze." *Journal of the Institute of Brewing* 83, no. 6 (1977): 356-360.

Van den Steen, Jef. *Het Pajottenland en De Zennevallei Bakermat Van Lambi(e)k en Geuze.* Leuven, Belgium: Jos Vandeputte, 2003.

Van Roy, J.-P. *Brasserie-Brouwerij Cantillon.* Brussels: Le Musée Bruxellois de la Gueuze, n.d.

Van Roy, Jean, personal communication, 20 April 2004.

Verhaeghe, Karl, personal communication, 7 April 2004.

Virant, Madja, and Duscia Majer. *Hop Storage Index—Indicator of Brewing Quality.* Zalec, Slovenia: Institute of Hop Research and

Brewing Zalec, 2001. Available at: www.czhops.cz/tc/pdf/hop.pdf.

Webb, Tim, Chris Pollard, and Joris Pattyn. *Lambicland.* Cambridge, England: University Press, 2004.

Zoecklin, Bruce. *A Review of Méthode Champenoise Production.* Blacksburg, Va.: Virginia Polytechnic University Publication Number 463-017, December 2002.

Index

Page numbers in **boldface** refer to illustrations and/or captions.